SURPRISE!
SURPRISE!

SURPRISE!
SURPRISE!

HOW THE LAWMEN CONNED THE THIEVES

by RON SHAFFER and KEVIN KLOSE
with Alfred E. Lewis

A *Washington Post* Book

THE VIKING PRESS   NEW YORK

Copyright © The Washington Post Company, 1977
All rights reserved

First published in 1977 by The Viking Press
625 Madison Avenue, New York, N.Y. 10022
Published simultaneously in Canada by
Penguin Books Canada Limited

LIBRARY OF CONGRESS CATALOGING IN PUBLICATION DATA

Shaffer, Ron
Surprise! Surprise!

"A Washington post book."
1. District of Columbia—Police. 2. Receiving
stolen goods—Washington, D.C. 3. Larceny—
Washington, D.C. I. Klose, Kevin, joint author.
II. Lewis, Alfred E., joint author. III. Title.
HV8148.W32K56   363.2'32   77–3373
ISBN 0–670–38894–7

Printed in the United States of America
Set in videocomp Baskerville

Grateful acknowledgment is made to the following:
Paramount Music Corporation: From *That's Amore* by Jack Brooks
and Harry Warren. Copyright © 1953 by Paramount Music Corporation.
Paul Simon: From *Mrs. Robinson* by Paul Simon.
© 1968 Paul Simon. Used by permission

To "Seeburn"

ACKNOWLEDGMENTS

We are indebted to many for their full and generous cooperation in providing us with the recollections and documentation upon which this account is based.

A special note of thanks to Special Agent Edgar L. Seibert of the Bureau of Alcohol, Tobacco and Firearms, who opened his life and his home for endless hours of interviews; and to Special Agent Michael R. Hartman of the Federal Bureau of Investigation for reviewing the manuscript and enriching it with his own recollections.

We are particularly grateful to other persons:

FBI director Clarence M. Kelley gave the full assistance of his Bureau; his Special Assistant, Thomas Harrington, cheerfully arranged interviews and provided other help. Special Agents

Robert Lill and Thomas R. Easton supplied details of the beginnings of the Sting operation.

John Rowley, Special Agent in Charge of the ATF Washington Field Office, and Special Agent Ronald Hendrix, extended help when we most needed it.

Our editors at the *Post*—Howard Simons, Benjamin C. Bradlee, Leonard Downie, Jr., Philip Foisie and Herbert H. Denton—patiently waited and guided us while we toiled past every deadline. Christopher Little, a *Post* executive, gave us wise counsel that made a better book. Staff Writer Timothy S. Robinson guided us through the courthouse maze. Sue Challis, helped by Sharon Curtis and Fran Baker, transcribed hours of interview tapes and Challis and Pamela Elliott retyped the manuscirpt under seige conditions.

Our editor at Viking, Elisabeth Sifton, and her assistant, Victoria Stein, provided help and encouragement all along the way.

Earl J. Silbert, United States Attorney for the District of Columbia; and his assistants, Donald E. Campbell and Daniel Bernstein; and Washington police chief Maurice J. Cullinane gave freely of their time and expertise.

Many of those arrested in the Sting operation spoke openly about their lives. Their voices are throughout the book. Some who have helped us have asked to remain anonymous.

We indulged our families' patience and support beyond all reasonable limits.

Ron Shaffer / Kevin Klose / Alfred E. Lewis

Washington
April 1977

AUTHORS' NOTE

This account is drawn from many sources: interviews with lawmen and defendants, official files of law enforcement agencies, court records, trial testimony and exhibits, and police videotapes and voice recordings.

Unless otherwise noted, the names used are real. In some cases, fictitious names or known aliases have been substituted.

Much of the dialogue is verbatim from tape recordings made on the scene by the lawmen. Some conversations are condensations of these lengthy, taped incidents. Other conversations have been re-created from the recollections of participants and supported or confirmed by a general review of many tapes depicting similar scenes.

SURPRISE! SURPRISE!

1

Young Tony Hendley, skinny and black, was trapped like an animal and getting sick. Here he was shackled by the left wrist to a desk at police headquarters in downtown Washington, and instead of a sweet syringe he was getting the aches and tremors of heroin withdrawal.

In a few moments, the arresting officer would return from the records room downstairs, and he'd be mad because Tony had given him a phony name and address. Hendley's stomach knotted. The rollers had charged him with armed robbery; he might not be back on the street again for years.

His head lolled on the desk, and his thoughts turned to the recent months of good money he had made by stealing things and selling them to the mob. That very night, in fact, a party was promised at the organization's warehouse for all the thieves who had made the Mafia's Washington operation such a success.

There would be women, booze, strong drugs. Awards to the

woman for the best sex. Door prizes for everybody. If he could just get there, he could somehow find safety. They had dope, money, and people who could take care of him. His kind of people.

He tugged at the manacle, snug around his wrist and attached by a short chain to a hasp on the side of the desk in the robbery squad room. He looked closer and a thought struck him. Draping his coat over the desk to hide his efforts, Tony fished a dime out of his pocket and began loosening the four screws that fastened the hasp to the desk. In a few moments he was free, the chain dangling uselessly from the manacle still locked to his wrist.

Hendley slid into his coat, hiding the police bracelet. He crawled to the open door, then got to his feet and strode purposefully into the hall. Within moments, he was safely downstairs, outside, and hailing a taxi from the broad sidewalk in front of Washington Metropolitan Police headquarters.

He headed north toward the dilapidated brick row houses and seedy commercial strips where he lived and prowled. Maybe he should get out of town fast, Tony thought, far away where he would be safe, unknown, beyond the reach of the D.C. police. But to do that he needed money.

Pasquale (Pat) Larocca, counterman at the P.F.F. warehouse, had plenty of money. For months, Tony had been bringing Pat credit cards, typewriters, television sets, purses—whatever he could steal—and he had been paid well. Some of the easiest money Tony had made in his twenty-one years. Pat was the best fence in town. He had said so again and again, and Tony believed it. Pat had never been touched by the police.

And now there was the party. Pat had personally given Tony an invitation: "7:45 P.M. Saturday, Feb. 28, 1976" was scribbled on the Mafia business card that read "P.F.F. Inc., 2254 25th Place, N.E., Washington, D.C. Phone 526–4032." "This is my chance to impress the Man," Pat had told him. "Don't embarrass me by not showing up. My boss will be here. He wants to meet you."

Things would be loose and easy at the P.F.F. party—with a chance maybe to lift some of the drugs, Hendley thought. After all his months of bringing stuff in there, they would never suspect he would do that. I'll rip 'em off, sky up and split, he thought.

When he got near home, Tony scrambled out of the cab and headed for a telephone booth, where he called Pat.

"I got arrested!" he burst out.

"Tough, " Pat said.

"—But I got away!"

"Oh, yeah? In that case, you go on home and hide and then come on over to the party. We've got some people here to take care of you."

Tony got to the 25th Place warehouse about 8 P.M. wearing the dark leisure suit he had been arrested in, a print shirt with oversize collar, and a knit watch cap pulled down on his head to ward off the night's chill.

He was later than his appointed time, but figured they would let him in, since he was such a regular customer. Following the usual procedure, he telephoned ahead from a public phone booth at the end of the block.

"Hey, Tony, how ya doin', man!" Pat boomed on the phone, sounding especially happy.

"I'm down at the phone booth and I've got a problem. I gotta get off the street."

"Well, come on down!" Pat yelled.

Tony walked in the front door, setting off an alarm he could not hear, and climbed the metal stairs to the P.F.F. offices on the second floor of the building. He was a friendly figure, peering through the window of the locked P.F.F. door; his enthusiastic smile masked the beatings of his childhood and the years spent in foster homes and city institutions for homeless and troublesome children, and the stealing and dealing in drugs.

Tony held up his left hand. "What you got on there?" Pat shouted through the door. Tony's grin spread as he clenched his fist and shook his manacled hand in the window. "You got a handcuff on?" Pat asked, his voice cracking with amazement. "Come on in."

The door swung open with a buzz. At first, Tony saw nothing amiss. There was Pat, bearded, shaggy-haired, stationed behind the chest-high counter, gripping his carbine. This time, instead of fatigues, he was wearing a black bow tie, ruffled formal shirt, and dark maroon dinner jacket. The enforcer, Michael Franzino, stood as usual at a counter behind Pat, leveling a shotgun at Tony, the same way he had greeted every customer for months. From somewhere behind the wood-paneled walls, in the back reaches of the warehouse, Tony could hear the swelling sounds of the Commodores doing "Sweet Love."

"How'd you escape, man?" Pat inquired, pausing to buzz two other guests in. The fence's hands grabbed at the loose chain, fondling the links. "Hey, my man here just escaped," he announced to these new arrivals. "Did you see anything suspicious? Hey, he just escaped; we might have to hide him real quick." Pat nodded to one of his helpers and said something that sounded Italian. "ARRIBA-DEECH."

Angelo, swarthy and grim, with flashing black eyes and slicked-back hair, came around the counter and began patting at Tony's leisure suit. Angelo looked peculiar in a tuxedo, Tony thought. He hadn't seen a way to make a move yet.

"Angelo's gonna check you over," Pat said. "We gotta put protection on the boss. . . . You got any pieces on you? We'll give 'em back to you at the end of the party."

Tony was unarmed. "They already lookin' for me, you know," he said, glancing about restlessly and holding up his manacled arm. "You got a saw or something to cut these off with?"

Pat asked once more what he had done. Sometimes he got too personal, Tony thought, and then he began to explain.

"What happened man, was, like, I robbed someone . . . like . . . the girl was standin' there . . . she snitched . . . the rollers caught us."

"Well, they don't have any evidence on you?"

"Naw, naw, naw."

"Well, who did you rob?"

"I didn't even know the girl, really."

"Stick her up with a gun? You gotta piece, you wanna hide it?"

"I already threw the piece away."

"Where was this?"

"Fourth and N."

"Damn, I hope you don't bring no heat on us," Angelo said.

"No . . . they don't even know my real name."

"Well, then," Angelo said to Pat, "give 'em the door prize!"

This whole scene could be cool, Tony thought, but on the other hand here was Pat aiming a carbine at him and Angelo frisking him down, and this is supposed to be a party?

He decided he would take his chances running; he didn't want any part of this party.

"I want you to know you're gonna have a good time tonight," Pat beamed. "You're gonna meet the boss . . . that's him comin' now. . . ."

Tony could hear heavy feet pounding toward him. Just as he was about to bolt, a wall seemed to collapse behind him and suddenly the room was filled with uniformed men with riot helmets, flak jackets, shotguns, and pistols. They rushed forward, shouting orders, and grabbed him. He was spun around and shoved against a wall. They pulled his arms back and he could hear and feel a new set of handcuffs being clamped on his wrists.

"Tony!" Pat said, his voice cracking with glee. "You've just won the door prize! We're police officers—and you're under arrest!"

Tony scanned the room, speechless in fright. They really aren't police officers, he thought. They're Mafia men out to kill me because too many people know about the warehouse.

They couldn't be cops the way they'd given money to people for months. Cops would have arrested me the first time I came in there. Other thieves had sold these men guns and walked away with cash. He waited to hear a weapon cock.

They pushed him toward a small back room. If they *were* the cops, he was in trouble. Not only for the armed robbery but all the other things he had sold to Pat. And if they were Mafia, he'd be killed. Strangely, he found himself hoping they were police.

Quickly, he was downstairs where other party "guests" were lined up at processing tables and swarms of men stood around, some wearing blue jackets with POLICE stenciled on the back, others just walking around with cups of coffee. Man, he thought, I'm all right now.

He was strip-searched and led to a bench in another room, where he was handcuffed to a chain alongside other customers who had come expecting a party. Many hung their heads. As the finger-popping theme music from "S.W.A.T." boomed into his ears from a warehouse stereo, the truth broke on Tony Hendley: They've been hustling me for months—these guys aren't any fences! Pasquale Larocca and Angelo and all the other Italians at this place called P.F.F.—all cops!

At 9:30 the next morning, Sheldon Bennett, the aging proprietor of a maintenance yard next door to the P.F.F. warehouse, arrived for his usual Sunday chore: feeding the mongrel dog he kept there.

Normally he was the only person around. This time, three uniformed police blocked his entrance. Cars of every kind, many of them luxury models, jammed his lot. A Cadillac pulled to a stop in front of the deserted warehouse and a woman driver shouted out a man's name. No one answered.

"What's going on around here?" Bennett demanded of the policemen.

One of them looked at him blankly. "Beats the shit out of me," he said.

2

In late March 1975, while government leaders in Washington were preoccupied with the collapse of South Vietnam and a $30 billion tax cut, the city's policemen had a problem of their own—thieves were stealing millions of dollars of equipment from office buildings all over the nation's capital and the lawmen couldn't stop it.

Typewriters, calculators, computers, and other expensive electronic equipment were disappearing from empty offices, loading docks, freight elevators, and storage rooms. Thieves with stolen purses, wallets, and payroll checks were walking past security guards. Insurance companies, city businessmen, and federal bureaucrats were angry. And pressure was mounting on the lawmen to catch the thieves.

Theft was hard to stop, a crime that offered few clues or witnesses and sometimes went undiscovered for days. Another difficulty was that since both federal lawmen and city police operated within Washington, a single crime could fall within the jurisdiction of several different agencies. Not only were the law enforcers failing to stem the crimes, they often got in each other's way.

Summoned to one recent burglary in a government building, FBI agent Robert Lill found investigators from three different city police squads, the Federal Protective Service, and another security force. all grilling a hapless guard and pawing the scene for clues. He could barely get in the door. This is insane, Lill thought. He had cooperated successfully with city police on other crimes, and now he began talking to Lieutenant Robert Arscott, a veteran policeman who was in charge of office thefts in Washington's downtown area.

Arscott had his own problems—he had inherited a backlog of two hundred unsolved office theft cases. He was pushing his detectives to "get the meat on the table," as he called it, but people were still coming to work in the morning and finding their typewriters missing. Thanks to dogged investigation, detectives had identified quite a few suspects they thought were making their living by stealing, but they were seldom able to catch them in the act or with the goods. When they interrogated suspects they got either nothing or the answers the suspects wanted them to hear. There had to be a better way.

Some of Arscott's detectives thought they could break new ground by posing as criminals themselves. One of the most vocal on that point was Robert W. Sheaffer, Jr., an aggressive young cop with a flair for drama. He wanted to disguise a detective as a fence—as the criminal middleman who bought stolen goods from thieves and resold them to bargain-hunting citizens or to bigger fences. While Sheaffer was looking for a way to start a small-time fencing operation in a storefront, Lill and Arscott began talking about the same approach on a larger scale. Arscott, a seventeen-year veteran of the city police, was known as a hard worker, the kind of man who would knock on 250 doors to get his suspect. In 1973, however, a federal grand jury probing allegations of corruption in the police department, brought indictments against Arscott and several other officers. The lieutenant, charged with bribery of a public official and conspiracy, pleaded innocent, and after a long trial, Arscott was acquitted of all charges. The publicity had embitterd him.

Lill and Arscott, working on Sheaffer's idea, came up with an unusual plan to merge the efforts of the police department *and* the FBI—two rivals who normally jockeyed for credit in solving a local crime—in a fake fencing scheme to snare thieves. They had cooperated occasionally on murders and kidnapings, but never on something so routine as office theft. In August 1975 they dressed a city detective named Vincent Tolson in a mod suit, named him Al White, and stationed him in a tiny office at 1625 K Street, in the heart of Washington's commercial sector. The lawmen let the word get out on the street that Al White, operating from a firm called Urban Consultants and Research, Inc., was really a fence for stolen goods. Meanwhile a handful of FBI men and police staked out the office. The idea was for Al White to take customers into a nearby alley where the surveillance team could photograph them receiving money for stolen goods.

But after two weeks, the lawmen knew that Al White's operation was a failure. The customers they really wanted were staying away, uneasy about coming to a fence in the midst of white-collar Washington. Worse, some of the people who walked into Urban Consultants were men in business suits looking for jobs as urban consultants!

So the task force moved two blocks to a new storefront in the 1400 block of L Street, Northwest, along a street of seedy buildings frequented by prostitutes—a fringe area where maybe the thieves would feel safer and start dealing.

But as the days on L Street drifted by with no significant progress, Arscott and Lill began to be pressured from their superiors. *They* wanted the meat on the table. High-level police officers sought out Lieutenant Garrett T. Kirwin, an intelligence officer who had specialized in operations against fences. "Send them to Frank Herron of the New York City Police Department," said Kirwin. "He's the best fake fence man on the East Coast."

So on September 10 Lill and Arscott, with FBI agent Michael Hartman and police sergeant Karl Mattis, drove the two hundred miles to New York in an unmarked police cruiser to see a man they had never heard of before. It seemed a long way to go for what they felt certain would be a quick brush-off from a busy Manhattan police captain.

Lill, Arscott, Hartman, and Mattis arrived promptly at 9 A.M. the next morning, September 11, for their appointment at 1 Police Plaza, a brick monolith near City Hall and the Brooklyn Bridge. The four expected it would be a short session. They were mildly stunned at their New York reception.

Captain Francis R. Herron, a tall, gray-haired Irishman, greeted them warmly and took them into a conference room next to his office, where he introduced several staff members. Herron said his Special Projects Unit had been staging fake fencing operations for two years. The first one had started in October 1973, when they installed detective Ron Kwosca as the fake fence in a small office in Queens. Every illegal sale was secretly audio-recorded for use in court. A shotgun-carrying backup man was concealed near Kwosca, taking 16 mm silent films of the transactions through a two-way mirror. Other police were staked out across the street, ready to rush in if needed. But none of the planners had foreseen the sickening ease with which customers could overwhelm Kwosca. On Christmas Eve 1973 two men robbed the fake fence. Then they tried to execute him.

Herron turned a 16mm projector on for his Washington visitors. The film showed a near empty office and Kwosca sitting at a desk with his back to the camera. The setup looked startlingly similar to the Washington operation on L Street. On screen, two men walked in, oblivious of the hidden camera. They wore long coats and hats, and they towered over Kwosca. One of them pulled a pistol from his coat. Then the screen suddenly went blank.

"That's where the backup man dropped the camera and picked up his shotgun," Herron explained as the conference room lights came on. "I'll play the tape recording now."

Male voice: *Back away, Ron.*

Kwosca: *Yeah, okay.*

Male voice: *Stay on the floor, Ron. . . . Stay on the floor. . . . Put your hands up . . . hands up. . . .*

The two men spread-eagled the detective and removed his wristwatch and a ring, Herron explained, then rummaged through his desk for cash and found his 9 mm semi-automatic pistol. The backup man watched silently through the two-way mirror, his shotgun loaded and cocked. His orders in such a situation were to let the robbery occur. Herron wanted no bloodshed.

Across the street, the tactical squad waited tensely, listening to the robbers through microphones hidden in the office and planning to intercept them when they emerged.

Then, with no warning, one of the holdup men shot Kwosca in the chest. Kwosca screamed. His backup man, aiming at the ceiling, loosed a blast through the mirror in an attempt to drive the holdup men out; they fired back. The backup man threw himself down and the tactical squad rushed toward the office, firing through the windows.

Police (outside): *Come out!*

Robber: *He'd shoot! He'd shoot!*

Backup man: *I won't shoot—*

Robber: *—He'd shoot me!*

Backup man: *I won't shoot ya, ya motherfucker!*

BLAAMM. A shotgun blast.

Robber: *Okay, we give up, man.*

(Garbled commands to the robbers, followed by furious shouts from police. Grunts and moans. The robbers refused to throw down their guns.)

Police: *Kill him . . . Kill the motherfucker!*

(Another shotgun blast.)

The robber screamed.

(Another shotgun blast.)

Another moan, a fusillade of pistol shots, then silence.

Policeman: *Get the fucking ambulance over here. . . .*

The men from Washington sat stunned. The bullet had gone through Kwosca's right arm and right chest, Herron said, and stopped at the pericardium, the lining around the heart. He survived. "The bullet's still in there—too close to the heart to operate." Kwosca was retired on full disability. One holdup man was killed, the other wounded. Arscott, shaken, abruptly left the conference room. He called Washington and ordered Urban Consultants shut down immediately.

Herron thought that was the second smart thing Arscott had done that day. The first had been to come see him.

Frank Herron, a twenty-five-year veteran of the New York Police Department, was the godfather of phony fencing operations, the men from Washington found out. He had spent two years studying the projects and running his own. His Special Projects Unit, set up in the office of then Chief of Detectives Louis Cottell, had recovered millions of dollars of stolen property, arrested hundreds of thieves, and got headlines from the hardboiled press of the city. There had been no violence since the Kwosca shooting. Herron was a zealot on the subject of fighting theft. He had written a master's thesis for his advanced degree in criminology on methods of recovering stolen property and he willingly shared his expertise with other police departments. Now he told the Washington men how to snare their quarry and keep from getting killed.

"You never know when someone is going to try to take you off," Herron said. *"You must control everything in this operation."*

As Herron spoke, men from his Special Projects Unit were beginning another day of business as Commercial Messenger Service, a fake fencing operation in a storefront in the Bronx. The location was 2701 Decatur Avenue, a neighborhood of whites and Puerto Ricans where burglaries had skyrocketed in recent months. The large plate-glass window of the storefront had been replaced with bullet-proof glass. William Carreras, a veteran plainclothes detective with a gift for street gab, did business from behind a high counter built into a wall. The counter was too high to vault and bullet-proofed inside with thick metal sheets. Carreras could duck beneath it if shooting started.

"Show them a gun when they walk in the place. You don't have to aim it. Nothing to provoke. Just let them see it. You get complete control. Let only a few people in at a time, and know who's coming in."

Detective James Varian stood behind Carreras, holding a shotgun on the customers. A mirror on the opposite wall gave them a clear view of the customers' back pockets—and any guns concealed there. The Commercial Messenger doorbell also rang in an apartment across the street, where three other detectives were ready to rush to trouble.

"You're going to have hundreds of cases if the project goes right. A lot of paperwork. Coordinate everything with the prosecutor's office. Keep them cut in." An assistant D.A. directed all Commercial Messenger cases, while the detectives handled the property forms, charge sheets, and incidents in the case jackets.

"Tell only those who need to know. A leak can come from anywhere. When you rent space, don't tell them you're the police. The landlord might have a brother-in-law who's a hoodlum."

Not even Bronx police commanders knew that Herron's Special Projects men were operating on Decatur Street. Local cops steered clear when they heard it was a project of Internal Affairs, the police arm that investigates police. Fenced items from the project were moved at night by unmarked vehicles to an out-of-the-way room at a remote precinct house. The property was identified, tagged for evidence, and traced to owners.

"You can scout for your customers and hustle them inside. But make it clear you are fences, dealing in hot goods. Don't tell them they should go out on their own and commit a crime, or accept their offers to commit one for you. If you do that, they're going to have an entrapment defense. They're going to say you converted them to crime."

Herron's men scrawled the message "Hot goods—Commercial Messenger" on buildings around the storefront. Detectives scouted for customers by offering money if the person would carry a "hot TV" into the storefront, or would give a man a handful of "hot credit cards" and offer to split the fee when they were sold at Commercial Messenger.

"Customers are going to have many aliases. Get them to tell you who they are. Make it easy on yourselves." Herron's detectives sold raffle tickets to unsuspecting customers and took down their names and addresses in case they "won." They also asked people to supply their names and addresses if they wanted to work for the "organization."

"We now use videotape to record every transaction. It has sound and makes strong cases." Visitors to Commercial Messenger found their attention drawn to nude centerfolds pinned to the wall around a small mirror. On the other side of the phony mirror, a detective stood in a tiny soundproofed room, operating a small videotape television camera. It was linked to a monitor in the trouble squad apartment across the street.

"When the time comes to close down, there will be dozens of suspects. You can't round them all up at once—dupe them into coming to you, and arrest them as they arrive."

That afternoon, the Washington visitors toured a nondescript warehouse in Brooklyn where they found a nest of rooms-within-rooms, a design that could have come from a funhouse—or a fortress. There were false walls, surveillance peepholes, hidden entrances, apertures for listening and recording devices, and elaborate alarms. Hidden firing positions were lined with makeshift bullet-proofing—cinder blocks filled with gravel. For sophistication, inventiveness, and attention to detail, this was an effort far beyond anything the men from Washington had ever imagined. They scribbled furiously in their notebooks.

Many months later, Washington Police Chief Maurice Cullinane would say that Frank Herron had saved the D.C. operation two years of work.

On the drive back to the capital the next day, the four Washington men reviewed their notes and talked excitedly about the kinds of things they might do. The car filled with their laughter. None of the four had the slightest notion that they were on the verge of a five-month undercover operation that would draw headlines—and laughs—across the country.

3

During the third week in September, a late-model Cadillac with New York plates rolled to a stop next to a vacant building at 2254 25th Place, Northeast. A peeling sign atop the building advertised: "Warehouse. Available." Several men clambered out of the car and went next door to the small repair shop of Sheldon Bennett, a sixty-four-year-old maintenance supervisor for the Cafritz Corp. and the caretaker of its vacant warehouse.

"We're from New York," announced a stocky white man with gray hair. "We want to open a repair shop for typewriters and computers . . . saw your sign and wanted to take a look."

"Sure," Bennett said, getting out the key. He was impressed with their appearance; when men in business suits came to 25th Place, it was usually for a good reason. The warehouse was thirty years old, a compact brick building located amid various light-industry plants just off Washington's busy Bladensburg Road.

The whole area, well to the northeast of the Capitol and miles from the sleek downtown office buildings, was on the fringe of some of the most dilapidated, crime-ridden residential sections of the city. Windows in commercial buildings were protected with heavy steel bars, and doors carried warnings about alarm systems. Bullet-proof glass shielded bank tellers, and the screech of police sirens frequently interrupted the rumble of heavy trucks along Bladensburg Road.

Twenty-fifth Place was a narrow street running two blocks from Bladensburg Road to a dead-end at the embanked, fenced-off right-of-way for the Baltimore and Ohio Railroad tracks. The Cafritz building was one of a string of small warehouses lining the south side of the street. The entire north side was taken up by a municipal bus garage and parking lot, cordoned off from thieves and vandals by a high, chain-link fence topped with barbed wire. Several burned-out cars rusted along the sidewalk.

"This would be good," the visitor said. "Quiet neighborhood, and dead-end street."

The man's words surprised Bennett. The dead-end was routinely cursed by trailer-truck drivers trying to turn their rigs around after a stop. Bennett figured the out-of-towners might not know what they were getting into.

Sunlight filtered into the warehouse through grimy glass, falling on the somber grays and browns of concrete floors, cinder-block walls, and dingy ceilings. The building was about 40 feet wide and 120 feet long with two floors of small offices in the front and the rest of the place taken up by cavernous storage rooms in the rear. The visitors wanted to rent the upstairs office —a suite consisting of a single large room with two smaller alcoves and two bathrooms opening off it. "Maybe we could rent just the office first and if things work out, the whole place later on," the leader said.

"Maybe so," said Bennett. But he doubted it. Cafritz management wanted $2000 a month for the whole building. It had been empty for ten years, and there was no reason to think that now they would rent it halfway. He showed them a power-operated overhead garage door in the front that opened to an interior loading dock. "It's wide enough to handle two trucks or three cars," he said.

"Good," said the man. "We can drive our trucks in there, drop the door, lock up, and leave them overnight and not worry. Typewriters are expensive. We wouldn't like them stolen."

At the end of the tour, the men insisted on a quick decision from the Cafritz people, so Bennett placed a call to the company's main office downtown. Thomas Mackall, manager of commercial leasing, took the call from the New Yorker, who, he thought, announced himself as "Mr. R. Scott."

What was the R for, Mackall wondered. Was it Robert or Richard or what? He was nettled; the man had a first name, he ought to use it. Then as he listened more, further uneasy questions flooded his mind. Who needs a typewriter repair shop way the hell out there, miles from the offices where the typewriters are? Why come here from New York to repair typewriters? Aren't there enough typewriters in New York? He cut off the conversation, saying he would check with his boss. The next day when "Scott" called back, Mackall told him no, boss Ray Carter had decided against it.

Several days later, Carter was startled to see two burly men walk unannounced into his private office. One of them swung the door closed, stepped forward, and said, "I'm Lieutenant Robert Arscott of the Metropolitan Police. I want to swear you to secrecy. . . ."

Carter signed for the company on September 24 and told his boss, Cafritz President Martin Atlas, of the arrangement with the police. Despite Herron's warning against revealing the operation to any outsiders, Arscott had already been forced to make an exception. He agreed to pay $250 a month rent, and the company allowed him to make some "temporary additions" inside the office. Bennett was relieved to know that the place next door finally would be rented. His principal companion at the shop was

Rag Mop, a mongrel he had saved from starvation years before. Now he would have some company.

A few days later, Mike Hartman stepped into the Security National Bank branch just across Bladensburg Road from 25th Place and walked up to the manager's desk. The woman stared at him suspiciously through the bullet-proof glass separating them. Her gaze took in the cap pulled over his forehead, his straggly beard, and his olive-drab fatigue jacket. He had worn it to convince people that he was not a lawman and he saw by her hostile stare he was succeeding. In fact, the jacket was part of his uniform as a member of the FBI's Special Weapons and Tactics Squad—its S.W.A.T. team.

"I want to open an account," he said, pulling out $3000.

She riveted her gaze on the money. "Oh my God, you walked in here with that much money? I wouldn't even walk across the room with that!" She looked at him as if she were a high school principal and he a truant. "Where are you employed?"

"P.F.F. Inc.," he said earnestly.

"Oh, come on."

"Yeah. Those are the initials of my three kids."

"What do you do there?"

"Fix office machines. . . . It's right down the street."

The woman manager reluctantly approved the account, but kept staring at him like something was wrong.

From next door to the Cafritz building, Leon "Buzzy" Payne could hear the shriek of a power saw.

Now this is very strange, he thought, as he watched long-haired workmen come and go next door. A dumptruck had just backed into the double-bay loading dock of the Cafritz place and was unloading some fine, brown sand. What did they need sand for in a warehouse?

Buzzy watched for hours, mostly out of curiosity and loneliness. The W. D. Campbell Furniture warehouse, where he was assistant manager, was a solitary place most days, with the trucks and their crews out delivering office furniture. Some days the furniture in storage swelled with the humidity, making strange groans and creaks.

"Hiya," Payne yelled at last to one of the several tough-looking white men. The man scowled and went inside.

Buzzy's curiosity jabbed at him all morning, and at lunch he walked over to the Cafritz warehouse. The metal front door was open; he went in, down a corridor, and up a flight of stairs toward the construction noise. Halfway to the second floor he could see some men there building walls of some sort.

"What the hell do you want?" A man in overalls glared at him.

"I just work next door. . . . I wondered what was goin' on. . . ."

"Well, you see what's goin' on, don't you?"

"Yeah."

"Then you can get the hell on back now."

Payne retreated. These men were no good.

The warehouse caretaker, Sheldon Bennett, was not happy with his new tenants. They refused to talk with him when he said hello; they were making alterations inside the building with cinder blocks, sand, wall studs, and plywood paneling, but wouldn't tell him what it was for. Bennett had called Cafritz officials several times to voice his displeasure, but they didn't seem to pay attention.

Now the tenants had turned downright ugly. They refused to let the meter reader inside the building, and when Bennett called in an electrician friend to repair the automatic garage doors, the bearded men slammed the front door in his face. They had told telephone installers who were eyeing some nude cutouts that they were going to open a massage parlor. And they yelled at the mailman so much that he had stopped coming.

Bennett called Cafritz once again, steaming. "I been in charge out here for twenty-five years!" he exploded. "Those guys you rented to have got me real mad. Let's get 'em outta there!"

There was a momentary pause at the other end. Then one of the Cafritz bosses said, "Now wait a minute, Bennie. . . . Can you keep a secret?"

A few blocks northeast of the Capitol, Thomas Edward (Tee) Brisbon waited with his wife and a friend for a morning bus to take him downtown to the Civil Service Commission where he would see about getting a job.

Looking for work was part of his life cycle. A little hustling, a little jail time, and, when the pressures built from his mother or his wife, a little job-seeking. At the age of twenty-four he sometimes thought that holding down a job was the best way to survive. But something usually seemed to go wrong and he would find himself in court.

An Eldorado Cadillac with New York license plates pulled up and parked illegally at the bus stop. Two men in elegant suits sat inside smoking cigars.

"Anyone here like to make forty dollars moving some furniture?" one of them shouted. Tee looked around; others either pretended not to hear the question or turned away. But Tee was listening. Here he was, going to see about a job, and work was rolling right up to him.

"What do you have to do?" he asked.

"There's no more'n a half-hour's work," one of the men said. "We're movin' into a new office on Bladensburg Road."

"I'm lookin' for a job myself." Tee was suspicious that someone would pay so much for so little work, but it was money, and the job sounded respectable.

"We'll bring you back here; get in the car."

Tee left his wife at the bus stop and along with a pal, call him John, climbed into the back seat of the Cadillac.

"You sure do have some beautiful women in this Washington, D.C., Chocolate City," one of the men with cigars said. Tee liked that, for he was proud of Washington; three out of four Washingtonians are black, and "Chocolate City" bumper stickers, in the Afro-power colors of red, green, and black, are common. "This sure is a hip city," they went on. "Some businessmen like you, you must know some lovely women."

"I'm a married man; my fun is limited," Tee said. John started bragging about some likely bars and clubs.

Had they brought along any of that good New York dope? The men brushed past John's question. "The only thing I don't like about D.C. is the damn bus drivers," the man behind the wheel said in a sharp accent that sounded New York. "They take up the whole street." He rolled down his window to shout obscenities at a passing bus.

Tee quietly surveyed his two new employers. "What line of business are you all in?" he asked. The driver mumbled something about community relations.

From jump street, which is to say from the start, Tee had thought something might be wrong. These guys were just too clean-cut. New York is fast, he thought, but everyone he had seen from there had at least a little bit of dirt under the fingernails. These dudes' fingernails were clean.

At 25th Place and Bladensburg Road, N.E., the men stopped at an Amoco gas station and made a telephone call.

"Where the place we got to go to move that stuff?" Tee inquired. John started arguing that he wasn't gonna work all day and move a whole office for forty bucks.

"Take it easy," one of the men said, smiling at John. "I like you for some reason. You got gumption." He poked his companion in the ribs and chuckled.

The pay phone abruptly rang and one of the men answered it, talked briefly, and hung up. He jumped back in the car and they drove down 25th Place and pulled up in front of a warehouse. All four got out and the driver popped the trunk lid open. Inside were two new IBM electric typewriters.

"Man, this all we got to move and you gonna give us forty dollars?" Tee asked.

"Yeah."

They must be real big dudes in this business to be throwing around that kind of money, Tee thought. He and John each hoisted a machine.

"Wait a minute," one of the men said, reaching into the trunk and pulling out a sawed-off shotgun. This is it, Tee thought. He wanted to drop the typewriter and run. "Naw, it's okay, this ain't nothin'." The man smiled. He turned the shotgun upside down; Tee thought most of the guts were missing and the gun wouldn't work. He felt some strength ease back into him. They must use the gun to scare people away from their office, he figured.

The man with the gun opened the front door of the warehouse and led Tee and John up the stairs. His partner stayed behind, saying he owed the people inside $600. "If they ask me where I'm at, tell 'em I'm uptown," he said, lounging against the Cadillac.

Tee wondered whether he should find a way to excuse himself. These two dudes could easily carry the typewriters themselves; but then they must have plenty of money. They looked successful.

The stairs went up to the second floor, where they ran into a locked door with a large window in it.

"Who is it?" a voice shouted through the door.

The man with the cigar gave his name.

"Anybody with you?"

He named his helpers.

"Show your faces."

Tee, peering in the window, could see a long counter but not the source of the voice.

The door buzzed open. The employer pushed it back for John and Tee, who thanked him for his politeness.

They found themselves inside a small room with one cinder-block wall and three oddly angled walls of dark wood paneling. A wide counter about 8 feet long was built into the longest paneled wall. Pictures of calculators and office equipment were tacked below it. A bearded white man with sharp blue eyes stood behind the counter, staring hard at their faces. Tee tightened.

Another white man, pointing what looked like a shotgun, stood a few feet behind the counterman and was mostly hidden by his own counter. He wore a beard and had dark sunglasses that hid his eyes.

Tee spotted a large mirror—surrounded by pictures of nude women—set into the wall alongside the front counter, but he was too scared to dwell on them.

The entrance door locked shut with a buzz. At that moment, Tee thought he was going to be killed. He could bolt for the door, he thought, but he'd never make it. He wished he had never got into the Cadillac. He and John gingerly set the typewriters on the counter.

"Who is this?" the counterman yelled, riveted on Tee. They turned to their escort with an imploring look.

"Oh, this Tee and John, two of my buddies uptown." He smiled.

The bearded man gave his customers a soul handshake. "My name is Pasquale Larocca, and this here is Michael Franzino. Call me Pat. We're the biggest fences in the U.S. We take anything you got!"

A bottle of gin, a bottle of Jack Daniels, and a large fluted glass beer mug stood on the counter to Tee's right. At Pasquale's invitation, Tee poured himself a mugful of Jack Daniels. After he downed that, he helped himself to the gin.

"Hey, how you like those broads, huh?" Pat inquired, motioning Tee's gaze toward several large *Playboy* nudes plastered around a mirror.

"Nice, man, nice," Tee said.

Pasquale eyed the typewriters. "Well, what you want for it?" Tee looked nervously to the escort in the corner of the room.

"Gimme three hundred dollars," the man said.

"Man, I can't give you no three hundred dollars for this," the counterman said. The New Yorker then offered his sawed-off to Pasquale, who gave it to Franzino. Damn, Tee thought, I know the thing don't work. Can't the man see that for himself? "I'll give you two hundred and sixty dollars," Pasquale said, as if satisfied with the weapon.

"Yeah, okay," said the man with the cigar.

Pat doesn't know good from broken, Tee thought.

Pasquale produced a green tin box, dropped it on the counter under the noses of Tee and John, jacked it open, and counted out the money from stacks and stacks of crisp new tens and twenties.

"Where's the other guy at?" Pat asked the man in the corner.

"He's uptown."

Pat leaned over the counter and looked at Tee: "I know you're a good thief.

"Man, I don't do no stuff like that."

"I take checks, credit cards, money orders, pieces, anything hot as long as it's good. Tell your buddies about us." Pasquale handed Tee a half-dozen white business cards which said "P.F.F. Inc., 2254 25th Place, N.E., Washington, D.C. Phone 526–4032." In a corner of the card he wrote the name, Pat, in ink and underlined it. In another five months, Tee would learn that P.F.F. Inc. stood for Police-FBI Fencing, Incognito.

Pat gave Tee and John each a new $20 bill, and the remainder of the money to the man with the cigar. They parted over another soul handshake and smiles.

Tee felt pretty good. It had worked out; he had got some money for easy work, and found out about something that might bring him more money. Going downstairs, he expressed his relief to the man who had brought him. "Damn," Tee said, grinning, "and here I thought something was wrong with you, that you were the police or something!"

The man laughed.

They piled back into the Cadillac and pulled away, but John was getting a little hot. "Hey, you guys told us we'd each get forty dollars. Where's the rest?"

"Hold on, hold on, you'll get your money," they said, pulling out another $20 to each. "Be cool, be cool."

Hundreds of bucks for two typewriters and a gun that doesn't work, Tee thought as they drove back to Northeast. His confrontation with Pat and Mike had stimulated his senses; now, with the Jack Daniels and gin sweeping over him, he felt giddy.

In his soundproofed room at P.F.F. behind a phony mirror, Detective William F. Gately, Jr., who now called himself Tony Bonano, stopped his Night-Gard video camera, carefully re-wound the tape, and played it back. The small monitor filled with the black-and-white images of Tee and John. The mirror, mounted in a wall a few feet from Pat's head, was close enough to provide detailed closeups of the customer's faces. Their voices, picked up through hidden microphones overhead and in the countertop, generally were clear. Tony Bonano was elated. The system worked fine.

Each morning during early October, the two men who had picked up Tee and John, a detective and an FBI agent, prowled in their Cadillac for likely criminals, while inside P.F.F. the four white undercover men waited. The scouts cruised particularly along the 14th Street and T Street corridors in Northwest Washington, where thieves trafficking stolen goods looked for sales among packs of dope pushers, junkies, hustlers, kids, and bargain hunters lounging in smoky poolrooms or milling amid the litter in front of fast-food stands and armored liquor stores. The scouts found people stepping out of the shadows to listen to their pitch and look at their goods. Many suspected it was a setup and walked away. A few, like Tee Brisbon, went with them to the warehouse, carried the goods inside, and asked no questions. Slowly, the word was spreading that people could go to this warehouse and come back with money.

For the white men inside, the first days were stretched with tension. The men realized how vulnerable they were. Arscott, posing as a thief, had tested the operation just before it opened October 1. Although the men thought they had planned for every possible surprise, Arscott had stunned them when he simply reached across the fencing counter, grabbed the counterman, and put a gun to his head. The counterman couldn't drop clear and the other men were helpless. They could only hope that a customer would never realize this.

The men were also aware that the project, unique in scope and method, had the blessing and attention of Chief Cullinane and FBI Washington Bureau Chief Nick F. Stames—each was pouring thousands of dollars from tight budgets into P.F.F. to catch thieves. Arscott talked to his men like a football coach before the big game. "I want you to do this one for me, men, do it for me," he urged. None of the men in the warehouse was yet thirty. Some believed their careers could hinge on whether they succeeded or failed.

In the first weeks, Tony Bonano and Detective Robert W. Sheaffer, Jr., who now called himself Bohanna La Fontaine, almost came to blows. Bonano didn't think the two scouts were working hard enough and announced that he was calling Arscott. Some of the other men did not agree with Bonano's criticism. "Put that phone down," barked Pasquale, the counterman.

"Whaddya mean? I'm a detective, you're a detective—you're not my boss," Bonano retorted. He began dialing. Suddenly, the phone was coming down around his ears. Sheaffer had thrown a chair that knocked the phone set from the wall. "He said to put that phone down!" Sheaffer screamed.

"Okay, I'll just use the other phone," Bonano said. "You gonna knock that one off the wall, too?" Bonano was next aware of something hurtling scythelike toward his head. He ducked and Bohanna La Fontaine's forearm crashed into the wall. Bonano conceded the dispute. Franzino, the backup man, mentioned the scout problem to Lill and soon two more black undercover detectives, were added. Eventually, Bonano and La Fontaine went out scouting, too, to relieve some of the pressure.

On October 14, two weeks after the warehouse opened, the first customer walked in without a scout. It was Tee Brisbon, and he brought a friend, James Alfonso Washington. Tee, who had been to P.F.F. only once before—with a scout—greeted Pat and Mike as if they had been friends for years. "They down from New Yawk to organize D.C!" Tee beamed at his friend, savoring a big-brother role. "They pay the best prices in town." Washington asked Pat how he could get in touch with him in the future. "He'll give you his card, man, he's got a card," Tee interrupted.

Washington had brought movie equipment and Pat knowingly offered much more than they could get anywhere else. "Shit, man, you can do better than that!" Tee complained. Washington looked at his friend as if to lock his mouth up. It seemed to the lawmen he was after this connection and didn't want Tee messing it up. "That's fine, man," Washington said. After the two customers left, the P.F.F. men grinned. Half in jest they chided Pat for paying too much for the equipment. But they all realized, from the way they had been accepted by Washington, that they would not have to pay as much next time.

As the six scouts worked through the last half of October, the word continued to spread on the street, and by the end of the month, the scouts were no longer necessary. The trickle was becoming a stream. Customers began appearing on their own, bringing friends and coming back again.

Most of the thieves were streetwise drug addicts from black Washington. The four white men waiting for them in the warehouse lived in suburban Prince George's County, Maryland, and were part of a predominantly white police force for the District of Columbia. This was consistent with the rest of the law-enforcement picture in Washington: most prosecutors, judges, and defense attorneys are white; the jails, prisons, courtrooms, and drug treatment centers are filled with blacks. White dominance of the key positions in government, business, and the professions is a fact of life in Washington, even though 75 percent of the city's 700,000 people are black. That the four lawmen in P.F.F. lived in the suburbs was also consonant with Washington social and racial patterns. Most of the whites in the Washington metropolitan area live either in the Virginia or Maryland suburbs, or in an enclave in the Northwest quadrant of the city. The black sections, while dominated by law-abiding citizens in comfortable if sometimes modest residences, are also spotted with neighborhoods of boarded-up and broken row houses, dilapidated apartments, glass-littered streets, and vacant lots strewn with abandoned cars and furniture. These areas are home for most of the city's estimated 18,000 drug addicts who, police say, commit most of the crime in Washington.

To play the key role of counterman, Pasquale Larocca, Arscott and Lill selected a natural salesman, Detective Patrick J. Lilly, an energetic twenty-six-year-old with down-home roots from his West Virginia childhood. Lilly "could con a wino out of his wine," one fellow officer claimed. He had been a police officer since the age of twenty and had distinguished himself with excellent undercover work. Detective Robert W. Sheaffer, Jr., Lilly's partner and the man who had pushed the K Street operation, gave himself an alias, Bohanna La Fontaine, that he could pronounce but never could spell. Sheaffer, a burly two hundred pounds, ran the camera at first and worked behind the scenes at the evidence table, processing stolen goods brought in by customers. He was set apart from the others by his sense of humor and devotion to weightlifting.

William F. Gately, Jr., a.k.a. Tony Bonano, was a quiet, dedicated lawmen who soon took over the camera operation from Sheaffer and also helped process evidence. Gately, at twenty-seven, had received a Bronze Star and three Purple Hearts in the Marine Corps in Vietnam. He had once been shot and left for dead when his company was overrun, only to be found by body-counters three days later, and had escaped death another time when the medical evacuation helicopter carrying him to doctors crashed into the sea and sank with most aboard. He floated free while strapped to a buoyant stretcher.

Michael Hartman, a.k.a. Mike Franzino, was the FBI man of the warehouse four. He had the build of a thug and the enthusiasm for the part, but like most FBI agents, he had in fact never done undercover work. A former all-city high school fullback, he attended West Point for two years, then finished college at night at the University of Maryland while working for the FBI as a lab technician. He approached his assignment with some apprehension, although that quickly evaporated when he looked down his shotgun barrel at the first customers and realized they were much more tense than he.

What the customers saw inside P.F.F. was considerably less than what there was. The undercover men had built a room within a room. Behind the false walls, in passageways carpeted to keep the noise down, they could walk to the hidden camera room, the hidden evidence-processing area, or the hidden toilets. Bonano and La Fontaine silently prowled these corridors, armed and on watch—shock troops kept out of sight of skittish customers.

From behind a fake air conditioning vent that was mounted on springs and dropped at a touch, Tony Bonano or Bohanna La Fontaine could watch the backs of the customers—and any moves they might make to guns in their pockets.

A customer entering P.F.F. had only a small area to move about. He faced the counter, built into a partition of wood-paneled walls, about 4 feet high, 8 feet long and 2½ feet deep —making it too high to vault.

The inside front and top of the counter were faced with steel plate supported by cinder blocks filled with sand—the sand that had puzzled Bennett when it was dumped outside the warehouse.

Pasquale's colleagues fired a rifle into it before they were sure it would be safe for him.

The operation of P.F.F. had been designed so that the men themselves could exert maximum control, yet maintain the illusion of a fencing ring. Before a customer could enter P.F.F. he was instructed to telephone ahead from the pay booth outside the Amoco gas station a half-block away, at the corner of 25th Place and Bladensburg Road. Visitors could come up only after Pat called them back. He admitted one person at a time, or two or three if they were connected with the same theft. "I don't want you interruptin' anybody else's business, and you don't want anybody interruptin' your business," he explained of the required advance call. The customers said they understood.

The men rigged a dead phone next to the counter, and when Pat occasionally found himself speechless, he scratched the back of his head, and Franzino pushed a button that rang the dead phone. Pat then pretended to talk to some Mafia boss in New York, and thus gained some time to prepare himself.

The way they had worked it out, no one was supposed to be able to surprise the lawmen. When the front door—unlocked during business hours—was opened, it set off a high-pitched flutter-noise alarm audible only inside the P.F.F. office. Once up the stairs, the customer was instructed to show his face in the Plexiglas window of the door before Pat would buzz the electric lock and let him in. As the customer entered, Pat checked a mirror on the opposite wall that enabled him to inspect the customer's back pocket for a gun. If anything looked suspicious any of the lawmen could summon the others to battle stations by triggering a silent alarm system of red Christmas tree lights. The man in the camera booth also had a shotgun, and as a last resort could blast through the mirror.

The door to the camera room, locked each night, carried a sign to discourage prowlers: "Warning—High Voltage—Do Not Enter."

When they left, the men switched on a sophisticated alarm installed by the FBI that covered the P.F.F. office and the rest of the warehouse. Sound beams triggered a tape recorder wired into the phones that placed calls in succession to the FBI field office and the homes of Lill and Arscott and the P.F.F. men, announcing: "An important message will follow. . . . There has been a break-in at P.F.F. Inc., 2254 25th Place, Northeast."

For added security, Pasquale and Mike told their customers that P.F.F. was protected on weekends by a Mafioso armed with a shotgun. This New York Italian, Pasquale said, "had his tongue cut out in a gang war. He's crazy, he never sleeps, he just shoots people." In five months of operation, there was no indication that anyone ever broke into the warehouse.

As Pat and Mike gained more confidence, they pressed harder to find out who the thieves were. Pat would come right out and ask, "Who the hell are you?" and sometimes the thief would give his real name. More often than not, however, the men were left to identify somebody like "Squirrelly," "Bow-legged Skip," "Zorro," "Weasel," "Pumpkin Head," "Graytop," "Blind," "Claws," and "We" ("Just call me 'We,' like, We the People"). Others gave proper names that were made up. Customers picking up a glass of wine or Jack Daniels left fingerprints that were dusted off and taken after each visit. When the customers drove away, Tony Bonano, tracking them from the second floor with a set of binoculars, jotted down license numbers.

Some of the customers stared suspiciously at the mirror, trying to detect any secrets that might be behind it. Even from one inch away the mirror looked like a mirror. It was revealed as a window only when light got into the camera room, but the men made sure that the door stayed closed. Some customers combed their hair in the mirror. Others regretted not finding out about the warehouse sooner: "I wished I'd a known about you all," said one visitor. "I had a couple a sawed-offs yesterday, and I practically gave 'em away."

Pat and the other men in the warehouse talked freely of "the family," and their boss in New York, the capo of capos, the Don. "He sent me down to organize the city," Pat explained. "We got

33

some friends in the police department; they'll leave us alone." The place had a front as a repair shop, Pat explained, pointing to posters of office machines and calculators on the P.F.F. walls.

"I'm Pasquale Larocca—call me Pat. What's your name?" he asked the customers. "Speak up, SPEAK UP!" he shouted at people who mumbled. "I got shot in the head in a gang war in New York; I no hear so good in-a this ear—see the scar?" Gently he would lift some of his shaggy black hair and point at more hair. A few customers stared and nodded; others said, "Yeah," perhaps unwilling to admit they saw no scar. "Speak in-a this ear," he said, tugging at his right ear, which was positioned just over the hidden microphone in a dead electric outlet on the countertop.

The customers, locked in this warehouse in Northeast Washington with these armed, bearded men jabbering in Italian, had never experienced anything like it. "Eh, Mike, bacha-ma-gu, bessamacu, me-dee-chi, me-dee-chi," Pat barked at his enforcer, gesturing wildly as he made up what he thought were Italian-sounding words. "That's Michael Franzino . . . he's my heavy, my heat," he explained.

"Eh, Pat, simpatico, simpatico," Franzino yelled back, waving his Remington pump-action FBI-issue riot shotgun. He had heard the word from his wife's grandmother, an Italian; she used it to describe food, but he felt he could make liberal use of it anyway.

"Man," one astounded customer remarked, "this is just like on television."

"I've been looking for a connection like this for a long time," another beamed after Pat handed him some crisp green bills. To each Pat handed one of the company's business cards.

"You got something for me, you call me first," Pat told them. "And don't lose the card. We don't want the rollers to get it."

Within a few weeks Mike Franzino began surprising himself

at how real his Italian sounded. Some of the customers began to refer to Mike and Pat as "our Italian brothers," as they exchanged soul handshakes. "Arriverderci," Franzino would say to them as they left. "Ciao . . . !" After a while some of them replied, "Solid, man. Arriverderci."

5

Frank Herron came to Washington on November 18 to inspect the P.F.F. operation, and he liked what he saw. The lawmen were running it with flair and control. Then he went to the federal courthouse at the foot of Capitol Hill to talk to Daniel Bernstein, a young prosecutor who had been assigned to oversee all the Sting cases.

Herron found the main hallway of the courthouse nearly deserted. The air seemed antiseptic—no gamy smells of perspiring people or stale cigarette smoke—and the floors were spotless. A guard drooped behind his desk at the far end, watching an outside door through which no one passed. Where were the swarms of prosecutors, defense attorneys, defendants, witnesses, families, all shouting at each other—the scenes so familiar in the crowded courts of New York City?

The police captain turned to his escort, FBI agent Tom

Easton: "Tom, what *is* this place?"

"The federal courthouse."

"Oh, really?"

They rode an empty elevator to the fourth floor and walked down another quiet corridor. Large double doors of blond wood opened into cavernous, deserted courtrooms. Hey, Herron thought, you could roll a bowling ball down this hallway and not hit a thing.

He strode through a large outer office, quiet except for the pecking of two secretaries, and into Bernstein's office. His desktop was tidy: phone, calendar, light. No crammed files piled up, no in- and out-boxes jammed to overflowing. No telephone ringing incessantly. The poor prosecutors in Manhattan should see this, Herron thought.

Bernstein introduced himself and sat down for some talk. "Tell me, are you still in business here?" Herron asked with an impish grin.

Bernstein looked at him, expressionless.

For the next hour, the two men discussed the prosecution process in New York, where elected district attorneys and their hundreds of assistants handle local criminal cases; and Washington, where its status as a federal city threw most prosecutions into the U.S. Attorney's office, regardless of whether the crimes violated local or federal laws. Both men found the conversation interesting but the differences between the two cities were so great that precise comparison was difficult. And all the time, Herron found himself uneasy about the sleepy pace of business in the nation's capital. Bernstein conceded that he had not even been to the P.F.F. warehouse, an omission Herron found incomprehensible. He thought of Brent Blacksburg, an excitable assistant district attorney in Queens who would work right through a weekend alongside the police to make his cases, and George Mayer, another assistant D.A. who had worked so many hours on a Bronx undercover operation that his wife wondered if he had found another woman. Herron advised Bernstein to call these two men, for perhaps he could benefit from the things they had learned, and he left their telephone numbers behind. Bernstein never called.

Bernstein's phlegmatic, bookish manner seldom stirred the hearts of others; he may have appeared unenthusiastic to Herron, but Bernstein believed his planning was sound; he enjoyed careful preparation of cases and talked extensively with the P.F.F. men about how to catch criminals and avoid losing cases later in court.

A thirty-one-year-old native Washingtonian who had attended local schools and Georgetown Law School, Bernstein had spent his entire legal career as a prosecutor, working up from routine jobs handling grand jury presentations to the complexities of undercover investigations. He knew defense attorneys would be eager to try to show that police who posed as criminals had actually enticed innocent men into committing crimes.

Counterman Pat, he ordered, must never suggest that a customer steal anything. Instead, Pat should only say that he would buy hot goods. That way, he was not technically implanting the idea of stealing; he would only be catering to criminal intentions already in a customer's mind. Legally, that was not entrapment.

Bernstein wanted the P.F.F. men to draw admissions from the customers that they had committed specific crimes, knew other thieves, sold other items to other fences, and were contemptuous of police, courts, and the law. All this would provide the prosecutors with a "good fact pattern," as Bernstein put it, and help lead to convictions.

The lawmen knew from experience on the streets and in courtrooms that their quarry were chiefly hardened criminals who floated in and out of the criminal justice system; when they weren't locked behind bars, they preyed on people. They lacked formal education, but they held master's degrees in sliding through the courts and prisons and getting back on the street. After repeated arrests and convictions, the criminals knew which judges were most lenient and which were gullible to feigned attacks of remorse. They knew the nuances of plea-bargaining a felony charge down to a misdemeanor. They had learned that when the evidence was against them, it was to their advantage to postpone trials as long as possible by faking an illness or requesting mental observations. In the interim, witnesses sometimes disappeared or died or forgot key testimony.

The P.F.F. warehouse was attracting not only office thieves, but people who admitted to armed robberies, auto thefts, hijackings, stealing from the mails, and many different kinds of firearms violations. The customers bragged to Pasquale about how they had fooled the courts and how they could beat any charge. One man came to the warehouse during a noontime break in his criminal trial and fenced his defense attorney's wallet.

Bernstein and his boss, Donald Campbell, saw that the videotapes were the key to success. The lawmen would show judges and juries, once and for all, that the P.F.F. customers were laughing at the system and twisting it to their own advantage.

They had been skeptical of the videotapes at first, since both of them had lost cases because of defective or confusing tape recordings. Concealed tape recorders and transmitters sometimes pick up dog barks and make them sound like lion's roars, or coughs that sound like thunderclaps, interrupting crucial conversations. But the P.F.F. videotapes had none of those problems —the sound was clear and the black-and-white pictures were unmistakable. The prosecutors realized that these tapes would make it impossible for the suspects to escape jail.

In many incidents, the videotape evidence was so incriminating that the prosecutors thought the defendants would be left no choice but to accept whatever small concession the government might offer in return for a guilty plea—a somewhat lighter sentence, for example—and in return the government got a reliable, quick way to put suspects behind bars. A defendant voluntarily entering a guilty plea waived his right to appeal the conviction. His fate was sealed; only the sentencing remained.

The prosecutors viewed jury trials as expensive and unpredictable, therefore undesirable. Juries misled by artful defense performances had acquitted guilty men, setting them free to prey once more on the city. Higher courts overturned convictions of violent criminals because juries had been improperly instructed, or judges intemperate, or prosecutors flustered and forgetful. Carefully constructed prosecutions had collapsed when key witnesses perjured themselves or failed to show up. Sometimes defendants free on bail had simply not appeared for their trials. So the prosecutors considered the jury trial a necessary evil to be avoided wherever possible. Campbell conceded that this wasn't American justice as portrayed by high school civics books, which tout trial by a jury of one's peers as the highest form of justice. But this was the view of a man tempered by years of dealing with hapless victims, multiple offenders, angry police, and jammed court calendars. The prosecutors anticipated that when the P.F.F. operation was ended, defendants would be marched quickly through the courts and, they hoped, sent to jail for a long time.

Every day Pasquale Larocca and Mike Franzino studied their own performances on tape replay, looking for better interrogation techniques. They agonized when they realized they had left out some important line of inquiry. But by the end of November there had been more than two hundred separate videotaped transactions, and Larocca and Franzino had become accomplished in their undercover identities, handling their parts briskly and with assurance in front of the hidden camera.

On December 2, for example, when two customers called ahead with an item to sell, Pat took up his position behind the counter and Tony Bonano turned on the camera and videotaping equipment in the booth. Pat faced the mirror, holding up a small slate blackboard with a diagonally striped black-and-white wooden clapper on top, the familiar Hollywood invention for marking film scenes and takes.

"December 2, 1975, Location One, Incident number two-seventeen, actor Lilly," he said, clapping the board and stowing it beneath the counter.

Tony focused the camera on the wall at the other end of the room where a clock indicated 1:42 and an adjacent calendar read

"Today's date is December 2." For the record he now had the day and time of the incident, and the incident number of the clapboard, all coordinated with the suspect's entry.

The two customers hauled in something in a large white flour sack. They plopped it down on the counter, and Pasquale reached into the bag and pulled out a 22 cal. bolt-action rifle with a short barrel. "A sawed-off rifle," he announced for the record.

"Yeah, magnum," answered one of the customers.

Pat cocked the rifle, aimed it between the two men and pulled the trigger, the firing pin making a small metallic click. He wanted the camera to record that the gun worked.

"Is it yours?"

The man shook his head.

Pasquale stared at him. "What!"

"The dude's waitin' downstairs. . . ."

Pat glared. "Well, bring him up, man!"

The customer smiled.

"I'm serious!" Pasquale barked. "Go bring him up!" He wanted the owner and weapon together for the camera.

"Both of you go get him!" Pasquale commanded. "Talk to him! Tell him I want to meet him! He might have more of this good shit!"

They returned with a third man, and Pat gave him a soul shake. "I'm Pasquale Larocca."

"Fred," the newcomer said.

"Fred?"

"Yeah."

"You got any more pieces like this one?" Pat was trying right off for an admission that could lead to a five-year charge of illegal trafficking in prohibited weapons. But Fred did not answer. "You saw this off yourself?" Another five-year felony—unlicensed manufacture of weapons.

Fred nodded. "It was brand new, you know, about this long." He spread his hands along the counter to show the rifle's original length.

"This one?" Pat asked, to eliminate a possible later claim

that the customer was talking about a different gun.

"Yeah. Had to saw the piece of the back off, too," Fred said, referring to the cut-down wooden stock.

"How you come across pieces like this?" Pat asked, seeking other names which might lead to a conspiracy charge. He held the rifle at arm's length and snapped off a make-believe round next to Fred's ear.

"Well . . . mmm." The customer paused, and mumbled something.

Pat glowered again. "Well, in other words, would you run across them in quantity?" he asked, trying for an illegal arms dealer charge.

"No . . . well . . . every now and then, you know."

Pasquale wasn't going to be deflected. "Occasional?"

"Yeah, mostly pistols."

"We could use some of these."

"Yeah?" Fred asked.

"You want to make some money, then?"

"Yeah."

"Well, you got any pistols you want to get rid of?"

"Not right now. I'm gonna check this afternoon because I gave my brother-in-law one of them," he said, offering a potential lead.

One of Fred's friends mentioned typewriters that could be brought in. "IBM?" Pat asked. "What kind? Selectric?"

"Yeah, electric," Fred said. "I don't know brand names."

Pasquale gave him a business card and began trying for facts he might have missed. "Ah . . . you have much trouble sawing this sonofabitch down?"

"He helped me," Fred said, pointing a thumb at a companion. "I had a brand-new hacksaw, you know. . . ." He grinned. But he hadn't said he'd actually done the cutting. Pat moved to fill this crucial gap.

"You did a job, huh?" he said with a warm smile.

"Yeah," Fred said proudly.

Franzino suddenly spoke up: "We can deal with every gun

42

you can get. Typewriters, too. . . . Ever use this thing?" he asked, nodding at the sawed-off rifle.

Fred nodded silently; the camera recorded his admission on videotape.

Pat, careful not to raise Fred's suspicions by asking too many questions, now dropped the subject. "What you asking for it?"
"Seventy-five."

"Okay, it's yours." The transaction was interrupted by a phone call. "I got an important gentleman in here. . . . I'm rapping with him," Pat told the caller. "Call me back. See?" he said, returning to Fred. "He'd a been right up here, knowing your shit. That way, the stuff didn't happen and nobody can say, 'Pasquale Larocca fucked up.' " Fred nodded. The lawmen used plenty of profanity, figuring that it would help establish underworld credibility.

Pat snapped off the money from a stack of bills in his hand.

"Awwright, thank you," Fred murmured, scooping up the bills.

"If you got a friend you like, you trust, a dude you hustle with, you know, whatever, you can bring him up . . . and come back next time," Pasquale said.

Fred wasn't ready to go. "What about a floor-model color TV?" he asked.

Pat drummed his fingers on the counter. Here was a dangerous question. If he answered, "Yes," the defense could later try to say that Pat told Fred to commit a specific crime.

"What I've done for the past two weeks, I've slowed down on takin' that shit for this reason and this reason alone," he answered, moving smoothly into the standard cover story that would also show a jury later that Fred knew he was dealing with criminals. "We have a couple outlets in New York—ah . . . so-called legitimate stores—but one of them got busted and we got an overload of shit in another place . . . so soon as we reestablish that store, we can go ahead and you know, move that shit easier. What we do is . . . just to give you a brief idea of how big this thing is . . . we got stores and certain numbers of chains and this kind of shit, and we resell it to the market. You see?"

Fred nodded impassively. ". . . This is, uh, another thing . . . ," he began haltingly. ". . . This is, uh, like, um—" His face suddenly contorted, and he raised a clenched fist and thrashed the air as he struggled to describe the electronic mystery machine in his mind. "—It's a camera . . . like you could see yourself on TV . . . you . . . you take it?"

"Bring it in and I'll have a look at it," Pat said, this time skirting the entrapment issue by promising nothing. "Where is it?"

"I got it at home, you know?"

"Okay." Pat soul-popped the three men, and as they moved toward the door, said abruptly, "What's your name again?"

"Fred."

"Right. Gimme another street name, anything . . . I got fifteen fuckin' Freds. . . ."

"Al." It sounded like Owl.

"Al? A-L?" Pasquale repeated.

"Yeah."

"Okay, good enough, Albert," Pasquale smirked. "Check you all later."

As Al/Fred drove away, they checked his license plate and phoned it to central records. They were told the car was registered to an "Alfred Blane Perryman."

"Now that's a real clever alias!" the lawmen laughed.

Pasquale and Mike felt pretty certain, after eight weeks of success, that they had devised cons to handle every kind of customer. But when prostitutes walked in and demanded to know why the men wouldn't have sex with them, they were speechless.

Inez, as we'll call her, was the first. She showed up in November. "Don't you guys ever get out of here?" she murmered, lingering around the counter. The men were not prepared for a customer who wouldn't leave; in fact, they never imagined any of them would want to stay. But Inez had already sold her stolen credit cards, and it was clear what she wanted.

"Yeah . . . well . . . uh, you know how it is," Pat stammered. For a long time they just looked at each other like a couple out on a first date, Mike thought. She was a skinny junkie and had a boyish figure. How would a Mafioso handle this? The conversation drifted, and then suddenly she had her clothes off, and was pirouetting naked.

"Doesn't anybody want to do nuthin?" she whined.

Inez thought for a moment, and then bent over, shoved the butt end of a cigarette into her vagina, and began gyrating to keep it lit. Puffs of smoke rose in the chill air. The men's jaws went slack. ". . . Hey . . . that's real nice," one of them said, dumfounded.

They got rid of her finally by saying they had a truckful of stolen merchandise "comin' in real soon" and had to get back to work. When she had dressed and gone, the astounded men clustered around the camera room.

Bohanna came out with a sheepish grin on his face. "Forget it! She stuck around so long trying to talk to Pat, I ran out of tape fifteen minutes ago!"

They made sure the camera never ran out of tape again.

Of thirty women who came into the warehouse, five were prostitutes who exposed themselves for the men. Pat and Mike played their parts as Mafia gangsters to the hilt, but apparently never touched any of them. Too busy with their other work, they said.

The men never backed off when a woman began to strip— they wanted credibility with the prostitutes, who could be good sources of information and might even bring them some customers.

One woman was especially aggressive, calling the men one day from a nearby motel. "I got a room all day and I'm lonely," she said. The men passed the telephone around. Finally one of them told her they had work to do. But soon she was in the warehouse stripping for them. "Don't you guys want to jam?"

"Well, we got another truckload comin'," they said.

"You want it right now?"

"Problem is, Pat's a fag," they said.

"No shit!"

"Sure. That's what P.F.F. stands for—Pat's Faggot Fencing!"

Despite the elusive tactics of the Mafia men, the women returned several times. One of them brought her madam to try to convince them to take a break from work. When women stripped, the men telephoned their supervisors to let them know an unusual tape was on the way.

The yawning, the watering eyes, the yellow slime in his throat told Cockeye it was time to go creeping. He had been awake about a half-hour.

Credit cards were easy to come by: he was making easy money selling them to Pat. But that was not enough to keep the yawning away.

About midday, Cockeye pulled on his clothes and thought about the pictures on the wall in Pat's warehouse. Next to the *Playboy* nudes, there were leaflets showing various office machines. "What's that shit?" Cockeye had asked Pat the day before. And Pat had explained how much certain machines were worth, say, nineteen hundred or two thousand bucks. Cockeye didn't know what they were, but they had names like IBM on them and were "computers and shit like that." And he knew they were portable.

He thought about the machines while his bowels broke over

a toilet for the first of many times that day. Damn, he thought, I've seen some of them damn things in my travelings that I couldda had but never took the chance. He had been in government buildings several times a week in recent months, grabbing up purses and typewriters from unattended desks. No one had ever caught him. Now he wanted a computer.

At age thirty-six, Cockeye had spent half his adult life in prison, and most of his adolescence in correctional institutions. His right eye wandered independent of the left, a result of his lifetime use of heroin, and the flesh on his face sagged. To protect his heroin-dilated eyes from light, he wore sunglasses day and night.

Shortly after the lunch hour, he walked into the modern glass-walled main building of the Department of Health, Education and Welfare in Southwest Washington. He strode into a room where he had been before, a room that stuck in his mind because it was unattended and full of IBM equipment.

The thing he wanted was atop a five-foot machine. It was hooked into the larger machine and running all the time. It was big but it could be carried, Cockeye thought, and Pat would want it. But damn, a black man can't just walk out of here with that.

In an office where two dozen women in partially enclosed cubicles typed correspondence and memos, Ko-Rec-Type at the ready, Cockeye found a cardboard box full of books and correspondence. He dumped them onto the floor. One of the secretaries leaned over her partition and stared.

"I'm just gettin' a box." He smiled, waving the empty carton at her. The secretary nodded and returned to her typing.

It was usually like that in government buildings. No one questioned Cockeye so long as he didn't give himself away. No one was really concerned, except for the cleaning ladies. They were the most curious, and the hardest to fool.

Cockeye unplugged the machine he wanted. It was heavier than he expected, and he had to ease it off the top of the larger machine and cradle it against his chest, letting it slide slowly down his leisure suit to the empty cardboard box, which, he suddenly and sickeningly realized, was too small. The sides of the carton collapsed. "Shit," he said. His suit was clinging damply to him, more from the drugs sweating out of his system than from the effort of grappling with the machine. Cockeye felt like he had the flu.

He grabbed a large plastic trash bag and tried to squeeze the machine and crushed box into it. The bag tore and a corner of the machine poked out. He hoisted the whole heavy mess and shuffled down a corridor toward an exit, his body sagging. He moved deliberately and quickly, arms extended to his knees, unmindful of the white-smocked technician staring at him from behind glass walls.

Cockeye heard quickening footsteps behind him. He hoped they would go on by, but if he was stopped, he would cripple his pursuer. I'm not going to get caught, he thought. I'm going to throw this sonofabitch on his foot and get out of here.

"Excuse me," the white man said.

Sonofabitch . . . what does he want? . . . Maybe he saw me get it. . . .

The white man picked up the trailing cord, carefully tucked it into the plastic bag, and smiled.

"Thank you," Cockeye said.

"Wait a minute!" The white man scurried ahead, stepping on an electric mat that opened the door to the street.

"Thanks again."

"You're welcome."

The getaway car was not in sight.

Here I am standing in the street with this goddamned thing, and there's no car, thought Cockeye. But he found Short Rick a block away; they flipped forward the seat of the late model Super Sport, set the machine on the back seat, and sped off to the warehouse.

"Damn, where'd you get this from?" Pasquale Larocca said, peeling the plastic bag off the machine on his counter.

Cockeye told him the FBI building. Pat always asked that question, and Cockeye never answered truthfully.

"Man, you didn't hurt anybody, did you?"

"Naw."

"You mean you walked out with this? Damn! I know you had somebody inside. . . ."

"Naw."

Pat's questions annoyed Cockeye. It was a lot of bullshit that delayed him from getting the scratch. Why couldn't he just put the goddamned thing on the counter and get the scratch? Sometimes, while waiting at the phone booth, Cockeye and the others in line would shake their heads: "Damn, that man ask a lot of questions," they'd say to each other. But from their mutual mistrust, the men in line never told each other exactly what Pat asked, or what they answered.

"You all must be good thieves," Pat said, examining the IBM machine.

"What about the scratch?" Cockeye queried.

"How much you want?"

"Shit, what you gonna gee us for it. You ask me what I want for it, I might tell you anything; you ain't gonna gee it to me." Cockeye knew this particular item was a good thing. It was a machine, like he thought Pat wanted; it was relatively big and heavy, and it had been part of a bigger machine.

He and Short Rick (not his real name), another junkie, had talked about the price on the way over.

"What you think it's worth?"

"I don't know, man, a ball sixty . . . ," Cockeye had said, meaning $160.

"You think he'll gee that to us?"

"Yeah, that's right, maybe he'll gee us two hundred." Cockeye had been boosting himself, but he and Short Rick both knew that neither of them was going to lug that machine back out of the warehouse no matter how little Pat offered.

"I ain't gonna take less'n a ball forty. I'll take it right back out," Cockeye had told his partner just before they went inside.

Pat offered $200. Cockeye felt himself tingle. "Damn, I know that's worth more than two hundred, Pat."

Mike Franzino butted in. "It ain't like it's brand new."

Cockeye hated Mike. Mike was always making smart-ass remarks about things, like saying a typewriter was broken when it wasn't. Once Cockeye had drawn Pat aside and whispered testily into his ear: "If he's so goddamned smart, why ain't he doin' your job?" Pat had nodded understandingly, but gave Cockeye a look that suggested it would be better to humor the man with the beard and dark glasses who kept a shotgun leveled at Cockeye's chest.

"Now I know it's worth more than that," Cockeye insisted. Pat gave him $230, which he and Short Rick split—after Pat took back $25 Short Rick owed him. "Damn, I'm losin', I ain't got nothin' to do with him," Cockeye said. Pat gave him another ten bucks.

Outside, an uncomprehending black man in overalls, working in the warehouse next to P.F.F., stopped his sweeping and stared curiously—nosily, Cockeye thought—as he and Short Rick climbed back into the Super Sport and headed across town to see the dope man.

To the thieves visiting the warehouse by mid-November, the men of P.F.F. appeared to be the genuine Mafia. They looked Italian, talked Italian, had Italian names, and brandished weapons from time to time that looked like machine guns. They drove cars with New York licenses, and, most important of all, they paid cash week after week, and the police left them, and their customers, alone.

Once in a while a customer would come right out and ask: "You all in the Mafia?" And Pasquale and his men would wink at each other and say, "Man, we ain't no Mafia; everybody knows there ain't no Mafia." The customers understood. After such "denunciations" they were likely to see Pat pick up the dead telephone and say something like this:

"Hey, Mario, this is Pasquale. Yeah, I'm buyin' a big truckload of typewriters tonight; they'll be up in New York tomorrow. . . . Yeah, I bought that shotgun. I'm buyin' guns, yeah. I'm buyin' government checks, and we're sending 'em to Chicago." The lawmen watched the thieves, trying to suppress their amazement.

Some of the customers had heard of the Mafia, and had seen it depicted in movies and on television, but few, if any, could say they had actually ever met any Mafia people. In fact, the police and FBI had concluded that there was no Mafia in Washington, D.C.—no Don, no family, no traces of the organization except for some contact men selling heroin at the end of Mafia-financed pipelines from New York.

If Pat were an example of the Mafia, some of his customers believed, then the Mafia was good for Washington. It knew how to do things right. Clearly, Pasquale Larocca was the best fence in town. He paid the cash to prove it. Other fences in Washington might promise a thief $250 for an item—$50 down and the other $200 after it was resold—but the thief would never see the other $200. Pat paid $100 cash for the same item. He made no promises.

Not that he wouldn't cheat any time he could. In the first weeks of the operation, he learned how to jam a perfectly good electric typewriter by pressing several keys at once, and how to scramble a television picture by turning certain knobs when the customers weren't looking.

"This no good." He would scowl at the customer. Then, after putting the item behind his counter, he might give perhaps $10 to show that although the thief had brought in bum equipment, there were no hard feelings.

With some customers Pasquale turned to a stack of Sears catalogues kept on the counter for easy price reference on various items. He would pay a small percentage of the Sears list price. Unknown to the customers, the catalogues were about ten years old.

The lawmen quickly discovered that the thieves did not object strongly when prices were set absurdly low; apparently they feared the wrath of "the organization." Occasionally someone would demand, "Hey, man, what's this?" But normally they would shut up when Mike Franzino cocked his shotgun. In all, the men of P.F.F. were buoyed by the ease with which they were conning the thieves after only a few weeks of operation. It was no accident; they had taken precautions to stay on top.

They had decided from the beginning to keep in custody until the end of the operation every stolen item they bought, even if the police were able to locate the victimized owners. By retaining custody, they hoped to eliminate the risk of having their cover blown by a clever customer. Arscott and Lill were especially leery that some customer might fence something that was actually his *own,* and then see if police would return it or at least come around and ask questions.

This precaution paid off almost immediately. An early customer, who called himself "Skeezy," sold the men a credit card listed to Albert W. Worsley. When the lawmen checked Skeezy's identity, he turned out to be none other than Albert Williston Worsley, Jr. By the time they discovered this trap weeks later, the credit card was still in an evidence bag and Worsley, apparently relieved of his fears, had returned to the warehouse several more times with stolen items and with friends.

The lawmen were also concerned about snitches. Informers might tell their unsuspecting police contacts about the P.F.F. warehouse, and these police would then have to be told about the secret project, jeopardizing the cover. Worse, it was possible that police, acting on snitch information, would want to raid the warehouse. With tense, heavily armed men on both sides, blood could flow. There already had been one near-disaster when two P.F.F. scouts were mistaken for drug dealers by an undercover narcotics detective working the same turf. The scouts were knocked down in a muddy street and spent tense moments staring up at the muzzle of a pistol until their identity was made clear.

In early November one snitch did go to police with a story about a gang of New York Italians armed with sawed-off shotguns who were doing business as fences in a Northeast Washington warehouse. Federal agent Edgar L. Seibert heard about it in a telephone call from a long-time police friend who was unaware of the warehouse operation.

Seibert was an agent in the Washington Field Office of the U.S. Treasury's Bureau of Alcohol, Tobacco and Firearms, and he handled dozens of referrals from area police on firearms cases. But unknown to his caller, Seibert was also in charge of all gun cases from the P.F.F. undercover operation. Maintaining the secrecy of the project, he said nothing of this to his friend, but said he would interrogate the snitch to find out more about these strange New Yorkers. A city policeman from 1959 until 1970, when he resigned to join ATF, Seibert over the years had made hundreds of arrests and testified in scores of criminal cases. Now forty, he had spent much of the last five years for ATF buying bombs and guns while posing as a Mafia hit man. In the P.F.F. undercover operation, however, he had been given a peripheral role, so far removed from the operation that he did not even know the address of the warehouse.

Seibert was used to manipulating snitches; he had extracted information from them in the past by terrorizing them—busting in on them with his gun drawn—or by paying them money, sometimes from his own pocket. He wanted to shut off this informant and protect the secrecy of P.F.F. "I'm interested in this operation," he told the informant in a small office in a police precinct house, "who these people are and what they do." The informant was interested in trading his information for leniency from the police on a pending felony charge.

"They got a sawed-off," the snitch said.

"What do they look like?"

"They're fences, and they come out of New York, and I think they're part of the Mafia."

"What kind of property do they handle?"

"Everything," the snitch said.

"Do they sell drugs, do they deal with stuff?"

The informant fidgeted. "I don't know 'em too well; I've only been there once or twice—"

"Too bad."

"—But if you get a search [warrant], you gotta be careful

because they'll shoot you, I'll tell you that."

"I need more information," Seibert said. "We want you to get back in and get a better description of this gun. It might not be a sawed-off. It might not even be a shotgun. We want more information about them."

The snitch was not enthusiastic.

"I can get a search warrant for the place and knock it off, but you gotta be right, you understand?" Seibert cautioned.

The snitch nodded. The meeting broke up; Seibert went back to his ATF office and called Arscott.

During his years as a city policeman, Seibert had gained an uneasy respect for Arscott, regarding him as a resourceful, professional officer who would push his way past others to get what he wanted. Seibert never felt comfortable around him. Now he couldn't pass by the chance to take the offensive in some verbal jousting.

"Bob, this is Ed Seibert."

"Yeah?"

"Well, I just found out from a snitch where your place is, Bob."

"There isn't any need for you to know," Arscott shot back.

"Well, this guy wants to be a snitch, and that's what he gave me, you know," Seibert replied smoothly. "Says it's the mob, and they got sawed-off shotguns. I just don't know what to do, Bob. Maybe I ought to get a search warrant and knock your place off."

"Hey—!"

"I mean, damn it, I'm short on cases. I need some cases, Bob."

"Hey, we gotta work this out!"

"How about if I call Pat and work something out with him?" Seibert asked.

"Yeah, go ahead," Arscott sighed.

Seibert dialed the warehouse. "Pat, there's a snitch, and he's told me and the police about you guys."

"So . . . what are the choices?"

"We blank him out and say don't come back, or we play along with him, string him along for a month. Those are the choices."

"How would that work?"

"Well, I could pick him up and say, 'Hey, how about taking some stuff in and prove they're fences for us.' You know, back and forth like that. Keep him strung along. 'Hey, I don't know enough . . . I can't prove you're reliable,' or 'I can't do this or that.' And just keep him going."

"Yeah." Pat sounded unconvinced. "He might not go along too far."

"That's true, bud."

"Why don't we just scare the hell out of him?"

"It's the easier way," Seibert agreed. "Then if it doesn't work, if he comes back to me and says, 'Yeah, the place is still there,' then we can try the other way and play him out as long as we can."

"Okay," Pat said. "Let's work it out."

When the snitch called the P.F.F. from the phone booth at the Amoco station a few days later, the lawmen were ready. "Let's go," Pat yelled into the back room when the customer hung up.

Bohanna La Fontaine and Tony Bonano ran out of the office and disappeared downstairs. A few moments later, the informant arrived at the upstairs door and peered in. Pat buzzed him through and gave him a big soul pop. They got down to haggling over the stuff he had brought in.

Bohanna and Tony now stormed in. "Well, we downed the guy, Pat," Bohanna huffed.

"Good work," Pat said. "These are two of our enforcers," he added, turning to the snitch, "Bohanna La Fontaine, Tony Bonano." They gave the visitor a quick look.

"We got him in the trunk of the car down in the driveway," Tony said. "What the hell do you want us to do with the body?"

"Put it in the warehouse, stick it in the freezer for a while," Pat suggested.

Bohanna eyed the informant, whose forehead was beginning to wrinkle. "That's what we do to snitches," he grinned.

"Ya know, Pat, I want to apologize to you for that rubout last week," Bohanna went on. "I had to take the old lady out, too."

"It's okay, man, you gotta do the best you can," Pat said, handing the burly hit man a package. "Here's some acid for the next time. Throw it in the guy's face."

The snitch's eyes widened, and Bonano thought he could see his heart beating.

"This damn guy tried to set us up for a bust with the police," Pat explained in an aside to the snitch. "We found out about it, you know. I told you before; we got some heavy people inside, man. We find out." Bohanna and the smaller, darker Tony mumbled their agreement. "So, we ripped him off," Pat continued. "I can tell you, you're not going to see the body again. We'll take him out in the country, stick him in a hole and put some lye on him, and you're lucky if you'll find the body in twenty years."

Pat pulled an envelope from beneath the counter. "Here's two thousand dollars for the next job," Pat said. "If you have to take the family, too, do it."

Bohanna carefully counted the bills. "Do you want him completely taken out or just mangled?" he asked.

"Take his head off!" Pat commanded.

A few hours later Seibert heard from his police friend that the snitch had recanted. "He said he got it all wrong, that it's really a straight place. Not at all what he thought it was."

"Yeah, I thought his information was poor," Seibert said. The snitch never came back.

As the weeks passed, lines of thieves formed to use the phone near the Amoco gasoline station on Bladensburg Road. Richard B. Mathis, operator of the station for twenty-six years, soured at the sight of these men dressed in leather coats and turtlenecks, loud colors, and elevator shoes—merchandise at their sides or in their cars—waiting to use the pay booth that stood on public property not more than thirty feet from his office and cash register. Sometimes they'd wait an hour at the booth before going down to the Cafritz warehouse.

Seeking consolation, he turned to his long-time friend Sheldon Bennett: "Bennie, what do you think of these people?"

Bennett seemed strangely unconcerned. "It's okay," he said. "I'd just leave them alone."

Mathis was perplexed; he and Bennett usually shared suspicions. He instructed his hired help, mostly teenagers, to keep special watch on the rolling tire displays and the cash register. The kids derided the hustlers: "Hey, dude, whatcha got in the bag today?" they would say, and go on pumping gas. At one point one of them put an "Out of Order" sign on the telephone; when that failed to keep them away, another employee threw a dead raccoon inside the booth. The P.F.F. customers tossed it out in the street.

The customers, under surveillance from the second floor of the warehouse, didn't seem disturbed by the long wait to get inside P.F.F., although a few complained that they had their pockets picked while standing in line.

From the driveway of the W. D. Campbell Co. warehouse next door, Buzzy Payne apprehensively watched the people streaming into the Cafritz warehouse where he had been thrown out a few weeks before. The visitors brought televisions and typewriters and similar equipment and never took anything out. He believed these men were hustlers, living by their wits on the edge of the law.

He knew the type. He had grown up with kids like that in the brick row houses of his Northwest neighborhood. As a teenager, he had wanted to be out on the street with them, but he had a father who'd pull out his belt for a strapping in the blink of an eye. Once, when he was fifteen or sixteen, Buzzy sneaked out to hang around on the street, spending the evening being cool with the fellas and raising some hell with them that night. When he returned home and backed himself inside through the basement window, his father was waiting for him with a belt and laid it to him before his feet hit the floor. Buzzy didn't go out with the fellas any more after that.

Now, at age twenty-seven, he was married and the father of a six-year-old girl. He made $4.05 an hour at the furniture warehouse, and he lived in a one-bedroom apartment downtown. His dream was to move to rural Virginia, where there would be peace, fresh air, room, and he could get away from everybody.

By December, eight weeks after P.F.F. had opened, Cockeye was doing very well with the machines. He found he could "get it over on somebody" in three hours and sell enough to keep his ever-expanding drug habit going.

The timing was very important, because if he exceeded three hours and had no more money to go cop, and could find no other dope fiend to loan him a bag, then he would get very sick, too sick to go creepin. Desperate, he might do something violent.

As it was, he had just enough time. He would rouse himself from his row home in far Northwest, travel to the government buildings downtown, and get it over on somebody for a machine. Then it was off to the warehouse, in Northeast, listen to Pat's bullshit and Mike's smart-ass remarks, pick up a ball or two, zip over to the Strip to cop, rent some works for a buck in the nearest shooting gallery—stepping over nodding people who hadn't been outside in days—and push the used needle around until he struck a vein and saw the syringe of boiled heroin begin to fill with his own blood.

With the money he was getting from Pat, Cockeye's habit soared to $300 a day. No longer did he have to pull armed robberies or yoke people for the money; he could steal machines, which was safer, and sell them to Pat for the money he needed. In a street sense, he had become a white-collar worker. With Pat's money, he oiled five times a day, retiring at 3 A.M. and rising shortly before noon, sick and penniless, to go creepin again.

Cockeye frequently brought Pat machines that were beyond his description. He found a lamplike machine in Washington's old Post Office building, a turn-of-the-century, fortresslike structure on Pennsylvania Avenue. The machine was sitting in a storage room and he took it because he thought it would bring some money.

Pat didn't seem to know what the hell the machine was. He kept putting a picture of a nude woman over, under, and between the glass discs, trying to reproduce a picture.

"Naw, you don't do that, you put it in, slide it around," Mike rebuked.

"I know how it works," Pat said. "Something supposed to come on the wall." He showed Cockeye the direction it was supposed to shine.

"Something you ain't doin' right there," Cockeye said, although he didn't have any suggestions.

Pat turned the broad's picture around.

"Damn, where'd you get this at; how'd you manage to get this out?" Pat asked as he worked. Cockeye fed him the first thing that came to mind.

Pat gave him a ball twenty.

In the back room of the warehouse an officer tagged the machine: one opaque projector.

Cockeye's biggest regret about all his creepin in offices was that he never got a Xerox machine. He'd always wanted one, figuring it was the most expensive portable item he could take.

Once he almost got one from a Howard University library. It was plugged into a wall and had wheels on it.

Cockeye had been wrestling with the cord when he noticed a woman behind a desk eyeing him suspiciously. He knew when a broad was about to come up and say something to him, or be nosy. He stood up, shook his head, lifted the rubber top, peered down through the clear glass, then turned the machine around and crouched behind it, like he was busy at work. The woman was still nosy.

He wiped his face with his handkerchief. When she turned her back Cockeye pulled the plug and rolled it toward his car. Damn, I hope the thing fits, he thought. The woman behind the desk, he assumed, figured he couldn't fix it on the spot and was taking it with him.

Short Rick, waiting at the car, looked disgusted. "Man, what you doin'? You can't fit that thing in the car."

"Man, we can at least try."

"Naw, I'm tellin you."

Cockeye trudged back to the library with the machine, plugged it in, and went down to the basement with Short Rick.

In an administrative office they spotted an IBM typewriter; a secretary was busy using it. Cockeye wondered if it was bolted to the desk. "Naw, it's not bolted," Short Rick reported after walking into the office and asking the secretary for directions.

"Okay, I'll get her out the room while you beat for the typewriter."

Around a corner Cockeye read a bigwig's name off a door, picked some papers off an unoccupied desk, and returned to the secretary.

"Mr.———asked me to come round here and see if he could get you to run these off the Xerox machine," Cockeye said, thrusting the papers at her.

The secretary appeared startled: "Well . . . there must be some mistake. . . . I'm not his secretary. . . ."

"Well, apparently she's out and he's a little short-handed now, you know," Cockeye said wearily. "I don't want to be bothered with this, would you mind just tellin' him that? Don't put me in the middle."

"Yeah, I'll be happy to!" the secretary huffed, trooping out of the office stride for stride with Cockeye. "Ain't he got a nerve to ask me?"

He glanced around as they approached the bigwig's door. "Look, you take them in there, I don't want to hear all this, I'm goin' to lunch." The irate woman barged ahead.

By then, Short Rick about had the thing in the car.

"I got an IBM," Cockeye told Pat over the telephone.

"Well, bring it on over."

Pat plugged it in and started throwing his fingers at the keys.

Cockeye didn't know whether Pat could type or not; all he wanted to see was the damn thing movin'.

"What you think about it, Mike, how much you think?" Pat asked his enforcer.

"Aah, a ball and a half," Mike said. Mike Franzino enjoyed his role as the heavy. He was intentionally critical and cheap with the customers so that Pat would look good.

Shit, Cockeye thought, that's why Mike's over there holding a gun, 'cause he don't have no sense of value. He was careful to keep his bitterest thoughts to himself, though, because the man had no eyes behind those shades, and he could be on dope or drugs.

"Well, what do you think?" Pat said, fixing his blue eyes on Cockeye.

"Well, I dunno, but I know damn well it's worth some money, it's IBM and shit," Cockeye said.

"What about two hundred?"

"Solid."

Cockeye's companion on another day was a man we'll call Sugarfoot, a tall skinny junkie whom he had met around 13th and T streets and got on with because they had much in common. Like most of his acquaintances, Sugarfoot seldom used his real name. He certainly didn't use it when he signed papers and checks; and when somebody came calling after him by his christened name, chances were he didn't want to see them.

Cockeye and Sugarfoot strolled into a large concrete office building, one of several that houses federal government agencies around 7th Street and Independence Avenue, Southwest. They didn't know which building it was, or what agency worked there, and didn't much care.

This particular building Cockeye remembered because he had taken a typewriter off the first floor a month before. He also remembered that it was crawling with "them damn cleaning women." It was easy to get things out of there if he could just get by the cleaning women. Traveling down the fourth-floor corridors, Cockeye found one room with three typewriters and no people.

"Let's get all three of 'em."

"Naw, man, them nosy bitches out there," Sugarfoot said, nodding toward a uniformed black woman with a sponge, a sentinel at the end of the hall.

Cockeye could see her way down at the end of the hall, on her knees, looking up real nosy. But he knew what to do. Making sure she saw him, he walked deliberately into an office. "Er, excuse me, ma'am," he said to the woman inside the office. "How do you get to Room 608?" When the secretary had finished her directions, Cockeye stepped out into the hall. Sure enough, the sentinel was gone, no doubt reassured by his purposeful stride into someone's office. He went back into the room he had planned on entering in the first place.

He was wrapping the cord around the typewriter when Sugarfoot, from the doorway, hissed through clenched teeth. "Don't come out, man, the old biddy's back there, peepin' at you."

"Just go on down there where she at then. Maybe she'll watch you."

Cockeye lugged the IBM out the door, away from the cleaning lady, and set the machine down around the corner. Returning for another, he met his companion.

"Man, like, we better make it out of here," Sugarfoot said, "the old bitch nosy as hell."

"Okay. Let's split."

They got halfway down the staircase with their machines when they spotted another cleaning woman sweeping the stairs with a broom. It was four more flights to the bottom, and to the safety of their getaway car parked in an alley behind the building. If I walk past her carrying this, Cockeye thought, she's subject to getting on the phone. That's how them damn cleaning women are.

He wheeled back upstairs, leaving Sugarfoot to make his own way out, and lugged the typewriter down a long corridor to the other end of the building. He wobbled down four flights to the main hallway, spitting some of his yellow slime on the way, and then struggled a half city block back along the main corridor to the exit. He didn't want to be walking the sidewalk with a typewriter and have the police be all over him. Better to use the hallway.

The exit he wanted was guarded by two men in the navy-blue uniforms and silver badges of the General Services Administration police—the Federal Protective Service—who are responsible for security in most federal buildings. Cockeye ducked into an empty office, filled a manila envelope with some papers he grabbed off a desk, and rested this on top of the typewriter.

Now, if the guards looked unusually alert and questioned him, he could begin sauntering away down a corridor, claiming he was just returning a repaired typewriter.

When the guards met his smile with relaxed grins of their own, he knew he wouldn't have to do that. His clothes soaked with sweat, he put the typewriter down next to them and pulled out his handkerchief, slowly dragging it across his forehead and inspecting it at arm's length for saturation. "It don't even make sense," he wailed. "I can't get nobody to help me. They jus' wanna work you."

"Brother, you tellin' the truth," the guard said.

Cockeye pulled out a cigarette. "Give me a match, man, mine's wet as the devil."

"Yeah. They must really got you goin' there. . . ."

"Do they? You know anybody lookin' for a job?"

"Well, I don't know nobody, but if I do, how can I get in contact with you?"

"Naw, I better not, I might wind up blowin' my job," Cockeye said.

They talked and smoked, and told each other how they'd be damned fools if they didn't quit their lousy jobs.

"Well, man," Cockeye said, picking up the typewriter, "I'd better get on and gee this white man his eight hours."

"Take care," the guard said.

As he left, Cockeye mused over the value of using race in describing imaginary bosses. He knew from experience that had the guards been white, he could've made it out just as easy, yelling something like: "Man, I swear these niggers gettin' on my nerves. You know I can't live with 'em no more. They such simple niggers. There's one thing I hate is a nigger, you can't tell me 'bout them niggers, man." The white guards, Cockeye had found, would be hushing him, fingers to their smiling lips, their faces reddening with embarrassment as he walked out the door with his loot.

Pretty soon, Cockeye felt he had become invincible in his role as a repairman. One of his best performances occurred in the Government Printing Office at 14th and Independence Avenue, Northwest, a building he never really cared for because people were suspicious and usually kept their doors shut.

He had been bending down, trying to unhook an IBM machine from a floor socket, when a supervisor walked in.

"Oh, you finally got here, huh?" the supervisor said. "Do you think you can fix it?"

Cockeye blinked and paused only a moment. "I dunno, you know, I'm probably goin' to have to take it to the shop."

"Ah, if you havta, I guess you havta, you know," the man replied laconically.

Cockeye wondered if he should take the damn old broken thing. Naw, let him keep it. If he brought that to the warehouse he'd never hear the end of it, especially from smart-ass Mike. "Well, I tell you what," he said, turning to leave for good, "I got one more thing to try here; if that don't work, I'll have to take it in. I'll have to go get it out the truck."

"Okay," the supervisor said, "I appreciate you comin' as soon as you did."

"Anytime," said Cockeye. "That's what we all about."

7

Pat boasted that he would buy anything, but he hadn't bargained for the volume and variety of stolen goods flowing into the warehouse by early December. Thieves were bringing not only the fruits of office thefts but other things as well.

They fenced expensive hi-fi components and complete home stereo consoles in polished wood cabinets; color and black-and-white portable and console televisions; digital clock-calendars, clock radios, check-writing machines, postal meters, slide and movie projectors, and cameras. They sold knives and swords, an acetylene torch rig, and a bowling bag containing ball and cork-soled shoes. Credit cards, savings bonds, and checks—welfare checks, Social Security checks, emergency assistance checks, and government checks for burial expenses.

Weapons ranged from cheap, small foreign-made handguns —known as Saturday Night Specials because of their lethal role in domestic shootings—to expensive, high-quality sport shotguns, target rifles, and pistols.

With the customers bringing in more goods than expected, Tony Bonano and Bohanna La Fontaine found themselves swamped with work. Each item had to be logged into a large police property book and described in detail on a police department recovery form. Small items like credit cards had to be put into property envelopes with a description on the outside. The larger things had to be tagged. The men took a back-room Polaroid photo of the items in each transaction to help in processing. Pasquale initialed the checks and engraved his initials on guns and appliances to leave no doubt that these were the items fenced to him.

Michael Franzino took long notes on each transaction, and between visits and after closing hours he wrote them up on FBI 302 forms. Meanwhile, either Tony or Bohanna had to operate the camera. They found themselves staying later and later at night to get all the paperwork done.

Sergeant Mike Harrigan, one of the men who helped build the warehouse, dropped in to help from time to time, and in November Sergeant Karl Mattis was added to supervise the enlisted men. Mattis, one of those who had gone to New York to talk with Herron, helped with the paperwork, moved evidence, kept in touch with Arscott, and generally provided advice and instructions.

In the morning either Tony or Bohanna would move the evidence to Second District headquarters miles across town. To the hustlers waiting in the chill morning outside the Amoco station, the blue van pulling away was just another of the Mafia's New York vehicles. The P.F.F. men knew it as the "Heidi Fletcher van," named after the daughter of Washington's former deputy mayor, Thomas Fletcher. She and two men had used it as a getaway vehicle in a sensational 1970 bank robbery attempt in which a city policeman was gunned down. The three were arrested and convicted; ATF agents confiscated the van when they found a sawed-off shotgun in it.

The van delivered the stolen goods to a basement room at the Second District station house, where Detective Larry Cunningham and a handful of assistants attempted to determine the owners of every piece of stolen property. Sometimes a theft interested several police agencies. A gun stolen in the suburbs, for example, involved city and county police, the FBI and the Bureau of Alcohol, Tobacco and Firearms. U.S. Postal Inspector J. C. Lee, a flinty veteran of major postal probes, handled mail theft, and Steve Lord, a Secret Service agent, investigated stolen bonds and government securities. The police test-fired the weapons for ballistics data that might crack unsolved gun crimes, and together the lawmen and clerks searched thousands of crime reports, mug-shot books, court records, and rap sheets in their attempts to send the P.F.F. customers to jail. Before leaving Two-D, Tony or Bohanna would talk with Arscott and pick up $2000 to $5000 for the day's P.F.F. fencing purchases.

Soon the stolen merchandise jammed the racks in several storage rooms at Two-D. There could have been much more, but the P.F.F. men refused some items, like auto tape decks and citizen's band radios, because they were easy to steal and P.F.F. would have been swamped with them. "We got too many of these already; we can't get rid of 'em," Pat would say. "Get the hell out."

Some customers seemed to be stealing solely *because* of P.F.F., making the lawmen uneasy—they didn't want to cause crime. They hatched ruses to shut off these customers. Thaddeus McRae, Jr., for instance, steadily fenced government property, credit cards, and items stolen from Georgetown University where he once worked. The men wanted to cool him off. When he called one day, Mike got the phone location, which he knew to be outside a bank. "We're busy. We'll call you back soon as we're free," Mike said. Franzino then called Fifth District police headquarters nearby and offered an anonymous tip: "There's a suspicious-looking guy casing the bank from a pay phone," he whispered. Within moments a police cruiser roared up and officers spread-eagled and frisked McRae, questioned him, then left.

Franzino called back. "Thad, we're ready now."

"The rollers just frisked me, man," McRae said excitedly, after he arrived at P.F.F. "They didn't search the car or they would have found an adding machine!" Franzino said he was sorry, but since the police were watching him, McRae had become too hot for P.F.F. "You better stay away from here," Franzino said. "Don't come back for a month." McRae didn't.

Another customer, Robert Steven (Bobby) Turner, brought the men stolen cars. He told them he knew a parking-lot attendant who would let him steal them. The men in the warehouse paid $100 per car. They used one of Frank Herron's suggestions to explain the low price: they were going to use the vehicle only once, for a hit, and then it would be burned. The men got rid of Bobby Turner by refusing to pay more than $50 for the last car he brought in.

But still the torrent of goods increased, and the men in Operation Sting were beginning to stagger under the load. In early December Lill and Arscott agreed to add another agent. Waiting for them was Edgar L. Seibert, the Bureau of Alcohol, Tobacco and Firearms agent who had helped them cope with the snitch. Seibert was regarded by prosecutors as one of the city's best undercover men. He had posed as a drug dealer, hit man, gun runner, and Mafia mobster. He had lived for weeks in the squalid Whitelaw Hotel, known to many city police as Washington's most notorious shooting gallery. Seibert had been processing the gun cases made at P.F.F., but he longed to get closer to the action. On December 2 Arscott and Lill selected him to help relieve the mounting burdens in the warehouse. It was the beginning of Angelo Lasagna, P.F.F.'s specialist in guns and jewelry, who became known to some customers as the man with the silencer.

"I know a guy who wants to sell a truck," said the mustachioed man on 14th Street.

Richie Parker (not his real name) listened intently.

"I heard that you know these Mafia-type people. Do you want to sell a truck?"

Richie weighed what he heard. He knew the mustachioed man, saw him regularly around 14th Street, and his instincts told him the offer was good. The man said his friend, Stan D. Robinson, wanted $500 for his hijacked truck, and would pay Richie a commission for introducing him to the Washington Mafia.

Nothing wrong with that, Richie reasoned. He had been in the warehouse before and got commissions. He was simply a middleman. It was Stan's truck, Stan's problem.

"Yeah, I'll call my people," Richie said. This Mafia leader, Larocca, had told Richie he would buy all the hot merchandise Richie could get.

At that moment, Richie Parker felt confident about himself. He would match his wits against anybody. He felt comfortable with the people of 14th Street and with his ability to deal with hijackers and Mafia fences. This scene was all part of Richie's world, the familiar cement corridors along U and T streets and 14th Street, an aging and decaying part of Washington that was still scarred by the destruction of the 1968 riots; an area of abandoned buildings, slum apartments, bars, small clothing stores, tourist homes where prostitutes took their customers, pawn shops, soul-food restaurants, and mom-and-pop grocery stores. It was a haven for junkies, dope pushers, backroom gamblers, petty thieves, robbers, and armed men hunting money and other people.

Here people lived by their wits and instincts, preying off merchants, outsiders, and each other. Here people constantly tested one another to sort out the weak. Everybody here seemed to be hustling for money like Richie; in street jargon, they were "in the life."

Richie had not always been in the life. He had been raised in the neighborhood, but there was a time when he wouldn't steal. His parents had been so strict that when he first told a lie he thought he would go to hell. They had made much of the neighborhood off-limits, but what he saw as a child fascinated him. How could a person let himself get on dope? Look at the junkies, beaten down, out of it. In a stupor. Sitting on the curb. How could that ugly-ass whore prostitute her body? Or rather, his body, since it was a man in drag?

Now, at age twenty-six, Richie had lied and had stolen. He had been a forger and had sold dope. He had decided some time back that the system—the government, the establishment, society —only stood for the haves, the rich. It was geared against him. Since the system wasn't going to give to him, he would take from it. Now he was trying to figure out how to cash in on a stolen truck.

He had started in this direction after dropping out of tenth grade from boredom—he was too intelligent for the classes, he believed—and joining the army. While he was stationed in Europe, the army refused to let him go home on compassionate leave to be with his dying mother. He had once gone AWOL to be with her, and so the colonel wouldn't sign the paper as she lay near death. He was still in West Germany when she died. Richie left the service an embittered man, and enrolled at Federal City College. This was supposed to be the institution of higher learning built by the District of Columbia to educate Washington's black people. He found it second-rate—teachers, supplies, facilities, books. Everything used. Hand-me-down furniture. A lot of black-awareness classes, but no substantial courses, in his view. At the same time, the best job he could get was as a forklift operator, and that was just temporary. By now he was twenty-one and married. Without a high school education, he couldn't get a good job.

Richie began exploring the areas that had been off-limits to him as a child, particularly the poolrooms around 7th and T streets, Northwest. Fourteenth Street was where the dopers hung out, the washed-out people too weak to make it in the life. Seventh and T was where the talent was. Soon pool was devouring him. He poured his energy into it, playing out of love and fascination. If you hit a ball a certain place, it had to go a certain place. It was all in his hands. That was the way life should be.

At first Richie would run all the balls on the table. Then, when people stopped playing him for money, he realized that showing off was cutting into his winnings. So he went into strange pool halls and began intentionally missing shots during warm-ups. If he gave eight to five—that is, with him having to make eight balls to his opponent's five—he would wait for the other man to sink four balls before he put in his eight. That would give the victim the idea he could have won, that Richie had only been lucky, and that he should try again.

Richie became the Kid, slim, handsome, alert, expressive, taking on gnarled veterans with rumpled skin and nasty teeth. "Like, I don't usually bet," Richie would say to them, "but, like, I gotta go see the dentist at five o'clock and it costs fifteen bucks,

so I'll go you five a game." Or, "Five a game! That's pretty steep
—but fuck it, I just got paid, come on."

He didn't expose his game, only showed as much of it as he
needed to. If his opponent pocketed seven balls in a game to
eight, Richie would run seven, and then intentionally miss the
eighth, yet place it in a position that made it impossible for the
other man to make it. If he did, Richie would back off—no sense
lockin' horns with a pro. Still, he found plenty of victims, people
who wanted to win so badly that they lost all their money trying.
"I know I can beat you," he would say, playing for fun with one
of the fish. "Shit, you lucky as shit to make that."

"That ain't lucky. That's a skill," the potential victim would
say. "Put your money where your mouth is."

He was making between $60 and $70 a day at his peak. But
after a while there weren't that many new people coming in to 7th
and T, and he knew he either had to move up or get out. He tried
to move up and he lost $836 to the dude Monksey. This was a
different caliber player, in a league with Strawberry, the best
player in D.C., who took on challengers from out of town and
whose picture hung in the pool halls at 7th and T. Richie wasn't
ready for them, he decided, and he drifted back to 14th Street.

There was very little to be made hustling pool there, among
the dopers. Before long, he started using heroin. A dude mentioned to Richie discreetly that he had just scored, and invited
him to join in. "No, man, I'm cool," Richie said at first.

But as they talked, the dude's argument seemed stronger.
Besides, Richie wasn't doing anything. The heroin filled the
empty time. Like the others, he used part of a matchbook cover
for a quill, spooning the heroin onto it, placing it to one nostril
and holding the other, vacuuming it to the back of his brain. At
first he found it disagreed with his system, made him sick, but
after several sessions he found it gave him confidence, and he
liked that.

Things soon started going sour with his woman. She was
carrying the financial burden and he couldn't get a job, at least
not the kind he wanted. He had to decide whether to make his

living legally or illegally. He believed he didn't have any skills to offer because of his lack of training. Illegal activity, on the other hand, could get him a decent income. He began selling drugs and quickly picked up an arrest record. Then in late 1972 his infant son died in what was supposedly one of the best hospitals in the city. The staff failed to recognize the pneumonia, he believed. Another example of life's double standards for blacks, Richie thought. A white baby would have been given much better care.

Right after his son died, Richie began forging checks. He could make money that way—not from any person, but from the system. He would walk into a busy bank with a newspaper under his arm. Underneath the top page were sheets of carbon paper. When someone at the work counter needed a place to write, Richie told them to pay no attention to his newspaper. "Go right ahead," he would mumble while he fiddled with various forms. After the customer left, Richie usually had their name and bank account number imprinted on his newspaper, underneath the carbon. Using that information he could get blank checks payable on the customer's account; he found that banks gave out substitute checks without question. Any street veteran knew where to get good identification to back up credit card purchases and blank checks. One could go to the D.C. Department of Motor Vehicles with a stolen wallet, pulled out the victim's Social Security card and two other forms of identification, and tell the clerk he had lost his driver's license. Within minutes, the veteran had a "replacement" license that matched his own photograph with someone else's name. Cost: two dollars. Meanwhile, the real owner found himself scrambling for proper identification to prove who he was so that the very same clerk could also issue *him* a replacement.

In the banks Richie became a doctor or a lawyer. He knew he couldn't impersonate them in hospitals or courtrooms, but in the banks, his act worked very well. He wore three-piece suits, walked erect and deliberately, and treated tellers with impatience. "I'd like four hundred dollars forthwith," he would say, believing he had impressed them with the legal term. Sometimes he would drop a lawyer's business card.

Forgery paid like a good job. Richie found he could get as much money as he wanted, but he settled for enough to take care of his family. He told his wife he was an insurance salesman in North Carolina, and hoped she believed that. She knew he was a good salesman.

After two months, Richie was juggling numerous accounts belonging to other people. He maintained careful records of how much each customer had, and kept up to date by asking for balance checks. Sometimes he found a customer with only a little money, say $6, in his checking account, and would feel sorry for him, so he would transfer money to that account from one of his wealthier customers. He was delighted with himself for his benevolence.

In November 1972 Richie got arrested. It was his own carelessness, he believed. He reached into the wrong pocket.

He had the ID and blank check for, say, Mr. Dobbs in his right pocket and, lets say, Mr. Smith, in his left. He knew Mr. Smith didn't have any money because he had just withdrawn it all, but by mistake he presented Mr. Smith's check and ID to the teller. He couldn't very well ask for Mr. Dobbs's money after presenting Mr. Smith's ID. So Richie asked what the balance was, hoping he could claim he forgot there was no money in it. To his surprise the teller said there were several hundred dollars in Mr. Smith's account. Richie decided to go ahead and remove it all again.

Only it was a trap. Police and bank officials had been alerted by the real Mr. Smith. They had tricked him, and Richie was upset. They had given him false information.

He was let out on personal bond pending trial. He was going to jail, he figured then, so he might as well get as much as he could while he was out. He went back to the banks. The system makes so much money . . . they insure it, and get it all back anyway, he figured. "I'd like my balance, please," Richie announced to a teller.

She dialed a computer, and said that it was more than

$15,000. Richie was stunned. None of his numbers had ever paid off like this. "Is this a personal account or a corporate account?" the teller asked, curious at his hesitation.

Danny knew nothing about corporate accounts, but he figured this must be one because otherwise she never would have asked. "Corporate," he said.

"Are you authorized to sign for this?"

"Yes," he said smoothly. "Of course."

The teller counted out the money, fifteen thousand and some odd dollars, to the penny.

"Yes, that figure tallies with what I had in my files," he said, carrying it away in an envelope.

He bought a new wardrobe. But buying anything he wanted for himself and his family was getting boring, and he began to draw satisfaction from giving money to friends, relatives, and strangers on the street. "Oh, those shoes you saw last week, babe —I'll get 'em for you." If they asked for $5 he was likely to give them $500. A couple of girls needed abortions; he paid for them. Friends and friends of friends approached him.

"If you see anything you like, just tell me and I'll get it," he told them at Christmastime. His relatives got motorbikes at $400 apiece, including a junior model for his sister's youngest son. He had become, in his view, the Godfather of 14th Street, and the prestige pleased him.

Richie shopped with his wits, passing off worthless pieces of paper. Everything was on paper and didn't mean much anyway, he reasoned. A bank says it has assets of $50 million, but it doesn't actually have $50 million. Most of it is on paper. The trick was getting people to accept his. He convinced department store clerks to accept his checks by handing them his wallet, with his fake ID and several $100 bills sticking out, and walking away. This showed that he was a man of substance and that he trusted the clerk. They usually hit the back of his bogus check with their rubber stamp, filled in the routine information, and returned his wallet with a smile.

In January 1973 Richie got caught again. An FBI man was

in the bank, and Richie's actions raised his suspicions. "Wait a minute, I want to talk with you," the FBI man said. At the time of this second arrest, Richie figured he had gone through at least $20,000 since he started three months earlier. The judge released him again, this time on $3000 bond.

Now more certain than ever of going to jail, Richie threw his forging operation into third gear, cashing checks and spending all he could before his trial date in D.C. Superior Court.

Now and then a clerk would resist, but Richie usually won. A woman clerk at a big department store bucked when he tried to buy two recliner chairs and take them away in a U-Haul trailer. She wanted it delivered to the address on the check—probably because she wanted to give the check a chance to clear.

"Look, I need this today," Richie said. "I'm giving a house-warming and I don't have any furniture in my apartment." She wouldn't buy it. Richie marched to her superior but he appeared more interested in backing her up than in listening to Richie's pitch. So Richie went to the vice president. He listened, and looked at the amount on the check. He doesn't give a fuck about those two people, Richie thought while he spun his story; he's just interested in making money, and I'm spending a considerable amount of it. The vice president approved the check; Richie trooped downstairs and hauled off the recliners.

By March things were going so well he was beginning to get sloppy: he went to Garfinckel's, one of the most expensive department stores in Washington, wearing only a casual shirt and casual pants. He knew better: to buy a $50 item you wear $50 clothes; to cash a $500 check you wear the clothes to match. But it was Saturday and he didn't feel like changing. He was after a leather jacket for a friend. He had bought two others there on Thursday, and since he was using a different name he halfway worried about seeing the same sales clerk this time. Ah, the salesman probably doesn't work on Saturday, he convinced himself. He remembered, bemused, how the salesman had put his bad check in the cash drawer without question on Thursday. He assumed it was because he was so convincing, and because

Garfinckel's deals with richer clientele, and wouldn't want to insult them by asking questions about identity.

"Can I help you?" The same salesman rushed up to Richie.

"No, I'm just looking," Richie said. Shit, he thought. After a while the salesman left, and Richie followed him out the door to make sure he was gone. He figured he was going to lunch. He ran back upstairs and bought the leather coat. Just then the salesman came back, walked up and looked over his shoulder at the check he was writing. He's noticing the name is different, Richie thought.

The salesman's mood seemed to change; he started to stammer. "Uh, you'll have to get that check approved on the ninth floor, sir," he said.

Richie knew that Garfinckel's only had eight floors; he figured this was the signal to other clerks to call the police. "Are you sure this is necessary?" Richie asked. He wouldn't panic. He didn't want to back off too suddenly, because the man might sound an alarm. Besides, Richie believed he could play out of it. "This is ridiculous," he huffed. The salespeople looked in other directions and he slipped out. As he left the store, Richie noticed police detectives coming in the front door. There must be a thousand people coming in here and stealing every day, he thought, maybe they're coming to arrest one of them.

He headed uptown and got some narcotics, which boosted his confidence. But he had to face it. He would have to go back to Garfinckel's to get his ID back. Because of his recent dealings with the metropolitan police check and fraud squad, they would be sure to recognize his picture on the phony card.

Richie got his friend, the one he was buying the leather jacket for, to drive him back to Garfinckel's. The detectives must be gone by now, he figured. They had no way of knowing he would be coming back. Still buoyed by the drugs, he went to the eighth-floor credit office.

"Oh, yes, we were wondering what happened to you," the manager said.

Richie recognized a setup, but he was high, and in his fuzzy thinking he just wanted to get to where his ID was.

The manager opened the door to his office. "Go right in," he said.

"After you," Richie said, smiling.

"Oh, no, after you," the manager said.

"After you," Richie said, sweeping his arm toward the office.

"After *you,*" the manager said.

Well, Richie had already said "after you" twice, and he didn't want to say it again and sound like a fool, so he went in first. The manager quickly shut the door and locked him in. Just as he thought, they had tricked him.

Richie ran to the window, but it was eight floors up. He pulled some blank checks out of his pocket and, after thinking for only a moment, tore them into little pieces and swallowed them. It felt good, considering what those pieces of paper could have done to him.

This time the judge revoked Richie's bond and held him in jail without bail. Richie pleaded guilty to two counts of forgery and was sentenced to a maximum of eighteen months in prison. At the D.C. jail, he asked for and got a job in the finance office.

Within a year Richie had been sent to a halfway house in Washington, and in December 1974, a year and a half after he entered prison, he was released.

I'm not going back to the life; it ain't worth it, he decided. So he took a job as a laborer in a scrap yard. For $100 a week he crushed cars with a machine.

One day in November 1975 a fellow told him that he knew a dude who had typewriters to sell. Richie had already heard about some kind of Mafia fences in a Northeast warehouse, and he figured he would put these people in touch with the warehouse for a commission. Nothing wrong with that, Richie figured. He hadn't stolen the typewriters and he wasn't going to fence them. He wasn't going to do *anything* that would violate his parole. On this particular deal, he knew he was in good shape.

Richie wound up taking three typewriters in. He assumed he

wasn't selling to undercover agents, but even if he was, he figured, it would definitely be entrapment. And since he had nothing to do with the crime itself, he felt the only thing he could be charged with was receiving stolen property—and that would be questionable, since he had never "received" it, or if he had, it had only been for two or three minutes.

Inside, the counterman bought the typewriters and directed Richie's attention to the *Playboy* nudes on the wall.

Richie told them his parole officer was pressuring him to get a job. The backup man agreed to tell the parole officer that Richie worked for them.

A few days later Richie told his parole officer that he worked for P.F.F., Inc., and gave him Pasquale Larocca's card. The parole officer called to check. "Yeah, that's true," Mike said. "He works here all right. He brings me a lot of good business." The parole officer hung up, without bothering to ask what line of work Mr. Larocca was in. He told Richie he was satisfied.

Three weeks later, on December 4, 1975, Richie placed a call to Pat to tell him about Stan Robinson's stolen truck.

"Yeah, bring it on over, let us take a look at it," Pat said excitedly.

Stan Robinson was sick. That was obvious to Richie on the ride over: it was about noon and cold outside, and Stan was sweating heavily. Richie leafed through the manifest and saw that the truck was carrying some toys. No value there—some dolls or shit, he figured. But Pat still ought to be willing to give Stan his $500 for the truck, and Richie ought to be able to get a commission.

The truck wouldn't fit inside the garage so they parked out front. While Stan waited behind the wheel Richie took the key around back with Pat to look at the cargo.

"Damn," Pat said excitedly as they opened it up. "Great work, good job, where'd you get it?"

"Damn," Richie said. His mind began racing. There were not just a few toys, as he had imagined, but hundreds and hundreds, a whole truckload, including stacks and stacks of expensive air-hockey games. This ought to be worth more than $500. Why not give Stan his $500 and keep the rest? "Go on down to the corner and wait," Richie said to Stan. "I'll take care of this." The driver wandered off.

Richie eyed all the toys. He wanted to keep a few for himself and give some to friends and relatives. These guys wouldn't miss a few toys. "Sure, go ahead," Pat said. "After all, it's Christmas!" Richie took some toys for infants, and some of the air-hockey games. "Come on, hurry up," Pat prodded.

"Thanks," Richie said, feeling a little ridiculous, since he could have helped himself to anything he wanted before he brought the truck over.

Pat, Richie, and Mike, toting his shotgun, walked upstairs to talk price. Richie asked for $5000. Pat slipped away and called Arscott.

"No, get them down," the lieutenant ordered. "Don't pay that kind of price. They got a truck, they've got to get rid of it. Get them down as close to the bottom as you can."

After some haggling Pat paid $900, which Richie carefully sorted into two bundles, placing one in his pocket and the other inside his sock. Stan wouldn't find out about that.

Pat said he would help Richie but insisted that Stan come on up so they could get the cover story straight. Richie stiffened. He argued that Stan shouldn't come up because then he would know what these P.F.F. men looked like and someday he might finger them. Even after he got Stan, he continued to argue, "If he don't know who you are, then even under extreme torture he couldn't tell."

Pat told him to bring up the toys that Richie had left on the loading dock. "They'll be safer up here," Pat said. He really wanted the camera to record them. Richie reluctantly complied.

Pat and Mike had trouble getting Stan's name out of him. "Empty your pockets and gimme your wallet," he said, exasperated. Pat offered no explanation, but he moved so fast, jumping from subject to subject, and seemed in such command, that Stan handed over his personal belongings. Pat stepped behind the false walls and copied down the information from Stan's ID cards. Mike poured the men a bourbon.

"Now look," Pat said, returning Stan's wallet, "they're gonna be lookin' for you tomorrow—all the police! You disappear, your truck disappears, they're gonna know damn well you got the truck! They're gonna get a warrant for you and you're going to be getting locked up!"

Pasquale suggested that they go to their next delivery, and tell somebody in the store that the truck was just stolen. "Rough him up and make it look good. Drop him somewhere where it takes him a couple of miles to walk."

His advice seemed sensible. Stan and Richie decided to go make out a police report. Since he had to catch a taxi, Richie left his toys and said he would be back to get them. "We'll take care of 'em for you," Pat said.

As Pat buzzed them out the door, he called after them, "Use your heads, men, use your heads. How d'ya think I got where I am? Gotta use your noggin. You don't use your head, they're gonna be lockin' you up." The two customers left.

He dialed Arscott. "Damn," Pat said. "He wants to take some of these toys."

"We got some stolen property, do we give the guy stolen property?" he asked, explaining the situation.

"No, no way," Arscott said. "You bring every bit of those toys in here."

About an hour and a half after he left, Richie Parker returned alone for his toys. They were not upstairs where he had left them. "I've come to get my toys," he said to Pat, somewhat annoyed.

Pat looked at the place the toys had been, and appeared confused. "Hey, Angelo," he yelled into the back room, "where'd you put the man's toys?"

"I put 'em on the truck," a voice said from behind the wall. It was Sergeant Mike Harrigan, who was on a brief visit to P.F.F. and that day played the role of Angelo.

"What'd you do that for?" Pat asked.

"Hey, what the hell do we want the toys around here for?"

"No, man, those were *Richie's* toys."

"Well, why didn't you say so, man? You know? You didn't say anything to me. I wondered what the hell they were doing up here, you know. I put them on the truck."

"Where the hell is the damn truck?" Pat seemed to be getting angrier.

"Man, it's on the way to New York, Pat. I'm sorry . . . I didn't know."

Richie's jaw was set and his eyes narrowed on the lawmen.

Pat wheeled around and screamed at Angelo: "HEY, COCK-SUCKER! THAT'S IT! YOU FUCKED UP!

Angelo looked dumfounded. "How the hell was I supposed to know, Pat? You didn't tell me. You didn't say a word to me, you know. If I'd known that you wanted these toys up here, I wouldn't have taken them. But you never said anything. Why take it out on me? Why fire me? Man, I've been with you a long time. You know, up here, we've been pretty tight. Are you going to fire me for some bullshit like this?"

"Hey, Mike, shut his fuckin' mouth up," Pat snapped. He turned to Richie sympathetically. "Look, man, I'm sorry about all this, you know." He picked up a stack of cash and peeled off $50. "Here, take this, it's the least I can do."

"Ah, that's cold, that's cold . . . piss on it," Richie said, grabbing the money and storming out the door.

Actually, Richie wasn't mad at all. When things didn't make sense, like this, he would stand mute and feign anger while he tried to figure things out. Something was wrong here, he thought, but he didn't know exactly what.

The P.F.F. gang, meanwhile, had another problem: what to do with the truck. They saw on the manifest that the toys, headed for drugstores and department stores, were valued at something like $17,000. If they kept them for evidence, what value would they have after Christmas? On the other hand, if the truck and the toys were suddenly to be returned to the owner, Richie and Stan might start to wonder about P.F.F.

Pasquale argued to keep it all for evidence. Michael Franzino and Angelo wanted to drop the truck off someplace so the firm could get it back. It was a problem.

At about 11:30 P.M. that night, December 4, Heinz Gross received a telephone call from Stan Robinson. Gross, president of L and H Sales Co., one of the largest toy wholesalers in the country, couldn't believe what he was hearing. Robinson, one of the part-time drivers he had hired for the Christmas rush, told him his truck had been stolen. It happened about noon, he said. "Someone held me up with a gun." He said he had reported it to the police.

The story sounded fishy to Gross. In his thirty-three years in the business nobody had ever hijacked a toy truck. Everybody knows stolen toys have no resale value. Besides, why had Robinson waited nearly twelve hours to notify him? "You're fired," he said calmly. Gross did not anger: it was Christmastime, and he was working eighteen hours a day. He had many trucks, many drivers, and he did not have time for anger.

In the end the P.F.F. gang left the truck parked off the side of Interstate Route 95 between Washington and Baltimore, the ignition key in the cab, the emergency lights flashing. The next day it was still there. One of them called the Maryland state police. The state police checked it out and told the toy company that they had recovered the toys and would return them.

On a later visit by Richie Parker to the warehouse, December 10, Pasquale was not very friendly. "You sold us a bad truck," he snarled. "We get halfway to Baltimore and the truck breaks down. We go to get it fixed, and by the time we get back, the state police are there. We got to leave it."

Richie appeared unfazed by this development, and stood expressionless until he caught sight of Angelo standing in the wings. "Hey, I thought you fired him," he said to Pat. Angelo smiled sheepishly.

"Well," Pasquale said, winding up, "you know Angelo's been with us a long time, and besides, we're blood relations. I got back to the man in New York, and he just couldn't fire him. It was partly my fault anyway."

Angelo stepped forward. "Man, I'm sorry the thing went down like it did," he said, "but you know, that's the breaks of the game."

9

In early December the P.F.F. gang made two moves to provide more protection from a customer's bullet. The FBI installed for them a spy camera behind a partition in the downstairs hall and connected it to a small television monitor beneath Pat's fencing counter. Equipped with a wide-angle lens that took in the entire hallway through a tiny hole drilled into a partition, the camera let Mike Franzino see whether thieves inside the building were pulling guns to come upstairs and rob P.F.F. From the windows the men could see people coming up the street to the warehouse; the new spy camera eliminated a blind spot that had worried them.

They also decided to disregard the inconvenience and strap on six-pound bullet-proof vests under their shirts. The Fiberglas vests could stop a magnum pistol slug fired at close range, according to the sales brochure. They wanted to be ready if one of the customers decided to use his gun rather than sell it. And when one customer finally tried something, they were.

Arnold Cleo Ford was a belligerent customer who angered the lawmen by squabbling continuously with Pat over money and sneering at his handshake. One day Ford called to say he had something to sell; Tony Bonano took up his position at the fake air vent and readied himself. Ford entered, carrying a paper bag. The sight of a thief with a bag in his hand struck Tony as oddly false. He sensed something unpleasant.

As Ford began talking with Pat, Tony saw the customer's hand come down, reach around, and begin drawing a pistol from his back pocket. Instantly, Tony flipped a switch turning on the red Christmas tree lights concealed about the office that warned the undercover men of imminent danger, but Pat and Mike didn't detect them. Tony grabbed his shotgun and clicked off the safety.

Ford moved the paper bag to his side, shielding the stealthy movement of his hand from Pat. Tony tensed, about to drop the air vent to get a clear shot at him. Suddenly Franzino picked up the lights, thumbed the safety off his shotgun, and leveled the muzzle at Ford's chest. "What you got there, a gun?" he barked as he hunched down behind his bullet-proof counter.

Ford's hand stopped. The pistol was halfway out. "Hunh? What you talkin' about?"

Pat was on it now. "Look," he said calmly and firmly, "don't embarrass yourself."

Ford, a little startled himself, slowly shoved the pistol back down into his pocket, meanwhile haggling with Pat as if the price were the only thing on his mind. He returned several times, but never tried that again.

Not long afterward Eddie Seibert, now a permanent fixture in the warehouse as Angelo, brought P.F.F. a gift from home—an M-1 rapid-fire paratrooper's rifle. With wooden pistol grips under the trigger and forward beneath the barrel, and a cut-down stock, the rifle looked like a submachine gun. Pat cocked the weapon and waved it around when customers came in, delighted that now he, too, could scare the hell out of the customers, just like Franzino.

87

"Angelo's my weapons expert," Pasquale told customers with guns to sell, as he summoned the ATF investigator out front to inspect a weapon and suggest a price. Pat was right—Angelo had extensive knowledge of firearms: he could discuss the relative merits of a .32 versus a .38 as an assassination weapon, knew minute differences of dozens of different makes of guns, and was familiar with street prices for fenced weapons.

Between transactions, Angelo talked weapons with Pat to improve his recognition of different kinds of guns. They expected to buy many sawed-off shotguns—the favorite terror weapons of Washington criminals—but one weapon played in their imaginations as no other: the submachine gun. If they could buy one of those, they would be providing yet another trophy for their operation. But they didn't hold out much hope. Angelo knew of only a handful in Washington, and it was a major accomplishment to confiscate one. They decided that if anyone ever brought one in to P.F.F., they would buy it no matter how high the price. "You'd have to take it," Angelo told Pat. "It would look terrible if we let one get out of here and we had the money to buy it."

On the off-chance that they might someday get the opportunity, Angelo gave Pat tips on how to distinguish between real submachine guns, which were illegal, and a variety of other guns that looked exactly like submachine guns but were in fact rifles and therefore legal. Angelo pulled out his weapons books and pointed out that the key difference was the presence of a selector switch that allowed a real machine gun to fire fully automatic, spraying a stream of bullets with a single pull of the trigger. A gun without the switch was nothing more than a rifle, which was legal. There were a number of other marks and Angelo went on to explain them.

On December 15 Bobby Ray Crawford walked into P.F.F. with a Thompson submachine gun to sell. Angelo was away on an errand and Pat had to handle the transaction without him.

When Angelo came back later that afternoon, Pat crowed, "We got one! We got one! We got a machine gun!"

"Oh, come on, you're bullshitting me!" Angelo played straight man to boost Pat's jubilation.

"No, we got it!" Pasquale yelled and disappeared into the back room. He suddenly bounced out, crouching with the gun in his hands, aping Elliott Ness.

Angelo stared at the weapon—the real thing! Elation swept him. "Beautiful, Pat!" he shouted. "Beautiful! You got the sucker! Got him!"

Pat proudly handed him the gun, and Angelo hefted it, feeling the weight of the metal and the heavy hardwood stock, the balance of the weapon with its long black 30-shot clip extending below the breech. He scanned the gun for the genuine Thompson identifying marks that had to be there and the selector switch for full-automatic firing. He looked again, then stared at Pasquale. He could see that there was no selector switch, and engraved on the top of the barrel were the words "The Volunteer Arms Co., Nashville, Tenn."

"Oh, shit . . ." Angelo said in dismay. "Pat, you fucked up good this time!"

Pasquale gawked. "What do you mean!"

"This is a semi-automatic—a Commando Mark III! It's not a machine gun!" He showed Pat the receiver above the trigger: COMMANDO MK. III was cast into the metal. It was one of the differences he had explained to him.

"Oh my God!" Pat wailed. "How in hell am I gonna explain a thousand dollars for a semi-automatic rifle!"

Angelo thought Pasquale was joking. "You're putting me on. . . . You didn't pay that for this piece of shit!"

". . . Yeah. . . ."

"It's a joke!"

". . . No. . . ."

Angelo's head was whirling. The gun Pat had bought was worth no more than $150 new! He could see the thieves returning to their friends and saying, Man, are these guys idiots! Worse, ATF was paying for all the guns, and he would have to explain this to his bosses.

"Jesus, Pat, a thousand dollars for nothing! A legal weapon!" Angelo cried angrily. "You dumb sonofabitch, I just got through telling you about these differences!" He paced around the cold room. "How am I going to put this down on paper?" Visions of the bureaucratic review at ATF assailed him.

Pasquale was in despair, downcast and furious at himself. "Well, I'll make it up," he said. "I don't know what we're going to do, but we'll figure something out."

Angelo was almost beyond reach. The mistake was incomprehensible to him. He wandered back toward the camera room and found Franzino and the others rewinding the tape to show the transaction again on the small monitor in the video room, as if somehow they could understand the blunder better if they saw the tapes. Angelo watched disconsolately as the rerun began. Pat buzzed the door open and Angelo saw a familiar figure walk into the room. He stared now with interest at the face glowing on the screen, and then he dashed out of the camera room. "Pat! Pat!" he shouted. "You didn't fuck up! You got one hell of a man! You paid a thousand dollars and it was worth it!"

Pasquale rushed over.

"The guy that sold you the gun is Bobby Ray Crawford," Angelo said.

"Yeah, so what?" Franzino asked.

Angelo explained his belief that Crawford was being investigated by other federal agencies. And here he walks right in and we got him on a gun charge."

"Oh God . . . ," Pasquale said. "Is it going to be okay . . . ?"

"I can walk this one right on through," Angelo beamed.

From the day they opened P.F.F., Lill and Arscott knew that the few thousand dollars they had amassed could not pay for the operation through the entire five months. They applied in mid-October for a massive, confidential federal grant from the Law Enforcement Assistance Administration to underwrite the project, but by late December the application was still being processed and the P.F.F. coffers were almost empty.

Knowing the LEAA money would soon come, Angelo stepped in. He controlled a special ATF weapons account at a nearby Falls Church, Va., bank, and in late December he withdrew $3,000 in cash and brought the thick packet of bills to the warehouse, where he found Pasquale doing business with two customers. Grim-faced beneath a full Van Dyke beard and dark cap, Angelo swaggered in, pulled out the wad of money, and flipped it up on the counter.

"I got it all, Pat," Angelo muttered. "You said get half of it. You send me out to do a job, Pasquale, I get it all. And I didn't have to break a leg. . . . I didn't have to break an arm." Angelo glanced at the customers, and they looked away.

"Good, good," Pasquale said, tapping the wad on the counter.

"You ought to be a little more careful who you lend money out to, Pat."

"Yeah, yeah," Pasquale replied amiably, as if humoring the grim hit man.

"If you'd notice, I got the *vigorish* in there."

"The *vigorish*," Pat said, tapping the wad some more. "The interest."

"Yeah, it's all there."

"Good work, Angelo," Pat said. "That's one of my enforcers," he told the customers. "Guy don't pay a bill, why we got our ways."

"Just be more careful, wouldya?" Angelo said, unable to suppress a grin as he disappeared into the back room through the P.F.F. door to the right of the counter.

The ATF money lasted through December, and in early January the LEAA grant money flowed into P.F.F. Seibert was repaid, and he restored his ATF account to its previous level.

Still, handling P.F.F. money was a nightmare for all the lawmen. They knew that their own careers as well as the P.F.F. project could be ruined if large cash discrepancies turned up at the end of the operation. So they went to unusual lengths to

ensure that their ledger books balanced. Mike and Pat worked for hours detailing the smallest transfers of cash.

Angelo spent a tortured weekend in midwinter struggling to discover a $75 error in the thousands of ATF dollars spent buying guns. Pat kept careful logs detailing his expenditures and was greatly distressed one day to find he had overpaid someone by $30. Thereafter he cracked each bill with a snap of his fingers to be sure none stuck together. When Bohanna found a paper bag full of cash in the trunk of a customer's car, he called Angelo to witness him counting it so there would be no doubt about the amount later.

Angelo was bemused. Just a few years before, it seemed to him, there would have been a good chance that the money—not to mention the car itself—would have disappeared, no questions asked. As a rookie in the late 1950s, Angelo had known plenty of cops on the take. One, with a second job as a house painter, stole all he needed from a supply store, and "hoodled" (slept) through his night patrols so he would be fresh for the painting job in the morning. A corrupt watch captain earned himself a new Oldsmobile Starfire every year by seeing to it that his men didn't interfere with a gambling casino that operated a few blocks from the Capitol. Many patrolmen routinely got half-pints from bootleggers who wanted no interference from police. For a time, Angelo had wavered, too. But under the tutelage of an older policeman, he had preserved his honesty.

In the years since, the department had made strong efforts to cleanse itself, with investigators of the Internal Affairs Division constantly probing for wrongdoing. Angelo saw that Pat and Tony and the others were different from the men of two decades before, and he felt good being with them.

10

From time to time in his travelings through government buildings, Cockeye would beat a woman out of her purse. In his world, beating somebody out of something did not mean using force, but winning by con or by stealth. When Cockeye found he really had to beat someone physically he would "steal on" them. That meant trying to put his fist through a person's face when that person was not expecting it. Once Cockeye got into a bitter argument with a man we'll call Goon. During the height of the bitterness, Cockeye abruptly turned his back as if to walk away and just as quickly swung around and threw his knuckles full force into Goon's jaw. "Man, I stole on Goon, and he didn't even get up."

Sometimes, especially when he was in prison, Cockeye felt he had to commit stealin' on—even over trivial or imagined differences—lest the other man steal on him first. The best time to steal on a man, Cockeye learned in prison, was when the man was on a drug trip or asleep. The important thing was to get the job done. So it is, in the life, that to beat is to steal and to steal is to beat.

In one office building Cockeye beat ten women out of their purses. He did it by wheeling a delivery cart into a sparsely populated office and making rounds, pulling papers off some desks and delivering them to others. In between he picked up purses. He knew from experience that women generally left their purses in the lower right-hand desk drawer—usually the only one large enough for a purse—or supposedly out of view inside the chair alcove. They would cash paychecks for $300 or $400 or more and then walk away down a long corridor to powder their noses or get some coffee, leaving the money behind in their purses. Amazing.

One day before Christmas Cockeye found himself in a federal office building at 4 o'clock, a bad time to be there, he believed, because workers were scrambling for elevators and doors to get home. Anyone lingering or heading in a different direction from the exodus was likely to be stopped by a guard or reported by a cleaning lady. But he was there, dressed in a suit and tie and carrying an empty briefcase, because he had been lazy and got off schedule, and now he found himself with no money and the urging need to oil. He called it his panic-button time.

Standing in a corridor while people rushed past, he noticed one plump young woman moving back and forth between offices. He fixed a stare on her, mainly to determine if she threatened to interfere with any opportunity that might present itself. She caught his stare, and smiled.

Cockeye watched her swish into a large, empty office and then disappear into an inner room, which soon filled with the methodical grinding noise of a mimeograph. Quickly he was into the office, but before he could move further the woman stepped out of the inner room and confronted him. "You followin' me?" she asked warily.

"You know I have to be crazy if I ain't," Cockeye replied, grinning. "Like, I'm not tryin' to be fresh or anything, but I know you from somewhere." He was surprised she had come out of the room so fast; he had figured she would continue at the mimeograph, so that he too could get on with business.

"Where you from?" she asked.

"Northeast," he lied.

"Where about?"

"Oh, around Dix Street, 15th and H, around that way. . . ."

"I don't think we've ever met, you know."

"Why?"

"I'm from Southwest."

"Well, aren't we all from Southwest?" Cockeye asked. It was a sly question with a special meaning in black Washington. In the 1960s, thousands of blacks were resettled from Southwest to other parts of the city, and their old ghetto slums had been bulldozed and replaced by more expensive townhouses and apartments now generally occupied by whites.

She named some parties where they might have met. All the while, Cockeye was eyeing a white woman moving in and out of the office. "Wait a minute, I'll be right back," the black woman said, and she walked over, chatted with the other woman, and returned with her. "We're goin' to this party, a Christmas party they givin' here," the black woman said. "What you doin'?"

"I'm on my way to the party, too," Cockeye said sweetly. "What you think I been doin', jus' standin' out in the hall?"

"Well, I got a few more things to type up, then we can all go together."

"Yeah, okay, that'll be good." He couldn't tell how much she was attracted to him, but it didn't matter: he hadn't had any interest in sex since he started oiling again in the summer.

"Now you don't go nowhere," she smiled, hurrying away, after having told him her name was Marilyn.

The white woman went on to the party, and a few moments later Marilyn reappeared, carrying some papers. "One more trip and I'll be right with you," she said, scurrying down the hallway and around a corner.

Cockeye went directly into the inner office. There, sitting on a desk, he saw two big fat pocketbooks. Quickly his right hand moved to his briefcase and snapped it open. His method was to sweep the purses quickly and unobtrusively into the briefcase and snap it shut on the way out.

As he moved toward the purses he heard murmuring. Wheeling around he found that in a further section of the room a half-dozen men were sitting around a conference table, apparently swapping stories. From their manner, he could tell they had been drinking.

Cockeye went directly to the desk and grabbed one of the purses. "This is Marilyn's, right?" he said, holding it up.

"Yeah, that's it right there," one of the men said. "And the other one's Alice's."

"Thanks," Cockeye said, collecting them both. He looked out the door and nodded and smiled, as if the women were waiting for him, then quickly moved out, dropping the purses into his empty briefcase.

In the hallway he met Marilyn.

"You ready?" she beamed.

"Yeah, I'm ready, babe," he soothed. They went to the party, in a large room nearby where several dozen people milled about among homemade cakes, cookies, and punch, and a three-foot plastic Christmas tree.

"Just make yourself comfortable," she said. "Everybody's friends here."

Cockeye chatted with Marilyn and her friends for several minutes, laughing at their inane remarks, until she went for their drinks. Then he eased out of the party and out of the building, stopping in an alleyway to open the purses and run his fingers across one hundred and twenty odd dollars, and three credit cards he could sell to Pat. He threw the purses into a trash can. Ordinarily Cockeye would have tossed away the credit cards, too, but Pat was paying up to $20 apiece for them, which didn't make much sense to Cockeye.

Until Pat came along, a person could find credit cards in the street. People were always running across wallets in Cockeye's world, particularly the junkies. They walked a serpentine line down their streets, moving along the curb for a while to peep into parked cars and see what the owner might have left behind, then weaving over to the middle of the sidewalk so as not to attract too much attention. Sometimes unsuspecting victims left wallets for them—white men from the suburbs or out-of-towners at a convention, blurry-eyed men who came to the cheap rooming houses on the Strip, their arms propped around a black hooker. Other desperate men lounging nearby would seize the opportunity and with knives and coat hangers break into the john's car in a minute. The john usually left his wallet in the car because he was afraid to take it into the cheap hotel lest he be robbed. It could be found under the front seat, or on the floor carefully covered with a newspaper. Cockeye's friends usually looked under the newspapers first. When the money had been fished out, the wallet and its credit cards and identification—all considered incriminating evidence—were likely to be tossed away. Sometimes they would be left under the john's car, and after he returned from the rooming house and discovered his loss, and cursed himself or lapsed into embarrassed silence, he would drive away, and in the gas-bright glow of the anticrime lights overhead, passers by could see his emptied wallet and credit cards scattered in the street.

But ever since Pat came to town, it was very difficult to find credit cards lying around. The P.F.F. people insisted that the victim's ID be brought in along with the stolen cards. It would be easier to pass the cards in New York if they had the identification, they said. Cockeye's friend, a man we'll call Hard Rock, later had someone hold his feet and lower him headfirst down inside a storm sewer so he could pick out some credit cards and IDs he had once thrown down there.

Besides the money for credit cards, Pat was paying crazy money for other things, too. Like the ring Cockeye picked up one night. He had thought it was a pretty nice gold-and-diamond setting, but when he took it to a pawnshop, the man told him it was worthless. So he was left with a useless ring and no scratch to cop with. "Damn, maybe we got to go out hustling," he told a man we'll call Hard Rock, examining the ring at arm's length. "Think maybe Pat will take it?"

"Shit, I dunno, but it won't hurt to find out."

Cockeye always liked to hear the P.F.F. phone ring more than once. That meant the recording would not come on, the one that automatically clicked into operation after the first ring and said something like "This is Pasquale Larocca of P.F.F. . . . We are not in at this time. . . ." The recording meant that Cockeye would have to wait to get the scratch.

Pat got on. "What's happening?"

"Like, I got some diamonds."

"Okay, bring 'em on over."

"What you got?" Pat said after buzzing them into P.F.F.

Cockeye took the ring out of his handkerchief and dropped it into Pat's hand. "Yeah, it looks all right," Pat said. "Hey, Angelo, come out here for a minute."

Cockeye felt uneasy. He knew the ring wasn't worth anything, but he hoped Pat and Angelo wouldn't catch on. The ring looked expensive—it had what looked like ten little diamonds glistening in the setting. Even if they did find out it was no good, he thought, they should give him some scratch just for coming all the way over to the warehouse.

Angelo put the ring up to the ceiling lights. "Mmmm, yeah, it looks all right," he said, squinting.

Cockeye and Hard Rock exchanged quick looks. The P.F.F. boys were falling for it.

Angelo walked behind the false partitions and returned with a magnifying glass. He began studying the ring at different angles.

We dead as far as gettin' any scratch, Cockeye thought. "Damn, we done fucked up," Hard Rock mumbled.

"Where'd you get this?" Pat asked, furrowing his brow.

Cockeye made up an address. "We done took it out a metal box in the bedroom." What the hell, he figured, the people wouldn't have kept it in a metal box if it wasn't worth something:

"I thought you didn't do no housebreaking," Pat said.

Hard Rock had got the ring, Cockeye said, which also was the truth. Hard Rock eyed him strangely, stupidly, Cockeye thought, because he would take care of everything. He always did.

"You ain't had to hurt nobody . . . ain't had to take it off someone's finger?"

"Naw, man. . . ."

" 'Cause I don't want you bringin' me any hot stuff like that, you know what I mean?" Pat wanted Cockeye to know that he didn't approve of violence.

Cockeye recounted some imagined details of the housebreaking, enough to deflect further questions. As he watched Angelo pondering the ring, he figured that when Angelo announced it was worthless, he would tell him something like "Damn, I ain't no jewelry. I don't know what the hell we're stealin'."

Actually, about all Angelo knew of jewelry was what looks nice and what doesn't. He noticed that the inside of the ring had "14K" on it, so he figured it wasn't too cheap. Where the hell had Cockeye stolen it? Did he cut somebody's hand off to get it? That's what he thought of Cockeye. "Let's see," Angelo said, "you got twelve points here . . . a little flaw . . . a very small, minute flaw . . . but it shows blue-white, so it's gotta be pretty good stuff, Pat."

Damn, he ain't no jewelry, Cockeye thought. He ain't sure of himself.

Pat interrupted, pointing to a shiny cluster of gems on a gold ring on his left pinkie. "Your ring looks good, but it ain't like this one here!"

Pat's ring was a story itself. Angelo had used it as part of his undercover guise for ten years, and he had loaned it to Pat a few days after he joined P.F.F. "Hell, you're the counterman, you're up front, go ahead and wear it," Angelo had said, putting it on Pat's little finger over his protests. "Boy, that's some kind of nice," Pat had said, admiringly. The ring was 21-karat gold featuring three large cut diamonds in the center and a dozen smaller ones flowing down the side. It had been a present to Angelo from relatives, and had been appraised at $3,500. A lot of thugs had asked him about it. "As long as I got the ring, I can make my bond," he told them. "You ever see me and I don't have my ring, you know I've been in trouble."

Yeah, your ring looks good, Cockeye thought. Just like the shit I'm bringin' you.

"If it had this, there wouldn't be no doubt," Pat said, talking some technical term about his ring to Cockeye. "We're goin' to have to send it up to our jeweler in New York," Pat said.

Cockeye had heard that one before. "Now look, man, you know how we are," he said firmly. "Now all that sendin' to New York, waitin' for your money type thing, you know, I ain't go for that, takin' my stuff and sendin' it somewhere else and ask for approval before you gee me my money, you know . . . like we can come over with something and you can do what you want with it. I'm sellin' it; I don't want you to send it noplace."

Pat paused for a moment. "Well, what you want for it?"

"Well, like two hundred dollars."

"Yeah, that's pretty fair, pretty fair," Cockeye heard Pat say, quite matter-of-factly. Cockeye and Hard Rock looked at each other and smiled.

"How do you want it?" Pat asked. He handed them each a new $100 bill.

Damn, we done got over decent, Cockeye thought, heading for the door.

"You all take it easy," Pat called after them.

All Cockeye wanted to do was get out. He needed that scratch. The goddamned gas hand was nearly on empty.

As the temperature in the warehouse dropped below freezing and stayed there, the men learned how to play cards, eat meals, and write reports with their gloves on. Three space heaters that Mike bought did little to cut the chill. The P.F.F. gang came up with a new name for their quarters—they called it The Hole.

They piled on new layers of clothing and Angelo, with a

lively wardrobe built up over years of undercover work, became the best-dressed gangster, wearing a long black leather overcoat that made the others, with their lumberjacks and combat jackets, warm with envy. He loaned it to them, but it never looked better, he was sure, than when he was wearing it himself, with a dove-gray fedora he had bought years before. When Angelo wore that combination, he believed that people took one look and felt a cold chill of recognition—here was a Mafia hit man.

As Angelo pitched into the evidence-processing job, the threat of a paperwork crisis receded. From his police years, he was familiar with the department's forms and soon had the tagging-and-identification process well in hand.

He also saw a way to improve P.F.F. At his request, ATF technician Noel Haera hooked up a second monitor to the video-tape camera so the men handling evidence could see the thieves Pat was talking to. The new monitor paid an unexpected dividend —they tuned in "Hollywood Squares" or reruns of "All in the Family" or other favorite shows to pass the time between transactions. Angelo also began making Polaroid photos of the suspects from the monitor, giving the processors at Two-D a chance to compare and upgrade the shots of some criminals in their mug books. However, the camera operator couldn't know exactly when Angelo was about to take a photo off the screen. Angelo solved this with bogus long-distance phone calls:

"Hey, Mario, hey, how ya doin', hah? How's the family? Now look, Mario, on this deal, we wanna sharpen up the focus of it, right? Hey, Mario. . . . Move in a little closer, okay?"

With the paperwork difficulties eased, the men now found themselves with leisure time on their hands. Angelo helped solve that, too. One boring afternoon in late December he threw his buck knife at Pat. The weapon thudded into the wall near the counterman.

"Not bad!" Pat said. "Do it again!" Angelo threw it a second time and now the others were gathering. Soon they were all trying, cheering and jeering each other when the knife stuck or bounced away, clattering to the floor. When the paneling around

Franzino's counter began to show deep scars, they moved into the cavernous downstairs warehouse rooms at the back of the building, setting up a target of centerfold nudes tacked to scrap lumber. The place filled with their shouts. Soon the knife was flying all over P.F.F., zipping through doorways to land in a wall across a room, or suddenly appearing with a loud thud near Mike or Pasquale, bringing hoots from the men backstage.

No one was safe, even during the transactions. Someone might whisper, "Psst—hey Mike!" and as the backup man turned, a knife would fly out from the wings and stick in the wood paneling next to his head. The customers peered with mystified expressions at the quivering knife while Franzino glanced casually at them. Occasionally he would turn his shotgun on his pesky colleagues backstage—"Yeah, what do you want?"—and watch them dive for cover.

Once, Pasquale was presented with a tightly wrapped bundle by a thief and he absently called, "Hey, Angelo, got something to cut this with?" Angelo appeared around the edge of the false wall and fired a knife into the wall near Pasquale. Pat nonchalantly pulled it out and sliced the strings while the customer goggled.

11

On December 23, 1975, the last day of business at the warehouse before the Christmas break, Loretta Butler came up the stairs. She had been at P.F.F. earlier in the month—and had fenced some stolen credit cards. This time she brought along a stack of stolen government checks she had got from her boyfriend, a mailman.

"You have any more credit cards?" Pat had asked her at one point.

"Mm, I think so," she said. "He's not finished deliverin' the mail yet."

"What's your main thing, what are you into mostly?" Pat probed.

"Nuthin much," Loretta replied.

"Really? I thought if maybe you (told me), we'd know know what to talk to you about . . ." "You don't go creepin' into any offices or anything?"

"I did that like . . . last week . . . and yesterday . . . but not every day." Loretta gave Pat a small grin. "The main thing I been doing, really, is workin' on the streets at night . . . trickin' . . . that's mostly what I been doin . . ."

"Why don't you go into the call-girl thing? . . . On the street you gonna get busted."

"That's what I want to do, but I—"

"—Did ya get busted before?"

"No, I never been busted. I had one place where they had a house, but you know, the business wasn't steady enough."

"Yeah, but you get the business to call you," Pat offered. "That way it's safe . . . That's why we plan our opeerations out. Everything we've done in our organization, we've planned it out. And that's why over the past years that everything's cool. . . Same way with trickin', same thing. . ."

Loretta nodded her agreement. She looked chic in a turtleneck and wig and had a pleasant face. Her smile suggested she had been around and, coupled with a sly stare from the corner of her eyes, seemed to announce that no one could put anything over on her.

"Hey, my man here needs a good deal," Pat said, motioning toward Franzino. "Where you trickin' so he can pick you up?" Pat wanted a little more information on Loretta before she left.

"He can call me up at my house," she said, eyeing the backup man. "He's not gonna have that machine gun with him. . .?"

"Nah, he'll have a different type of gun. . .It's called a one-shot derringer."

"Yeah—one shot," Franzino piped up.

"He's kind of funny though," Pat continued. "He goes in for head jobs and that kind of shit," he said, using street slang to describe oral sex. "Nuthin wrong with that."

"Most of 'em do," Loretta said.

"All right, look—" Pat said, reaching for the buzzer to let her out.

"—I have a district attorney, you know. . . and that's all he wants. . ."

"What's that?"

"He's a district attorney down at court."

"Yeah?"

"That's all he wants."

"Is that right? Who is it?"

"Um. . . his name is Robinson. . . Donald Robinson. . ."

"He likes head jobs?" Mike inquired.

"That's all. He don't want nuthin else."

After a pause Mike asked if she were carrying a gun. Loretta said she wasn't and she was buzzed out. The P.F.F. gang could barely conceal their excitement. "Play it back!" they whispered at the cameraman. "Play it back!"

On December 29, after the Christmas break which the P.F.F. gang had spent at home with their families, Loretta Butler returned. She was whining. Someone had stolen one of her stolen government checks while she waited in line at the phone booth. "He's gonna bring it up here; that's not right," she wailed. "He stole it from me. . . . Then he's gonna come up here and get money for it. . . . He took a check from me for two hundred thirty-two dollars. . . . I'm out there by myself. . . . I had it all together and he just took it from me."

Pat said he would see what he could do. "Now, I got a question to ask you," he went on. "This attorney that you know. We want him in our pocket."

"The district attorney?"

"Yeah. Can he be bought?"

" . . . I think so, because he's thirty, thirty years old, and he's complainin' about not makin' enough money."

"Try callin' him right now. . . ask him if he'd be interested in a business deal."

The P.F.F. gang spent New Year's Eve at Bob Arscott's home in Camp Springs, Maryland. There, amid the warmth of a family setting, the men and their wives chatted, drank, and nibbled snacks. Lilly and Shaeffer fretted about an upcoming sergeant's exam they were taking, and Seibert counseled wryly: "It's a snap. Just look at the question and whatever you wouldn't do on the street, that's the answer they want."

As the year came to a close, the men raised their glasses and beer cans and delivered the favorite toast of the night: "Here's to Sting!"

Meanwhile, at an elegant Italian restaurant elsewhere in suburban Maryland, Donald E. Robinson, Jr., an assistant United States attorney for the District of Columbia, was enjoying dinner with his wife, Beth, and three other fellow prosecutors and their wives.

Robinson had been an assistant prosecutor for two and a half years and now was assigned to handle felony trials in the city's Superior Court, the principal criminal court in Washington. His large face, with deepset expressive eyes beneath fair curly hair, gave no hint that he now was wrestling with an alarming incident.

The day before, Robinson had received a call from a man who had offered him what sounded like a $10,000 bribe. That was bad enough. But worse—much worse—was the fact that the man had been introduced on the telephone by Loretta Butler, a woman Robinson knew intimately.

He thought for a while during dinner that one of his colleagues, Joseph Guerrieri, might have made the call. Guerrieri was a prankster who liked to fake Marlon Brando's Godfather in phone calls to office mates. But when Robinson casually questioned him about it, Guerrieri's replies seemed genuine. So perhaps the call was no joke. Robinson returned to dinner, and afterward he and his friends toasted good fortune in the year ahead.

12

"Hey, man, like I got something heavy for you," Cockeye whispered into the telephone.

"Yeah? What is it?" Mike Franzino asked.

"Like, I ain't sayin', man—but this is sure enough heavy!"

"Hey, there ain't nothin' too heavy for us! Bring it on over."

A half-hour later, Cockeye entered the warehouse without a word and dropped fifteen stolen government checks on the counter.

"How much is it?" Pasquale asked.

"Heavy," Cockeye mumbled.

"What's the amount?"

"It's heavy. . . ."

"What's the *total* amount?" Pat asked, his voice growing a little impatient as he began to riffle through the stack of checks.

" 'Bout a million."

"A million dollars—oh, I see." The number seemed to go

right past Pat—until he began to look at the denominations on the checks: $109,991; $128,168; $119,424. . . . "Yeah . . . you do," Pat said, barely masking his astonishment.

Jesus Christ, Tony Bonano said to himself as he zoomed in on the checks from the camera booth. I have enough trouble locating *my* paycheck. Where'd this guy find a *million dollars* in government checks?

Pat fumbled with his calculator, totaling the checks. "Twenty-three million, two hundred ninety-seven thousand, six hundred thirty-seven dollars," he announced. Pat usually punched the wrong buttons in order to cheat the customer with a lower total, but in this case he apparently was so flabbergasted he boosted the amount by $22 million.

"Naw, two million," Cockeye corrected Pat, but still missing the correct figure.

In fact, the checks totaled $1.2 million—exactly half the $2.4 million in stolen property that would be recovered by the P.F.F. gang during their entire five-month undercover operation. Cockeye had obtained them as easily as he had all the other things he brought to the warehouse. Earlier that afternoon, January 6, 1976, he and a woman hustler, let's call her Marie, had removed them from an office desk in the Government National Mortgage Association, a part of the Department of Housing and Urban Development that assists the public in first-home financing.

"You see that?" Cockeye had asked Marie as they prowled the corridors of the sprawling GNMA building at 451 Seventh Street, Southwest.

"Yeah, I see it too," she whispered. They had both spotted a telltale brown envelope with the little window in it and the green government checks peeping through.

"How we gonna beat 'em?" Cockeye mumbled.

"Let's play it by ear," she said.

Walking into the office Cockeye saw several white men and women sitting at desks; one of the men was looking directly at him and talking on the telephone. The white women sat up, startled. They always did, Cockeye had found. Any time a black man like him walked into a roomful of white secretaries they always stopped their work and stared at him like he was a wild man and was going to jump on them or something. They all waited to see what he wanted.

"I have an appointment with Mr. ——," he said, picking one of the names off an executive door. Out of the corner of his eye he saw the checks lying on a desktop.

"What's your name?" one of the secretaries asked. Cockeye told her whatever struck his mind, one of his routine aliases, like James Walker.

She looked up from her appointment book, a little puzzled. "What time is your appointment for?"

"Two-thirty, but I came a little early." She scanned the book again. "I'm sorry but I don't know anything about that."

Cockeye feigned indignity. "Like, you gonna tell me you don't even have it? . . . I just talked to the young lady earlier and she told me to be down here before two o'clock!"

About that time he heard a quick, soft shuffle of papers over his shoulder and he knew that the checks were gone. While he had been talking with the secretary, Marie had been moving carefully about the office, a sweater draped over her arm. The secretaries were all watching him, he figured; they usually didn't pay any attention to a woman.

"I'm sorry—I'm quite sure there's been a mistake," the secretary said.

"That's all right," Cockeye said, calming again. "Just tell him he can call me."

As they drove away Marie reached into the sweater she carried and pulled out the envelope; Cockeye could feel the stack of checks inside. "Damn . . . we got over pretty decent." He grinned. "Now all we gotta do is bust 'em."

He checked his watch; it was getting late in the afternoon and the Treasury Department would close at 4 or 5 P.M.— he'd better rush over there. Cockeye frequently cashed stolen government checks at the Treasury Department, using a stolen government check-cashing card. He had found that he could replace the signature tape on the ID card to match whatever stolen check he had, and could then scribble in a supervisor's signature, walk into the Treasury Department's cashier's office, and have his money counted out in brand-new bills.

"Well, have you seen Mr. —— today? How come he ain't working this window?" Cockeye would say to the teller, trying to distract him while he pushed his stolen checks across the counter. The teller, turning the check over to see if it was endorsed, would explain that Mr. —— was busy in the next booth. Cockeye's attempts to keep the teller from asking for further ID usually worked: "Give it to me this time in ten twenties, maybe four fifties, eight fives, and forty dollars' worth of change in quarters and nickels," he would say hurriedly. He carried a briefcase and acted as if he did this routinely, which in fact he did.

Now Cockeye fumbled over the HUD checks and worried about getting to the Treasury before it closed. He and Marie had oiled that morning, but they were beginning to come down. A sickening chill swept over him as he looked more closely at the amounts. *They were six-figure checks—made out to companies and corporations!* He could never cash these at the Treasury; for that, he thought, he'd have to be white.

"Damn, these things ain't no million dollars," he wailed, throwing them onto the front seat. "What the hell did some cat make out a check for a hundred thousand dollars for? . . . What're we gonna do with this shit?"

"You're right. Goddamn," Marie said. "It's a goddamned shame." She mulled over their misfortune for a few moments and then began complaining that she was tired and getting sick. "What about Pat?" she said in desperation.

"Those dudes ain't gonna take these damn things," Cockeye cried. "What the hell they gonna do wif' 'em, you know?"

"Let's at least try," she said. "If we get over there maybe we can borrow some scratch."

Cockeye went to the telephone; he didn't want to be specific for fear Pat would reject the checks right then, so he said he was bringing something big. "Hey, there ain't nothin' too heavy for Pasquale." "Okay," Cockeye said. "I'm on my way now."

Pat really didn't sound like he was gonna take them, Cockeye was telling the woman on the way over. "We should've gone on and threw 'em down a sewer or someplace," he said. When Pasquale didn't seem too surprised at the amounts on the checks, Cockeye was pleasantly surprised. Damn, he thought, he really does want them!

"What do you want for all of it?" Pasquale inquired.

"I'm not gonna gee you a price," Cockeye snapped. "You the businessman. . . . I know you can't gee me no fifteen percent. I know that." Cockeye wanted Pat to lead so he could trump.

"You bust a safe?" Michael Franzino asked.

"Huh?"

"You a safe man?"

"Naw . . . I'm a creeper," Cockeye mumbled.

"They don't even know they're missing yet?" Franzino asked. "When will they know?"

Pasquale answered his question. "Oh, they'll probably know any day now." (Actually, the Government National Mortgage Association reported to the Treasury Department a week later that the checks were "lost, missing or stolen," and requested payment be stopped.)

"Just gee me a hundred dollars a check," Cockeye said. This thing was taking too long.

"Well . . . fifteen hundred's a problem," Pasquale said. "I'm interested to see what we can do with these motherfuckers. . . . Hey, Tony, lemme show you something."

Franzino, bearded and in a leather cap, peered down his shotgun at Cockeye. "It'd be better if you had more of 'em than less . . . so we can use 'em in a scam—you know what I mean?" he said. Mike was always saying something stupid like that, Cockeye thought. He hated Mike and thought he was a fool.

For their part, some of the lawmen hated and feared Cockeye. With his rimless glasses, wandering junkie's eye, and leather features cast in an impassive, unreadable mask, the grim visitor struck them as more dangerous and untrustworthy than other people they dealt with. Unlike many customers, he made no small talk, didn't laugh or joke with Pasquale. Whenever they knew he was coming, they chambered shells into their shotguns and waited tensely for the visit to end.

Tony Bonano had a special reason for disliking Cockeye. He had to fill out an individual evidence tag and form for each item Pat bought—and Cockeye usually had stacks of credit cards to sell. Tony regarded the thief as a one-man crime wave and wondered how, despite arrest after arrest, he could keep getting back on the street.

Now Bohanna La Fontaine chimed in. "COCK-A-SUCK," he said.

"Big sonofabitches," Pat said. "I just wonder what kind of a scam we can pull off . . . you know I think I might buy a couple of 'em, fifteen percent? Well, wait a minute—let me call New York."

I hope they do something with these mothers so I can get some scratch for 'em, Cockeye thought.

"It's totally impossible—there's nothin'," Franzino said.

Pat dialed the dead phone and staged a conversation. It was a routine ruse by now, one he used to talk out his thoughts and afterward convince a customer that whatever they were selling, New York didn't think much of it.

"Hey, Mario! Yeah, Pasqual! Pat! I got a guy brought me in some heavy checks, man. I'm talkin' about heavy. About two million dollars' worth of government checks. The fuckin' amounts on 'em range from something like a few thousand to, I dunno, several hundred thousand . . . whattya think, man? Yeah. Yeah. Uh-huh. Well, I tell ya what, let me hold on, you talk to the other boss, man. Yeah, I wanta find out something right now— Don't use that motherfuckin' language! . . . Yeah man, he's a cool guy. He brings in the best shit in the world. Yeah, man, Yeah. . . ."

From behind the paneled walls Cockeye could hear the rasp of a file across metal. The P.F.F. backup men often ran a file across a tabletop or door frame during tense moments to give the impression that guns were being filed down. Cockeye stood in front of the counter, impassive, a listless figure.

". . . All right, I'll see what I can do," Pat continued on the telephone. "I'll talk to you later. I'll be coming up there this weekend. Yeah, all right man, later." He slammed the phone down.

What about the money, Cockeye thought.

"Okay, I talked to 'em up there and they said that one of the bigger bosses is in Italy now, and unh, he sits on the board of trustees at many banks, and he's gonna call him to see if we can do anything with 'em, and in the meantime he's suggesting that I give you five hundred dollars, wheew, pardon me, fifty dollars a check, uh, if you're agreeable."

If he wasn't agreeable, Pat said, then the organization would buy a couple checks, at a hundred bucks a check, and see what they could do with them.

Cockeye figured he was in the driver's seat now.

He had come up there expecting nothing, but now that they had shown this much interest he decided he wasn't just going to give them away.

First he asked a favor. "I might need a hundred dollars in a blue moment," he said. "Oh, I'm not sayin' I'll come up Monday —I might not come up till two months from now." What he wanted was easy money on the days he had to go to court and didn't have time to get money for the drugs.

"Well, let me tell you something," Pat said. "I like that. And let me tell you something else. I like the way you handle business. We're having a party in February and we're choosing dudes to work. Now I make plenty of bucks. The organization makes plenty of bucks. That's how we stay in business—being careful. You dig what I'm sayin'?"

Here he goes again, Cockeye thought. This fool is bound to run his mouth.

"Some people try to be a fence like me, but they're not as good; they go out and get themselves over their head and they

113

can't handle it. My point is this: I like the way you handle yourself, conduct business. I might not return the favor as a hundred dollars. I might return the favor as a position. . . .

"The big boss is out of town; he'll be back next week, I hope, and of course at the party we'll announce who's going, but, unh, the way you handle yourself I'd be pretty certain that you're gonna be selected. I'm gonna be leavin' D.C. to go somewhere else, and where I'm going, we're gonna be workin' black areas. I need a good man. A good man and you might be that man. Well, whattya say?"

"Just gee me fifty dollars a check." Cockeye didn't want to hear all that nonsense. He wanted the scratch. Pat counted out $750 and gathered in the checks as Cockeye walked out the door.

Over the years, tens of thousands of dollars of other people's money had flowed through Cockeye's hands. He got it through armed robberies, theft, con games, and yoking people—strangling them until his partner had their money. Despite his success at crime, at age thirty-five he had no bank account and no possessions of any consequence. Almost everything that he stole went into his drug habit.

What Cockeye had done with his life, when considered step by step, seemed to make sense to him. Every time he broke the law it was for a logical reason, he believed.

He was ten years old the first time—stole a cap pistol from the five-and-dime. Everybody he hung around with seemed to be stealing. He soon felt that stealing was exciting. Most of the money went for clothes—he liked corduroy pants and high-priced sneakers and if his folks couldn't afford them he would steal enough to buy them. His first arrest was at age twelve after he had strong-armed a newsboy for money to go to the movies.

For a while after that Cockeye tried to make money in less risky ways: he shined shoes in the Trailways Bus Depot until somebody complained he was pestering people and the police chased him out and stomped on his shoebox. He returned to carry people's luggage for tips, but the porters got upset and he was arrested for having no license. Later he just stole the luggage.

At fourteen, after more arrests and detainment in less restrictive institutions, Cockeye was sent to the National Training School for Boys, a fortresslike institution in Northeast Washington. It puzzled him that he could not go home. When his mother visited, she told him she couldn't take him back. She was getting tired, she said, and if he didn't change, she wasn't going to worry about him any more. He knew he had done wrong, but he hadn't hurt anyone and besides, he felt he wasn't doing anything worse than anyone else. His mother cried and he cried.

At the National Training School Cockeye learned that the best jobs, like cutting the grass, went to whites, and the garbage jobs, like the boiler room, went to blacks. He stopped going to school because he figured there wasn't any future in it—he didn't think he would come out any better than he was. At mealtimes the bigger kids sometimes stole his pie. He shook it off and figured when he got bigger it would be his turn to take someone's pie.

His father and his mother, both working people, asked him why he was so bad, but Cockeye didn't have any answers for them. He didn't know why he did what he did and never knew what was going to happen to him until he got to juvenile court.

In 1957, at age seventeen, Cockeye was paroled from the National Training School to live with his folks in the family's modest, neatly kept row house .

Before long he had slapped a girl during an argument and knocked out two of her front teeth. He got a year in jail. His mother paid the girl's dental bill.

When he got out, at age nineteen, Cockeye began making his living by yoking people. He would come up behind a person and wrap his arm around their throat, clamping the windpipe until the person collapsed and his partner had snatched the wallet. Then they would run. Yoking was a great success—he was making a lot of money.

Sometimes there were squabbles over the money they stole.

Such as the night outside the bus station when Cockeye spotted an obvious out-of-towner and began walking down the block with him, talking about women he could set him up with. The man looked uninterested; when they got to a corner, Cockeye yoked him. His partner, rushing by, grabbed the man's wallet and they were off. Cockeye, running right behind, noticed the partner going through the wallet, something they should have done together later.

"Hey, what'd that man pay," Cockeye inquired when they stopped running. "A ball ten, eleven, something like that," his partner said.

"Man, like you sure that's all they was?"

"What you mean . . . you think I'm lyin?" the partner snapped. "You don't trust me! I'll never go hustling with you again!" The partner carefully pulled his pockets inside out, and glared.

"Yeah . . . what you got in your waistband?" Cockeye asked. The man appeared ready to fight; Cockeye figured he'd touched a sore spot. Just as abruptly the partner began grinning; he reached into his waistband and pulled out another $50. "Man, I was gettin' ready to burn you, but me and you okay," he said.

Cockeye nodded and accepted his share. He and his partner frequently went soft on each other with the money—that is, they said they had found $75 when actually it was $100. Cockeye felt this was part of the game, but he didn't want to know about it. He couldn't stand to see himself get cheated.

One day a junkie acquaintance challenged Cockeye to snort some heroin. "Well, can you handle it or not?" he asked. Although twenty years old, Cockeye had not taken drugs yet, mostly because he had spent so much time in institutions. "There's nothin' to it. I can handle this," he said. Snorting the white powder to the back of his nose, he felt nothing. "Ain't nothin' it can do to me," he said. After about a half-hour he started to feel funny.

Not until the third or fourth time did he feel good. It gave him a sense of content that he had never known, like taking a big weight off his shoulders. But it was expensive—$25 to $50 a shot, and to get more he stole more. From stores, by distracting the cashier and hitting the till; or slipping out with full shopping bags; from passengers at the Trailways depot by stealing their luggage. "Got change for a five?" he would ask a stranger on the sidewalk, and while the stranger fiddled with his wallet Cockeye's partner would rush by and grab it. Cockeye would suddenly get clumsy and get his legs tangled up with the victim's, and later he would meet his partner at the dope man's house.

Cockeye learned deception as well as force. He showed young men who were looking for a good time to a certain house of "topnotch whores." Once there, he cautioned them about getting ripped off and offered to help them avoid it—he sealed their money in an envelope and wrote the amount on the back. Now they could give it to the madam, who would return it because she wanted the men back. Just then, his partner made a noise in a nearby alley and shouted that the police were coming. In the confusion, Cockeye switched envelopes. It took only a second. The victims sometimes held the envelope of play money up to a light, thinking it was filled with their own cash. Some victims warned Cockeye they had been duped like this before and would get him if he tried anything. Others offered him money for his help. He refused—he had all their money anyway.

"You just go on up there and knock and tell 'em I sent you," he said. Actually, he was pointing out a home at random. By the time the victims found out, Cockeye and his partner were gone.

At age twenty, Cockeye was throwing bricks every day. In his terms that meant doing something he could get busted for. He knew that every brick he threw increased his chances of getting busted, but he had to have the drugs.

He picked up homosexuals, and when they took him to their homes for fear he was setting them up for a robbery, he robbed them there. He yoked the same man three times in one week. The man kept leaving his government job late, and Cockeye happened to be hiding in the bushes, looking for stragglers from the evening stampede home. "Please, not again," the man begged

Cockeye the third time. He took his money anyway, and left disgusted because the man had been carrying only $20.

When the operator of a Chinese laundry didn't hand over enough money and refused to tell where there was more, Cockeye pistol-whipped him. "Don't hit him," the man's wife begged, so Cockeye grabbed her, too. The man pulled out a tin box with the rest of his money.

By this time—it was late 1959—the police were knocking regularly on the door of Cockeye's parents. To escape the law Cockeye fled to Waterbury, Connecticut, where he had a relative. Within weeks he was arrested for stealing drugs and money from a Waterbury doctor, and a local judge gave him seven to ten years in the Connecticut state penitentiary.

Within hours of his release from prison in 1968 Cockeye filled himself with heroin. He had been dreaming about it every day for eight years. Shooting up again was like having a drink to celebrate.

Free and twenty-eight, he returned to the District of Columbia and went to work with his father, spreading tar on suburban roofs in Virginia. It bothered him to see how his father had spent his life: toiling at the whim of a white man, no pension, layoffs. It wasn't right. After seven months Cockeye quit. He had been staying up until 2 or 3 in the morning, bullshitting with the fellas, trying to catch up for the eight years missing out of his life, and he just couldn't see getting up at 5:30 and going out to tar roofs. Besides, the heroin he had been shooting before he left for work wasn't lasting any more, and he had been leaving the job at about 2 to go cop.

He turned away from yokings and robberies for a while because of the risk and made a living by cheating young émigrés from the South in cards and craps. "Bamers," he called them. These were people too naïve to hustle, who worked in places like supermarkets. He did whatever was necessary to win: if he felt he had a strong enough hand he would play it; if not, he would reach into his lap and pull out a better one. His winnings were averaging about $200 a day, enough to keep him comfortably in heroin.

He was addicted to the drug and the ritual of it. There was something exciting and stimulating about using his stealth to get money, then finding the dope man and making the buy. The tinfoil packet he bought for $50 contained exactly one teaspoon of dope—if he hadn't been cheated.

In the safety of his house, he wrapped a belt or the waistband of a pantyhose around his bicep again and again until it was pinched out of shape and discolored, and he fingered and thumped the veins, the ones that hadn't dried out. Like most junkies, Cockeye believed he knew every usable vein in his body—not only his forearm, but in such places as his neck, his forehead, his groin, and between his toes.

Next, he opened a disposable syringe packet, manufactured for insulin injections and bought on the street for a dollar, filled it with water and squirted it onto the powder in a wine-bottle cap. He cooked the solution by holding matches under the bottle cap, then drew the liquid into the syringe through a cotton ball to catch dirt and impurities and jabbed it into a vein. If he drew back on the syringe and nothing entered the hollow tube and his skin seemed to try to crawl into the needle, then he had missed, and he tried again. When he saw the syringe fill with dark, almost black blood, he felt as if he had struck gold. Then everything he had gone through to get the dope was worth it. He pushed the magic solution into his vein and drew the syringe full with blood again and pushed it back into the vein to be sure he had gotten every last drop of the heroin into his body.

After a few moments his voice would begin to thicken and his pains went away. It was like a hand had suddenly crept up and stopped the water running out his nose. His eyes drooped and he began to nod off, asleep but not asleep; he felt like someone was pulling a blanket over him and it would soon cover him up. It was peace and truth and goodness.

In one of these moments of bliss, Cockeye got himself messed up in an armed robbery that put him in prison for five more years.

Three men with whom he was sharing dope were talking

about pulling a robbery, but their mood had turned sour because one of them said he was backing out. They began arguing. Cockeye was listening, feeling quite content, and after a while he found himself volunteering to take the man's place.

Their target was the residence of Walter (Sweet Daddy) McCullough, head of the United House of Prayer for All People. The wealth of the church—said to be at least several million dollars—had been widely publicized during a squabble for control following the death of its founder. Sweet Daddy McCullough had won, and stories had circulated on the street about a safe in his home.

At 1:30 P.M. on October 17, 1969, Cockeye ambled up the front walk of Sweet Daddy's home, an elegant house in the exclusive "Gold Coast" section of Northwest Washington, long the residential center for the city's well-to-do blacks.

He was wearing a dark suit, which he referred to as his "trust me" clothes, and was carrying a sticklike object wrapped in a trash bag. The others had wanted to simply pull a pistol on whoever answered the door, but Cockeye told them that was stupid: what if someone came to the window? Then the others thought about pretending to deliver flowers, but Cockeye thought of something better.

As his two acquaintances flattened themselves along the wall by the front door, Cockeye knocked. "We got a special delivery for Bishop McCullough," he said to the older looking lady who answered. "It's a statuette." She unlatched the door and Cockeye walked in, pulled a stocking mask over his face, tossed aside the trashbag and leveled a sawed-off shotgun in the woman's face. She began screaming; the other two men burst in and slammed the door. The house and its contents were theirs.

But within moments the easy robbery of their daydreams began to evaporate. The bishop turned out to be away for the day, and none of the half-dozen church workers in the house knew the combination to a large walk-in safe the robbers found in the basement. Instead the men rampaged through the house, scouring for cash. In an upstairs bedroom Cockeye found a wad of bills rolled up carelessly on a dresser, and pocketed it. Well, at least this whole thing's worth something, he thought. But when he went back downstairs, he found the other two talking excitedly about waiting for the payroll to arrive in a little while.

"Damn, man, damn that shit," Cockeye said. "We already been here thirty-five, forty minutes. I don't like this shit. We can't get the safe open, let's get outta here."

"What about the payroll comin'?"

"Anybody could be comin'!" he shouted. Then a car drove up and a couple got out. Cockeye unctuously ushered them inside, closed the door, and trained the shotgun on the surprised man and woman. They found brown pay envelopes inside the woman's purse, then they sprinted out.

As Cockeye and his accomplices raced off in their Mercury Cougar getaway car, a police cruiser careened down the street toward them, screeched into a U-turn and tore after them. Now they were the hunted. At first, Cockeye wanted to leap from the car, but that meant he would lose his share of the payroll money in the purse the others were guarding. We gotta escape, he thought, seeing himself behind bars once more, getting sick with no dope. He cursed himself, remembering his own promise never to use guns again. Armed robbery meant big time. He couldn't believe he'd got himself hooked into this; he guessed it was because once he made up his mind, he went ahead and did something without thinking it through. As his frustration built, the police lost them. Suddenly, they were safe.

When the men stopped they divided the payroll—about $500. The others went on to get some dope, and Cockeye drew the moneyroll out of his waistband. Over $700. Shit, he thought, this whole thing wasn't that bad after all.

Five days later the police burst in on him at 3 o'clock in the morning. He was at his folks' home at the time, in bed with a woman. The woman moaned and tried to cover up when the police came in and pointed guns at them; Cockeye grumbled about them always coming in the middle of the night. On the way out his mother tried to catch his eye. "Oh my God, what you done now, boy?" she asked. He did not answer. They charged him with armed robbery, and his thoughts turned to how he could minimize his time in prison.

He had no room for feelings for the victims. He couldn't understand why they had cried—after all, the money didn't belong to them. And he had told them he wasn't going to hurt anyone. Now, in jail, Cockeye felt sorry for himself, and sorry that he had done it because he got caught. He always felt sorry after he got caught.

In 1970 U.S. District Court Judge Oliver Gasch sentenced Cockeye to eight to twenty-four years for the McCullough robbery and a variety of other crimes. He was taken to the city's correctional farm at Lorton, Virginia. Four years later Herbert Voyt, deputy chief probation officer for the court, wrote to Gasch about Cockeye; he had been a model prisoner, Voyt wrote, toiling on a federal housing project during a community-release program, working his way from maximum to minimum security, and faithfully sending $50 home to his parents every two weeks. "Perhaps some kind of consideration at this time to encourage and motivate him is indicated," Voyt wrote. Gasch reduced the minimum sentence from eight to five years. "You've got to give these guys a break when they work for it," Gasch said, several years later, of his decision. "You've got to try to rehabilitate them when you can." In 1975 Cockeye was released, having served the minimum five-year term.

This time he experimented at being a family man. He had met a woman at D.C. General Hospital while on the community-release program and she had visited him almost daily, encouraging him to change his life. He moved in with her, becoming stepfather to her three children, and she pushed him to go straight. But the only place he felt comfortable was in the street, where his friends were, where he could catch up on the five years he missed. And he couldn't turn the drugs down. Not chasing the dope man, not shooting up—it was freedom, but it was a void. Soon he was oiling over the bathtub, telling his wife he was busy and would be right out.

He was sure he could never make it as a straight. His whole life had been spent in one small part of Washington. He had never been fishing or boating, or gone for a drive. He had never even been to the Washington Monument, except when he stole someone's purse there. In prison he had seen magazine pictures of families on a picnic, but he felt if he had ever asked a woman to go out in the park and just sit she would've thought he was crazy. He had an opportunity to talk with a psychologist in prison —at group therapy sessions mandatory for parole—but nobody was going to talk in front of ten other people about what was troubling them.

Another problem was that Cockeye couldn't get the kind of job he wanted. He wanted one without much strain—definitely not manual work—and with women around him, working in pleasant company, doing something he liked to do, maybe working with kids as some kind of counselor. He thought it would be nice to wake up every morning knowing he would be working indoors, so he wouldn't have to be mad that it was cold or rainy outside. But even if he could find such a job, he believed, he didn't have the training for it anyway.

By September 1975 he was red in the eye, staying up to 3 A.M., shooting five times a day at $50 a time. He started out at 10:30 in the morning, seeing what he could steal, and shooting around noon, 4, 7, 10, and again before going to bed.

Without heroin, Cockeye ached and hallucinated. The symptoms are common: sweating and freezing, lying in bed, aching. There was no sleep.

To feel good again, he stole—from offices and department stores, selling the goods to street fences and, beginning in November 1975, to Pasquale Larocca.

Despite his caution and his savvy, the averages were against Cockeye's staying clear of the rollers. During 1975 he was arrested seven times, for such things as theft, petty larceny, receiving stolen property, and burglary. But he never stayed in jail, because once caught, Cockeye used the knowledge he had accumulated about the legal system to get out on bail and then to delay his trial as long as possible.

He had found it easy to postpone his trial dates: he could check into a hospital for narcotics treatment, or at least say he was going to; he could claim a sickness in the family; or he could simply fail to appear and later tell the judge that he got mixed up on the dates. Each excuse was usually good for a couple of months' delay because of the crowded court calendars.

His parole officer tried three times during 1975 to have Cockeye's parole revoked and was refused each time by the D.C. Parole Board. As the arrests multiplied and the parole violations piled up, Cockeye was out on the streets, prowling, stealing, shooting up, then reappearing in his "trust me" clothes to engineer another court delay for more freedom. He closed out the year with a flourish, pleading guilty in the District of Columbia Superior Court on December 18 to four crimes and then convincing the judge to let him go free on bond pending a later sentencing. The crimes included stealing a purse that belonged to the secretary of the Superior Court's grand jury and stealing a wallet while on the work-release program from Lorton in 1974. He was pleading guilty because he had run out of stalling ploys.

His attorney, Alan Soschin, asked Judge Fred McIntyre to allow Cockeye to remain free on bond until his sentencing in February. "It means a lot to my client to be out for at least the Christmas holidays," Soschin said. He pointed out that although Cockeye was pleading guilty on December 18, his original trial was not to have begun until January 6. "There is no doubt in my mind that he is going to refrain from getting in any more trouble," Soschin said, "[because] I think the government will take a very dim view—as well as the court—of any future trouble. He knows he is already vulnerable for a long period of incarceration."

Unknown to anyone in the courtroom, in particular his lawyer, Cockeye just an hour before had fenced a batch of stolen credit cards at P.F.F.

Judge McIntyre asked how long Cockeye had been out on bond, on the charges, and was told eight months. Had he committed any new offenses during that time? Cockeye stood up and told the judge he had—three other charges pending in suburban Montgomery County. Judge McIntyre recoiled, and said he couldn't possibly allow Cockeye out on bond.

Cockeye saw things going against him, and he moved to turn things his way. He wanted to be out on bond until the last possible moment. He asked the judge if he could speak. "You know, like, I got—me and my wife got a house we are buying. I told Mr. Soschin, like, the only way I am taking the plea, you know, is because of this. Not because of the bond. Otherwise I would go to trial."

"Just through the holidays, Your Honor," Soschin said.

"I cannot permit him to remain out."

"Can I take my plea back, then?" Cockeye asked.

The judge stopped him sharply. "It doesn't matter to the court one iota whether you plead guilty or go to trial!"

"I am not saying that, Your Honor. I want to plead guilty, Your Honor. I want to save the court the expense and everything."

The judge thought for a moment. "The only reason I will consider letting you remain out after Christmas is because admittedly I couldn't have brought you to trial. Your next trial date would have been January the sixth. That's the only basis on which I can justify permitting you to remain on bond. So, in fairness to you, you didn't have to come in and enter this plea until the sixth of January, so I will let you remain out until the sixth of January.

"You understand that if you don't return you will be subject to an accumulated total of five, ten, fifteen, twenty years of bail violations if you don't return on the sixth of January? Do you understand that?"

"Yes, Your Honor."

"Sign your order and you will be back before me on the sixth of January."

Cockeye did not show up in court on the sixth of January. That was the day he was fencing the $1.2 million in federal checks

125

to Pat. Judge McIntyre issued a bench warrant for his arrest. Cockeye appeared voluntarily on January 8 and told the judge that he had been confused about the date. Judge McIntyre quashed the bench warrant, set sentencing for late February, and released him on $5,250 bond.

Over the Christmas holidays Cockeye had brought stolen credit cards and savings bonds to P.F.F. four more times. Between his court appearance January 8 and his sentencing February 26, he made fifteen more trips to the warehouse to sell property that belonged to others.

13

The lawmen of P.F.F. moved smoothly through the bitter cold days of January, their fourth month, dispatching several unexpected problems and enjoying themselves in ways they had never imagined.

They were at times bemused and outraged at what their customers brought in, but they continued to work the transactions to come out on top. In the middle of the month a customer called to say he wanted to sell them a bear rug. Pat worried whether there would be enough identification to make it worth buying, but the rest of the gang didn't need any urging; as Angelo said later, "How many Sting operations in the country could say they bought a real bear rug? Not a one!"

The customer turned out to be Albert "Skeezy" Worsley, Jr., the man who months before had tested the fences to see if they were lawmen by selling them a credit card with the name Albert Worsley on it. He now arrived with a large bundle under his coat.

When Pat unrolled the rug, it had an $840 price tag in the ear from W. & J. Sloane—all the identification he needed. He admired the rug's lustrous dark fur and large size. "How much you want for it? Price tags don't impress me—I'll kill my own bear!"

"Three, four hundred."

"Hey, you know, be nice. What the hell am I going to do with a bear rug? Hey, wait a minute, I got this summer place up in New York—this would look nice in front of the fireplace up there. I'd like to buy it from you *personally.*"

Angelo, watching on the monitor, wondered how in hell he could get the rug for *his* own house. He, too, easily imagined the rug in front of a fireplace—his own. It was a whimsy that blissfully glossed over the fact that his house had no fireplace.

"Now, this is my own money and I can't afford much," Pasquale continued, hauling out the cashbox. "This is not organization. I'll be honest with you, give you what I can." He cracked off a hundred dollars, and the thief departed. Just before the next incident, Angelo grabbed the rug and draped it over himself, so the bear head and shoulders appeared in front of the camera. "GRRRRRHHH! THE NEXT INCIDENT IS ———!!!" he growled, holding up the clapboard.

A man brought in an electrocardiogram machine and a heart-lung resuscitator stolen from Prince George's County Hospital. "What do I need these for?" Pat asked. "I'm not a brain surgeon." But he bought the machines anyway after the customer told how he stole them: he simply put on white pants and a white shirt, walked into the hospital and rolled the things he wanted down the corridors, onto the loading dock, and into his car.

"You want an oxygen tent, or any stuff like that? I can get whatever you want," he went on. "I can get a portable X-ray machine, but I'll have to get a van to bring it over here."

"Nah, man, we really don't need it," Pasquale assured him. "We got our own family doctors."

"Well, how about sheets, blankets, pillowcases, stuff like that?"

"Nah, not now. Tell you what, maybe we can use some of that stuff some day when we take to our mattresses."

No one lifted a finger to help two young thieves the day they struggled up the P.F.F. stairs with two new electric ranges.

"Where'd you get these, off a construction job?" Pasquale inquired.

"No, man, we took them off a boxcar out in Maryland," said one of the thieves, his face glistening with sweat.

"Well, goddamn, they don't look bad, hey?" Pasquale paused. "What are they, gas?"

The thieves blinked. "Hey . . . no, man, they're electric."

Pasquale looked crestfallen. "Oh, well, you know, everybody's going to gas now. Electric is so damn high."

The thieves nodded, their faces wrinkled with doubt.

"Ah . . . how much you want for them?" Pat asked.

"Three hundred each."

"No way," Pat declared. "What the hell am I going to do with two electric ranges? Nobody buys these things any more. I'm doing you a favor buying them at all. I'm taking them off your hands."

The customers stiffened. "These are worth a hell of a lot more than that. . . . They're brand new!"

Pat glowered at them. "Well then, get them the hell out of here!" They stared at him in bewilderment. "C'mon! Get 'em out!" The customers exchanged glances and eyed the unwieldy stoves.

"Okay, I'll give you a hundred and twenty-five apiece," Pat said.

They sulked.

"Look, if you don't like that, I'll give you twenty apiece for them."

"We'll take a hundred and twenty-five."

Another day, when a customer brought in a small microwave oven, Angelo knew exactly where he'd got it—from a house in

Prince George's County. He had spotted a report of the oven theft in a recent newspaper article, and it was so unusual that it stuck in his mind. When Pat bought it, the lawmen were able to assemble an easy case.

But the microwave oven was not put on the evidence van the next morning for the trip to the Second District. Instead, the P.F.F. gang enjoyed freshly heated sweet rolls with their coffee and began to plan for better fare. They were having steaks a day later when a detective called from the district demanding that the oven be sent in the next day's evidence run. "We forgot," the men mumbled. "We'll send it tomorrow." But they "forgot" once again.

Their dreams of even more elaborate feasts ended when they got another call from Second District. "Get that oven up here!" They sent it off and went back to hotplate and electric skillet.

A few days later, Angelo dropped by Two-D to chat with some officials. The microwave oven sat on a table nearby, efficiently warming a TV dinner for someone. Angelo wasn't amused.

In early January, while the men were settling in for their fourth month, a new gang member arrived and brought tensions with him. He was a young sergeant, James Szewczyk (pronounced Sev-chek), chosen to replace Sergeant Mattis, who had injured his back just before New Year's while lifting a fenced typewriter.

The sargeant, with dark blond hair curling over his ears and muttonchop sideburns, came to be known as Rico Rigatone. Like Angelo, he brought a deadly gift for the P.F.F. warehouse—a semi-automatic .12-gauge shotgun made by the High-Standard Arms Co. especially for police. It resembled a large submachine gun, with a pistol grip under the forestock and cooling vanes around the shortened barrel. Mike Franzino claimed it for his backup position.

But unlike Angelo, Rico had a personality that seemed to grate on some of the men. Where Mattis had blended his authority with diplomacy, the younger Rico repeatedly reminded the gang that he was a sergeant and they were not.

To teach Rico that he didn't control them, the men began "initiating" him—stealing his pens when he wasn't looking, or picking his pocket as he walked past. When he caught on, he put his pen deep in a button-down pocket and held a hand over it. He didn't think it was amusing.

Then, when he continued ordering them around, Pat, Tony, and Mike began talking quietly between incidents about what to do. It had been a bad day for Pat, with Tony nagging him to do better, criticizing him for forgetting important questions. Finally, he blew up. "Get off my back, Tony!"

"Drop dead! You don't know how to do your goddamned job!"

"I'm sick of your criticisms!" Pat yelled.

Tony screamed back, his face contorted with rage as he stood next to Pat behind the counter.

"Haaay sergeant, you better come out here!" Mike called to Rico, who was in the back. "It looks like there's gonna be trouble!"

The two men up front suddenly leaped at each other and scuffled.

"Hey, calm down!" Mike yelled. "Sergeant, these guys are really going at it!"

They heard Rico lumbering toward them from the back room. Tony broke away from Pat, grabbed a shotgun, and threw it to his shoulder as the sergeant rounded the corner and looked at them. Tony wheeled on Pat and fired point blank into his chest. *Blam!* Pat shrieked and flipped backward.

Tony whirled toward Rico, and the sergeant flinched and ducked. Tony burst out laughing, and the others joined in as Pat picked himself off the floor. Rico, his face drained of color, sputtered at them. And he quit throwing his rank around.

But a few days later, he began suggesting that he run the camera for Tony. The job required some skill—focusing, zooming for closeups, balancing the sound system, and other demands, and Tony, a perfectionist, had enjoyed the work. He himself had replaced Bohanna, who was happy to cook, eat, lift the weights he kept in a back room, or delve into paperwork, and now here was a sergeant muscling in. He reluctantly gave way and Rico took over the camera operation full-time. Some of the lawmen resented this move and during free moments they got on him.

"How come you're filming for us?" they asked. "That's an officer's job, not a sergeant's. . . . Come on, don't bullshit us."

Rico threw up various reasons, but some of the men believed it was the overtime that kept him behind the camera—that Rico figured he would have to be in court extra hours to authenticate the tapes during the trials.

Tony scrutinized the camera logs for errors, and when he found one, he would sing out, "Sergeant, you screwed up again!"

The staples of the P.F.F. trade continued to be office equipment, credit cards, and government checks. The lawmen recovered hundreds of credit cards, including some stolen from a former Washington police chief.

The government checks flowed into P.F.F. in cycles, with a surge at the beginning of each month, when the mails in Washington—and every other community in America—are filled with thousands of legal-sized manila envelopes carrying financial aid from dozens of federal and local agencies to the elderly, sick and handicapped, the unemployed and the veterans. This immense flood of checks was too rich for the city's thieves to ignore. They battered mailboxes, jimmied locks, snatched purses, and mugged citizens to get them. In January the best fence in town was Pasquale Larocca, who usually paid 10 percent of the face value of any check.

A few of the mailmen themselves were among the best thieves. Two letter carriers became regular P.F.F. customers, periodically interrupting their rounds to fence some checks and walk out with extra cash. They also rounded up pilfered checks from other mailmen so that postal inspectors could never suspect a sole mailman. They told Pat how they had access to sorting rooms where they could grab up dozens of federal checks and drift out of the building unchallenged. The smart mailman, these customers said, spread his thefts among checks from various agencies to minimize the risk of being caught.

One mailman infuriated the lawmen because he refused to tell Pat his name. One day, in his haste to make a sale, he drove up in his red, white, and blue Postal Service mail truck and parked it at the P.F.F. front door. They quickly got the license plate. And the mailman had forgotten something else.

"Oh, hello, Badge Number——!" Pat shouted, singing out the identification for Angelo, who was processing evidence in the back room.

"Hey, why don't you tell me your name?" Pat cajoled as the mailman finished his business.

"No way, man. No way!"

Other customers told how they in turn preyed on mailmen who used their cars as a supply point for the day's mail. When the letter carrier had walked several blocks from his car, the thieves broke in and looted it.

The men of P.F.F. also came to know and despise a high school janitor, a federal messenger, and a city welfare clerk—men who depended on their obscurity within vast bureaucracies to commit crimes safely.

The janitor worked in the Prince George's County schools, a job that provided him with a special knowledge of the elaborate burglar alarm systems which the school board had ordered installed in order to stem vandalism and theft. On various Friday nights, the janitor turned off the system at a school while his friends helped themselves to typewriters. On Sunday night he would throw a rock through a window to make the theft look like a break-in. They kept P.F.F. busy, once bringing in twelve typewriters.

The federal messenger, who worked for the Equal Employment Opportunity Commission (EEOC), had a government sedan and government identification for access to dozens of public buildings. On the way to his car after deliveries, he would pause and sometimes notice on a loading dock the latest office gadgetry about to be trundled inside the building to speed the grinding papermills of the bureaucracy. He gave some of these items an unscheduled delivery—in the back of his car, to P.F.F. The lawmen collected machinery marked for the departments of Commerce, Labor, and Interior from this man, as well as for the EEOC. Once the messenger had so many new IBM Selectric typewriters still in their shipping cartons that he brought a small handcart with him to help unload them. The lawmen bought the handcart, too, easing their own work getting the typewriters back downstairs into the evidence van. When they finished reloading, they tagged the cart, threw it in the van, and took it along as more evidence against the messenger.

The city welfare clerk worked in a mailroom handling thousands of public assistance checks for the sprawling Department of Human Resources, Washington's social service agency. He bragged that his check thefts were nearly foolproof because he stole them before they were serialized and collated, making it virtually impossible for the city inspectors to determine where in the pipeline the checks had been grabbed. As he explained this one day, he pulled from his pocket forty-four unopened envelopes—checks to reimburse welfare recipients for burial expenses.

Pasquale pronounced his usual benediction: "You a good thief!" then began opening the envelopes to see what they totaled so he could pay a percentage of face value. Pat carefully split one end of the envelope and slowly drew the check out. He squinted at it. "Man, forty-two-fifty, right?" He turned the check around and flashed it under the customer's nose.

"Uh-hunh," the thief said as Pat rang up the amount on his desktop calculator and put the check aside. Pat repeated the procedure. "This one's eighty-seven-ninety," and pushed it past the customer onto the pile. When all forty-four checks were counted, he doled out $280 from the cashbox—supposedly 10 percent of their face value—except that the checks actually totaled about $8,000. In counting them, Pat had revealed only four digits—two on each side of the decimal point. The thief never saw that the checks were for hundreds of dollars each.

Pasquale had other ways to keep his costs down. When a thief brought in a federal check for more than several hundred dollars, Pat said, "Man, what the hell you doing? How you going to cash this? You take this thing to a bank and try to down it, six hundred bucks, and they're going to come after you."

As the customer nodded in surprised agreement, Pat tore the check up and threw the pieces in the trashcan.

"—Hey! What the hell you do that for! Goddam, Pat!"

"I'm doing you a favor, keeping you from going to jail. You bring me two-, three-hundred-dollar checks, I can handle them." While the customer grumbled, Pat pulled out the cashbox and cracked off a bill.

"You're so upset, here's ten bucks . . . just because I like you." When the man was safely gone, Pat retrieved the pieces, taped them together and sent the check back as evidence against the thief.

With the operation rolling along successfully, the P.F.F. gang began to create and enjoy frivolous moments at the expense of the customers and sometimes each other. This change in mood from the grim apprehension of the early months emerged not only from their growing confidence but from long hours of boredom and the close confinement that played on their nerves.

The hidden men—Angelo, Tony, Bohanna, and Rico—began more and more to come out from behind the false walls when they found that they, too, could help control the customers and at the same time enjoy new attention as Mafia personalities. One day a thirsty customer grabbed the wine bottle and the mug to pour himself a drink, then shoved the fluted glass stein at Pat. "I can't drink out of this, man," he said in outraged tones. "It's filthy."

Pat studied the dregs caking the bottom of the only glass they ever provided the customers and called Angelo out front.

"You got any clean cups back there? This good thief deserves a drink."

"Well, lemme see," Angelo said, grabbing the mug and bolting to the back. He wondered how a two-bit junkie who probably drank out of the sewer could object to some dried wine in the bottom of a glass. He returned a few moments later and handed the now-sparkling mug back to the customer.

"Hey, that's better," the customer said, examining the mug with a smile. He poured himself some wine and Angelo headed for the back room. Drink up, you bastard, he thought. He had rinsed the mug in the toilet.

The men in the back rooms helped add new cons to the operation. One day Angelo told a story that entertained the P.F.F. gang and quickly became a blueprint for Pat in dealing with a nagging customer.

Angelo related how his ATF colleague Bill Manning had tricked another agent, an obnoxious man named, say Charlie, for trying to steal an undercover informant. Manning, masquerading as a snitch, called Charlie and suggested they meet at 19th and East Capitol streets that night. "I'll put you next to a whole houseful of guns," Manning promised, in his best street voice.

"I'll be there," Charlie said eagerly.

Manning hadn't lied entirely: 19th and East Capitol streets is the location of the D.C. National Guard Armory. The next day he called Charlie again. "Hey, where were you last night? I waited out there for an hour and a half and you didn't show!"

"Oh, yes, I waited all night . . . at Nineteenth and East Capitol."

"What!" Manning snapped. "I told you *Seventeenth* and East Capitol, Jack. You screwed up, sucker!"

A few days later, Manning strolled by Charlie's desk at the ATF office. Charlie looked haggard from two nights of staying up. "You get yourself straightened out yet, sucker?" Manning said in his street voice.

The duped man wheeled, furious.

"That'll teach you," Manning said. "Never try to snatch another man's snitch!"

A few days later a customer came in who had been asking the P.F.F. gang to put him in touch with someone who had strong drugs. "You got the connection yet, man? C'mon, you gotta get it for me."

"Okay, you got it," Pat said. "I want you to go to the corner of Fifteenth and Eastern Avenue in Baltimore at eleven o'clock tonight and look for a black man in a pink coat. He'll be wearing an earring. You just have your money ready and tell him Pasquale sent you."

"Well . . . how good is the stuff?"the customer asked, somewhat astonished.

"Man, this stuff's so good you'll have to step on it seven or eight times before you can use it."

The customer returned the next day. "I never found that dude."

"Well, where'd you go?"

"Fifteenth and Eastern, just like you told me."

"You dummy!—I told you *Twelfth* and Eastern! I'll get hold of my man—you be back there tonight at eleven, and you wait there till you see him."

The customer eagerly agreed. The men in the warehouse never saw him again.

One customer told the P.F.F. gang he was jumping bail to avoid prison and heading for Philadelphia. "Call me collect once you get up there—let me know what's happening," Pat suggested. He wanted to keep track of the man so they could pick him up when the undercover operation closed.

A few days later the fugitive dutifully called and reported there wasn't enough action in Philadelphia, that he was going to New York. "Wait a minute—I'll give you the number of some friends of mine up there," Pat said, and he read off the address of Captain Frank Herron's undercover fencing operation in the Bronx.

137

Weeks later the fugitive reappeared at P.F.F. He told Pat he had stolen some credit cards in New York, and thanked him for sending him to the Bronx operation to fence them. "Man, I was a little worried when I went in that place, though," the fugitive said. "I'd have never gone in there if you hadn't said it was all right—they acted like they were the police."

Another time, when a thief hauled in a huge cardboard box of stolen goods, Bohanna joined in the con.

"What's you got for me?" Pat asked.

"Golf shoes."

"Golf shoes! You serious?"

"Yeah."

"Hey, Pasquale, see if you got size eight and a half!" Bohanna barked from the rear.

Pat tipped the box up and peered inside and fished out a pair. Not enough identification to justify a purchase.

"Hey, I don't need this shit," he announced.

"Pasquale, you got an eight and a half?" Bohanna persisted.

"D?" Pat asked, looking inside the shoe.

"C."

"Ah . . . I got D," he said, dashing the thief's last hope that something good might come from this. "I can't use 'em, man," he added, dropping the shoes back in the box. "I appreciate it."

If a customer haggled too long with Pat over a price, Bohanna or Angelo suddenly might shout through the walls: "You need help, Pasquale? Why don't we just take the stuff?" The haggling usually ceased.

Once when three customers fell to arguing about a fair split of the cash Pat had given them, Pat interrupted to warn, "Quiet. Show some respect for the Organization!" Just then there was a scream from the back room, and the sound of a shell being pumped into a shotgun.

"If I come out there, them goddam *tutsuns* don't have to worry about the money," Angelo shouted, using what he thought was a derogatory Italian slang word for blacks. "We'll divide it ourselves! Don't take-a no shit, Pasquale!" The customers charged for the door.

Sometimes the lawmen's threats were more serious. In late January three new customers arrived with some office equipment and began negotiating with Pat. Angelo, working the backup position that day, was uneasy—the trio was checking out the locks and doors and coldly staring at Pat while he rapped with them. They're setting us up, Angelo thought. He leveled the muzzle of the High-Standard shotgun at the nearest customer.

"Man, don't point none of that shit at me," the man said, glaring at Angelo. "What's with all these guns, anyway?"

"You're in our place, we do it this way!" Angelo snapped back. *He* would control this situation. In his rookie year, he had waded into brawls with drunken marines and sailors in bars all over No. 5 Precinct to prove to himself that he would never turn away. He had frequently spent off-hours stalking suspects in pitch-black alleys to control his fear and condition himself to keep absolutely cool. After fifteen years of street work, his responses were well trained.

"Goddamn, man, never put a gun on me," the thief warned.

"If you don't like it, get the hell out!"

The man turned for the door.

"Hey!" Angelo bellowed. "You go when we tell you to go!"

The man wheeled back to the counter, enraged. "I'll tell you something—a man has *never* pointed a gun at me and lived!"

"Yeah, well, I got one on you now," Angelo sneered.

"And I don't like it!"

"Tough shit!" Angelo hit the breechbolt and it snapped forward, jacking a shell into the chamber. "What are you going to do about it? You going to beat me up, huh? What?"

"Well, I don't know, man. I ain't going to do nuthin' now, but maybe I'll see you later when you ain't got that gun!"

"Oh, you want to see me on the street?" Angelo taunted, striding out from behind the backup counter. "I tell you what I'm going to do. I don't want to keep looking for you . . . I don't want to worry about seeing you on the street and you try to take advantage of me. I'm not as big as you. I might get hurt. So I think I'll take care of you right now, you know? We can just go ahead and finish this off right now!" He pulled a pistol from his waistband and leveled it at the man. It was a .32 cal. Baretta with an eight-inch-long double silencer on the barrel—an assassin's gun loaned to Angelo by a former federal agent.

The customer gaped. Angelo pulled the hammer back and wrapped both hands around the handle. "I could hit you with this and you wouldn't even hear it. You wouldn't even know you were dead."

The customer back-pedaled. "Hey, wait a minute, man. . . . I just don't like guns pointed at me."

"Hey, I don't like guns pointed at me, either. But you're there and I'm here. Pasquale pays me good money to do my job well, and I'm not going to see anybody harm Mr. Pasquale. Mr. Pasquale gets harmed, then I get harmed. And I ain't gonna get harmed. You understand?"

The customers left. Two weeks later when they returned, the belligerent man refused to identify himself. "Look," Pat explained, "I gotta know who y'are, because there have been cops nosing around here and how do I know you aren't a cop? Maybe you got a wire on you, or any shit like that. Now tell me your name!"

The man glared at Larocca.

"Tony! Search this guy!"

Bonano slid out the P.F.F. door, with Angelo's assassin gun down at his side. He smiled at the customer as he approached, then jammed the muzzle against the man's side. "What's your name, motherfucker!"

The customer's throat clicked drily. "I . . . just give my wallet to him," he said, pointing at Pat. Pasquale nodded; he was already searching through the papers and cards. The customer stammered, "I . . . vowed I'd kill any man that ever pointed a gun at me . . . , but I just changed my mind!"

"You a lucky sonofabitch!" Tony said.

The customer smiled weakly. "Shee-it, I thought stealin' this stuff was hard enough . . . but sellin' it is a whole lot tougher!"

When Angelo joined P.F.F., the police pistols were loaded with "ball" ammunition—shells containing a half-charge of powder and a 148-grain round-nosed lead slug. Officials said the shells were more humane than full-charge ammunition, but most street cops disagreed, contending the shells were more dangerous to police because they did not stop an assailant. Angelo had seen a police slug bounce off a car trunk and another stop halfway through a getaway-car windshield. But Angelo's own Treasury Department pistol shells were "hollow points," with a hollowed-out nose that spread on impact, and a full powder charge for more stopping power. The FBI, ATF, and most suburban forces around the city, as well as elsewhere in the nation, had shifted to hollow points. City police officials had resisted up to that time, however. (D.C. police began using hollow points in late 1976.)

Within a few weeks of Angelo's arrival, hollow points were being used. He and Pat soon found new uses for the discarded police ammunition. Using pliers and a door and doorframe for a makeshift vise, they extracted the lead slugs from the cartridges and poured out the gunpowder, leaving the small explosive primer behind. They now had a blank cartridge that would make a loud, harmless report and enough loose gunpowder to have some fun.

Bohanna La Fontaine, absorbed by his paperwork, was an early target. Angelo and Pat quietly slid a paper plate full of loose gunpowder under his chair and put a match to it. Bohanna leaped as the others guffawed.

They used the blank cartridges to "test fire" some of the pistols the customers fenced. The thieves reeled when Pat squeezed off a shot, and then they searched in vain along the opposite wall for a bullet hole.

The lawmen began using their shotgun shells for the same purpose. One day Pasquale slipped a blank shell into a shotgun brought in by two customers, casually aimed the weapon between the two men and fired.

"Uh . . . uh . . . ," one of the thieves staggered away from the counter and vomited.

"Yeah, this is a pretty good gun," Pat said nonchalantly. He shoved some paper towels at the sickened thief. "You made the mess. You clean it up," he said, and told the man to take the trashcan with him when he left.

Arscott called the next day and banned the blanks—he said he was worried that a jury might get the wrong impression of the lawmen.

At other times the men ate. Bohanna and Pasquale were particularly active trenchermen, Pat out of tension from handling the counter and Bohanna to replace energy expended weightlifting in one of the back rooms. Often they would gobble down prodigious amounts even if it was intended for someone else. When Tony's girlfriend, Anita Seldeen, sent down four dozen fresh-baked hot-cross buns, Bohanna and Pat, along with Rico, wolfed down forty-seven of them. "You oughta be ashamed of yourselves!" Angelo said when he discovered what had happened. He figured he would have the last one, and wandered over to the coffee urn. When he got back it was gone. Angelo looked at the empty plate for a moment, and at the grinning Bohanna, and walked away, feigning disgust.

On another occasion the men decided to cook up some special treats for their customers—meatballs, doused in hot mustard, with cores of salt. They brought them out for two unsuspecting customers, who took one look at the yellow oozing out of the meat and wanted no part of the snacks. "Hey, you. You have-a one of my spicy meatballs, huh?" Lieutenant Arif Mosrie said, holding the plate over the counter. Mosrie, who would head up the arrest teams at the February party, had come down to look at the operation.

As Giuseppe held the plate the customers started to turn away. "Naw, man, naw. I don't think so . . . I'm fine." Giuseppe glared. "You don' wanna my spicy meatballs? This-a special Old Country recipe!"

"Hey, look, I'll have one," Pat said, picking off one of the good meatballs the men had made for this purpose. "Hey! Those are damn good," Pat said. "Have-a meatball," Pat urged. "You don't have-a meatball, you hurt Giuseppe's feelings."

The customer bit down. His eyes widened in disbelief. "Very nice," he managed. The camera zoomed in for a closeup and the men in the back huddled around the monitor barely suppressing their chortles.

They served the snacks to other customers that day, and when the lawmen left that evening, they noticed remnants of meatballs on the sidewalk outside, and a few places where people had vomited.

When Angelo was announcing an incident and misread the incident number chalked on the clapboard, Mike playfully tossed a dart toward the slate. The dart glanced off it and pierced the heel of Angelo's hand. Mike jumped forward. "Damn!"

Angelo smiled at the camera. "Ladies and gentlemen of the jury, let the record show I have just been assaulted by a federal agent. . . . From the FBI no less." He held up his hand with the dart dangling from it.

"Come on, Ed, get rid of that thing," Mike begged from the sidelines.

"Hey, no way, Mike," Angelo replied. He pulled the dart out and began picking at the tiny wound to make it bigger.

The hidden television camera represented an audience, and the men found it seductive.

"Good morning, ladies and gentlemen of the jury," Angelo intoned, smiling at his reflection while Rico Rigatone focused on him from the other side of the phony mirror. "And now for the weather. It is thirty degrees outside and overcast. And here inside the spacious, luxurious establishment known as P.F.F., it is twenty degrees and we have the flu. . . ."

One idle afternoon, Bohanna and Pasquale busied themselves in the backroom, mixing peanut butter, salad oil, and

143

leftover potato salad into a gooey concoction that they piled up on a paper plate and deposited on the counter in front of the mirror. Rico manned the camera; Pat and Bohanna walked out to the suspect area.

Mike Franzino announced: "The P.F.F. Players are proud to present a little break from the routine."

The two men strolled slowly toward the camera.

"Hey, what's that there?" Bohanna said, pointing at the plate.

"Dunno," Pat replied. They approached and stared. Bohanna got down for a closer inspection.

"Looks like dog shit," he said.

"Yeah?"

He sniffed at it. "Smells like dog shit!"

"Yeah?"

He buried his face in it.

"It *is* dog shit! Be careful you don't step in it!"

The next day Arscott told the men they were wasting tape.

The cameras sometimes provided unexpected diversion for the lawmen by spying into the customers' most private acts.

A regular customer showed up one day with his girlfriend and a young man who was a casual acquaintance of the couple. Pat wanted to talk to the new man privately and told the other two to wait downstairs. They left and moments later appeared on the monitor of the surveillance camera in the first-floor hallway. They leaned against the wall and talked. As Pat's conversation droned on, Mike Franzino's attention flickered and then suddenly focused on the spy camera monitor, set beneath Pat's counter where Franzino could see it.

"*Botch-a-ma-gu . . . !*" he exclaimed, staring at the screen. "Hey . . . come look at this!"

Pasquale stepped back and the other lawmen crowded in from the back room. "I don't believe *this* shit!" Angelo declared, and they laughed and pointed. While the customer stood mystified on the other side of the counter, the lawmen watched his new friends standing against the wall downstairs, copulating.

144

14

While the men in the warehouse were getting their laughs in January, they were also up to something deadly serious. They were trying to check out Assistant United States Attorney Donald E. Robinson, Jr. And Robinson was spending more and more of his life trying to elude their grasp.

In their first telephone conversation, when Pasquale had posed as a man named Pete Smith, Robinson had seemed to them like he might take a bribe. With approval at the highest levels, the lawmen had pressed on to see how far he would go.

For Robinson the Pete Smith phone call had been the beginning of a nightmare. In trying to string Smith along, he was nearly suffocating in a web of deceit; he was lying to the men in the warehouse and to his bosses at the United States attorney's office, trying to keep his career afloat; and lying to his wife to keep his marriage intact. But Smith kept intruding, using the one person Robinson least wanted to hear about—Loretta Butler.

145

Robinson's crisis had started with an act of fellatio performed on him one afternoon six months earlier by Loretta, a black hooker and junkie who had been a government witness at one of his trials. He had lost the case and later he and Loretta talked by telephone about the verdict and about how she might make him feel better. They met outside D.C. Superior Court and he took her across the Potomac River to an Arlington, Virginia, Holiday Inn, where he rented a room under a false name. He had lost no more than an hour or so out of his busy schedule. He kept the incident secret from his superiors and from his trusting wife, Beth. He had virtually no contact with Loretta for months afterward, and considered the assignation forgotten.

But it was different for Loretta, a twenty-two-year-old hustler with friends like Tony Hendley, the thief, and Eugene Isaacs, a mailman who stole mail. Her sex act with an assistant U.S. attorney was something to boast about, and when she met Pasquale Larocca of P.F.F., she made sure he heard of her triumph.

By Christmastime Loretta was trying to get back into Robinson's life, leaving telephone messages for him. On December 30 she reached him from the P.F.F. warehouse and introduced a man who identified himself as Pete Smith. (Pasquale had given himself that name, figuring that if his own name really *was* Pasquale Larocca, he would not want to give it to a United States Attorney who might launch an investigation.) Smith's vague offer of $10,000 in return for some kind of business deal made Robinson uneasy. Pete Smith sounded like a criminal, and Robinson knew he was committing a crime—obstruction of justice—if he failed to report the telephone call to his superiors. But if he *did* report it, he risked revealing how Pete Smith had found him. And if he named Loretta they might uncover his secret. The U.S. attorney's office and stiff-lipped Earl Silbert were not going to condone his having sex with a witness! As for his wife, perhaps he could have explained it away if the other woman had been stunningly beautiful, but how could anyone from his world understand a union, however brief, between a pudgy black prostitute and a man like Robinson, with his Jesuit training at Fordham University and Fordham Law School, his experiences in the Peace Corps and with a prestigious Wall Street law firm, his current powers of prosecution, his wife and three children, and his new townhouse in the Maryland suburbs.

He thought about it for twenty-four hours and finally calculated a solution. He would tell almost, but not quite all, of the truth.

The next morning, December 31, Silbert received a call in his courthouse office: Arscott and Lill and several high-ranking police officials were on their way over—their undercover operation had turned up some alarming information about one of Silbert's assistants.

Robinson, knowing nothing of this, now approached one of his superiors, E. Lawrence Barcella, and floated a carefully thought-out version of the Pete Smith phone call, telling him that Smith wanted to meet him at National Airport and talk about giving him $10,000 over the next six months. He told Barcella everything except that it was apparently Loretta Butler who had given his name to Smith. Robinson said he thought it might be a crank call and thus he had waited a day to report it. Barcella, a driving young man who, like many of his colleagues, favored three-piece pin-striped suits and slicked-back hair, immediately suggested that Robinson strap on some recording equipment before going to meet Smith at National Airport.

Robinson recoiled. He feared the gangsters would find out he was a prosecutor. "Larry, I have a wife and three children! This is not what I'm trained to do." But Barcella saw little danger. The conversation ended inconclusively and Robinson returned to his office, where he got another unexpected call from Pete Smith, saying the airport meeting was canceled and that the big boss now wanted to come down from New York to meet him. They would be calling again and it could mean $10,000.

Meanwhile, Barcella headed for Silbert's office, where in the space of the next hour, the United States attorney heard versions from the police and from Barcella of the Pete Smith–Donald Robinson phone call that were alike in every important detail except one.

Silbert, a Phi Beta Kappa at Harvard, a wiry man who kept fit with tennis and wind sprints, had had bitter experiences with investigating official corruption. He had helped lead the original Watergate investigation that had stopped short of detecting Richard Nixon's White House coverup. Silbert's subsequent claim—that he couldn't believe an attorney general of the United States would lie to him—did little to blunt the congressional critics of his performance, and senatorial displeasure with his handling of Watergate matters had held up his appointment as the chief federal prosecutor in Washington for months. The criticism still rankled.

Now here were allegations that one of his own prosecutors was covering up a relationship with a prostitute and had fixed a trial for Loretta and one of her friends, Leon Black. The information was sketchy, though—none of the officials could tell him precisely what the hooker had said, nor had they looked at court records on the trial. So Silbert told Barcella and Barcella's boss, Donald Campbell, to study the videotapes and the case records and report back to him. It was decided that the police would continue their efforts at talking to Robinson.

No sooner had the meeting ended than Robinson called Silbert to report on the second telephone call from Pete Smith.

"Are you sure it couldn't have been a woman who told them about you?" Silbert asked.

"I don't know," Robinson lied.

That night, New Year's Eve, he sketched the details of the calls to his wife. Beth Robinson grimaced. "I don't want to get a call from someone at National Airport saying your body is in a trunk!" she said. She was furious that his superiors would suggest wiring him up and sending him off to meet with gangsters. The people he worked for, she believed, ought to have more concern than that for his welfare.

On January 5 Barcella and Campbell looked at the tapes of

Loretta Butler's visits to P.F.F. and told Silbert they believed Robinson was deliberately concealing Loretta's name out of fear they would discover he had had sex with her.

Silbert now ordered Robinson to put in writing all the details of his contacts with Pete Smith, including the names of anyone he thought might have directed Smith to him. If Robinson complied truthfully, he would have to disclose Loretta Butler. The prosecutors also looked up the files from the Leon Black case—but they sharply limited their efforts, pursuing only a few folders for fear that an extensive investigation would alert Robinson. What they did find was not enough to confirm or quell their suspicions that Robinson had somehow thrown the case.

Loretta Butler, Pete Smith—Robinson rolled them over and over in his mind. He wanted them to disappear quietly, but a resolution to his problem arrived unexpectedly just a few days into the new year when a relative called from upstate New York, to tell him that a district attorney there was interested in offering him a top position. Robinson leaped at the chance, and landed the job in a weekend interview in New York. It looked as if he himself could disappear.

More phone messages from Loretta were waiting for him when he returned to his Washington office on Monday, January 12, but now he figured he could ignore them and soon be safely out of town. On January 13 Robinson told Silbert he was resigning to take a big new job in upstate New York. He and Beth quickly spread the word among their Gaithersburg neighbors—their tidy townhouse would go on the block and they would move north in March.

His dream of peacefully slipping into a new life lasted one day. On January 14 Beth Robinson received a 7:30 A.M. telephone call.

"Hi, Robbie!" she said.

"I know you are alone," the voice said.

Beth was surprised to hear from her husband so soon—he had left for work only a half-hour before—but she knew he was a prankster and sometimes teased her on the telephone. "Of course you know I'm alone—you just left a little while ago," she said.

"I even know what you are wearing," the voice said.

"Come on, Robbie. What's going on?"

"Robbie won't be around," the voice said.

Beth Robinson insisted on knowing who was calling, and received an obscene answer. She slammed the phone down, locked the doors, checked on the children, and phoned her husband. Robinson demanded to know every word the voice had said, and reassured her that the telephone call was not significant. But he dwelled upon it, trying to place it in the stream of bizarre events that was threatening to scuttle his career.

No one ever did determine the source of that call, but Robinson at the time believed it must have come from Pete Smith—or one of his friends. Was it someone watching his home? The caller said he knew what Beth was wearing. And what about the suggestion that he, Robinson, wouldn't "be around" any more? Had "they" tried to reach him at the office and gone looking for him at home? If he continued to ignore them, there was no telling what they might do. He had asked Silbert if he could go immediately to upstate New York, but Silbert had refused to waive the required sixty days' advance notice. Robinson decided that for safety's sake he had to talk with these people at least once more before his scheduled departure on March 5. He would try to put them off.

Loretta called him on January 16 to say that Pete Smith would telephone him soon. This time Robinson had a plan. He would tell Smith he was tied up in a very important case and had a bodyguard assigned to him. That should scare him away. He would lie his way out of it.

In the FBI's Washington Field Office, Pete Smith, also known as Pasquale Larocca, a.k.a. Detective Patrick J. Lilly, tuned up for his phone call to Robinson. The men in The Hole at first were reluctant to try nailing a member of their own law-enforcement fraternity. "I don't want to ruin a guy's life, his family, his career, if he's just seeing a prostitute," Pat said.

But Mike insisted they had to dig into it. "A prostitute normally doesn't know what job a john has. But Loretta does. That's gotta mean something."

"Well, I don't like it. I'm no gink," Pat said, referring to the despised investigators for the police department's internal affairs division.

Angelo tried to offer support. He himself had once been a gink and he had hated it. Probing his fellow officers for wrongdoing violated the code he had known so well as a street officer —that clean cops didn't snitch on their buddies but simply looked the other way. Still, "If you got a prosecutor or a cop on the take, they're gonna hurt your reputation as an officer and hurt the department," he told Pat. "You don't want to walk with him. You gotta go ahead with it."

Now Lilly spoke into a telephone specially equipped with a tape recorder. "The date is January sixteenth, nineteen-seventy-six. The time is approximately four thirty-nine P.M., FBI Office, Washington Field Office." He dialed a number.

"Robinson?" Lilly asked when a voice answered.

"Yes," Robinson said.

"Yeah, this is Smith."

"How ya doin'?"

"Pretty good. Aah, Loretta told me to give you, uh, uh, call, you know. She said that she talked to you earlier."

Robinson tensed. He thought the way they were using Loretta's name right off meant that they knew what he had done with her in the motel and were threatening to disclose it. He decided to lead them on, and then ignore them.

"I want to find out if you're still interested in a business proposition," Pat said.

"Well, yeah, I am interested. Of course, I don't know anything about it yet."

"We might be able to use your kind of protection, if you can provide any."

"Well, it kinda depends on what kinda jams you might get

in, you know? Some cases I deal with and some cases I don't have much to do with . . . you know?"

"Well, I don't think at this point it would involve anything heavy that you couldn't handle. Like, what type of cases do you handle, Robinson?"

"Well, it all depends on what comes in the office. Uh, if you talk about, uh, income, tax evasion, stuff like that, I don't get involved in that. . . . It's not my, that's not my area."

"Yeah, yeah. Well, like, what could ya do for us?" Pat asked, trying to steer clear of any entrapment.

"Well . . . give me a situation and tell me what you need," Robinson said. "I mean, give me a situation where you got something that, you know, you need done and I'll tell you if I can do it. It's kind of a broad thing . . . really I don't know what we're talking about yet. . . ."

"Say a man is locked up for a gun—say a man is locked up for—shit, anything," Pat probed.

"That wouldn't be any problem, you know," Robinson said.

"What, a gun charge?"

"Yeah."

"Wouldn't be any problem?"

"No, that wouldn't be any problem."

"You sure?"

"I'm sure."

"Well, now. . . ." Pat paused a moment. He had just drawn a corrupt offer from the prosecutor; the door had opened to a serious criminal charge. "The thing is my boss up in New York said he'd be willing to meet with ya, ya understand? We'd be willing to shell out some money for your assistance."

"Uh-huh," Robinson said.

"The thing is, you could give us protection," Pat added.

"Uh-huh."

Lilly started talking about the Leon Black trial, remarking that Loretta had said Robinson threw the case. "You know, you can believe a bitch just so much, you know what I mean?"

Robinson said he would rather not go into it over the phone.

In fact, he had done nothing to throw that or any other case. Before he had gotten involved with Loretta and Pete Smith, he had considered himself an impeccably honest prosecutor.

"Well, hey, man, you in this thing or not?" Pasquale asked.

"Well, I'm in this thing," Robinson said. "But you never know [when] somebody's on the other end of the phone with a recorder or something like that; it ain't so hot to do that kind of thing over the phone."

"Dig it. I can understand that," Lilly said.

Robinson felt he had played the game long enough. Claiming he was involved in a particularly sensitive trial, Robinson told Pete Smith he had a bodyguard. "He kind of sees where I go and watches me and that's his job," Robinson explained, adding that he wouldn't be able to meet with anyone for a couple of weeks. Pat said he understood. They talked a little more and then hung up.

If these people were gangsters, Robinson figured, then the last thing they would want to do would be to deal with someone who was under some kind of protection.

By the end of the day, Robinson had completed the long-overdue memorandum to Silbert that was supposed to detail his contacts with Pete Smith. The memo failed to report the telephone call of that day, concealed Robinson's contact with Loretta, and did not report that she and Smith had left repeated telephone messages for him. Instead, Robinson wrote that he had heard nothing more from either of them since the December phone calls and that he had concluded the calls were "probably some kind of hoax/prank."

As he left for home, Robinson sensed he was rebounding. He had told Smith he would have a bodyguard for two weeks, figuring they certainly wouldn't call for at least a month or more, and by then he would be in his new job. He was relieved.

Silbert got the memo a few days later and added it to the Robinson case file. Then he authorized a formal FBI investigation of Robinson on suspicion of obstruction of justice. Silbert had concluded that by refusing to disclose Loretta's name, Robinson had at least impeded investigators who might want to arrest Pete Smith–Pasquale Larocca, supposedly a Mafia fence.

A few mornings later, the telephone rang in the Robinsons' quiet townhouse and Beth, unsuspecting, answered.

"Hi . . . it's me again—" the caller began. It was the same threatening voice.

Shaking with fright, she hung up and called her husband. He soothed her and tried to think what to do. Clearly, "they" must have found out he didn't have a bodyguard. Now he was sure it was more dangerous not to meet with them than to see what they wanted. They seemed determined to get him before he got away.

The call he dreaded came on January 26. Pete Smith told him the big boss was coming down from New York in three days and wanted to meet Robinson. Smith would tell him where to go to meet the boss. Robinson agreed to meet the man.

On January 28 Richard A. Genova, a broad-chested man of medium height with a pinched baritone voice and a peppery manner, flew into Washington from New Haven, Connecticut. In his late thirties, Genova spoke Italian and once had worked undercover as a chauffeur for a Mafia chieftain. Genova checked into a hotel and spent a quiet night.

Meanwhile Robinson had lost all doubt about who Pete Smith really was—he was convinced he was a Mafia man. If the telephone calls didn't make it clear, there were other reasons to believe it, including what was said by the woman who had got him involved in the first place—Loretta Butler.

"Loretta, who are these people?" Robinson asked as he drove her around late one afternoon during this time.

"They will tell you," she said curtly and looked away.

"Well, what do they do? Are they into drugs, these people?"

"No."

"Are they into pornography?"

"They will tell you what they do. You will find out."

A light snow was beginning to fall. Robinson drove aimlessly around Washington.

"Well, what are their names?"

"I think they are the Mafia."

Robinson paused and repeated the question.

"The first names are Mike and Pat," she said.

Mafia people with first names like Mike and Pat? That made about as much sense as the rest of this. As he questioned further, Loretta told him that they had some bigshots helping out already, judges and congressmen and people like that.

"You know, Loretta," he said, "if you know too much about what they are doing, some fine day you are going to find yourself floating in the river. Your grandmother and your mother won't know where you are!"

"You don't have to be afraid of them if you go along with them," Loretta said. "You'd better go there because if you don't you are going to be disappearing."

That confirmed his fears—there was no limit to what these men might do. Loretta told him she expected to be paid money for bringing him to Pete Smith. (Loretta had asked Pasquale what she was getting for her trouble. "Like . . . I don't know whether it's good or it's bad or who's right and who's wrong," she had said. "I just don't want it to come back on me." Pasquale had assured her that it wouldn't, that it would be between him and her, and that for her involvement she would "make some money." In fact, she never did.)

When Robinson had no more questions to ask, he dropped her off near her home and hurried on to Southwest Washington, where he taught a night class for the criminology school of the American University entitled "Introduction to the Administration of Justice."

On the morning of January 29, Richard A. Genova journeyed out to the Cafritz warehouse at 25th Place, Northeast, climbed the stairs to P.F.F. Inc., and was buzzed in. Now he called himself Frank Paccione.

At 9:15 A.M., Pete Smith called Robinson to tell him the meeting was all set. Robinson replied that he was due in court and didn't know if he could get away.

"Look, we brought the boss down here from New York," Smith said, an edge to his voice. "He has been down here once before and he is asking about you. Don't embarrass me. We want you here! We want you here around noon."

At midday, Robinson headed toward the strange address Pete Smith had given him. It was miles from any place familiar, on a dead-end street isolated in an area of garages and dingy warehouses. He pushed into the cold building and headed upstairs. At the top, he found himself in a chilly room being closely watched by two men—Mike, bearded and with a cap; and Frank, a balding man with a small moustache and a fast, authoritative manner. A third man emerged and identified himself as Pat.

. "How ya doin'?" one of them asked.

"Good," said Robinson. The thirty-two-year-old prosecutor, dressed in conservative suit and trenchcoat, had the rangy build of an athlete. Although nervous, he maintained the cool demeanor and glib tongue of a trial attorney.

They frisked him, just as he figured they would have if he had gone to National Airport. He was glad he never thought about wearing a tape recorder into the warehouse. (The search had been Paccione's idea—to convince Robinson the Mafia was worried about his carrying a recorder, even though *they* knew he didn't have one. It was the Mafia that had the recorders. The deceptions turning within themselves delighted Mike Franzino; they appealed to his sense of the comic. For this transaction, he had left his shotgun in the back of the warehouse—they were certain Robinson was no threat, and didn't want to scare him away by showing too much force.)

"Well, Mr. Robinson, what we want to know is if you could help us," Frank said.

"Everyone has said the same thing over and over, and I have no idea what we're talking about," Robinson protested.

"Well, let's get specific, that's why we're here," Frank replied. "Okay . . . we talked to Linda. . . ."

"Loretta," Pasquale corrected.

"She told us that she's a friend of yours."

"Yeah."

"She also told us that you helped her out."

"Yeah."

"What we're interested in is can you really help us?"

"It depends on what you're talking about. I still don't know. How do you mean, help you?"

"I want to know, how did you help Loretta? . . . What position are you that you can help us more than a regular attorney I'm sure could help us?"

"Well, if you get a guy locked up with something, I'm the guy who's in charge of whether he gets charged or how the case gets put together. . . ."

"Let's go back to the case," Frank said, trying for strong incriminating admissions from Robinson. "That's the only case I know, and it's the reason I'm here. In other words, would you be able to help us as well as we can help you? Now in this case with Loretta—how did you help? That's what I wanta know. And if I can see that, then I can see maybe you can help us in other things. . . ."

Robinson preferred to speak in generalities. He described how he could bounce cases back to police. ". . . On a burglary case, a stolen property case, narcotics case and stuff like that, I mean, you say, 'Look, your search was bad. I'm sorry.' "

Pat leaped at this. "In other words, you could stop it?"

"Yeah."

The lawmen in hiding were becoming alarmed. Robinson was studying the mirror. They knew that the slightest light leak into the camera booth would make the mirror transparent. He has somehow hawked Rico taking his picture, Angelo worried. There was little they could do except wait and hope.

"Can I ask you a question?" Frank Paccione said at one point, leaning over the counter and feigning warmth. "Now we've bullshitted about Loretta and I think we know where we stand. What exactly did you do for that one? Be honest with me. Now I think we've got a certain rapport going back and forth. . . ."

Robinson eventually felt he could not stall them on the point. They had asked him again and again; they were the audience and he was on stage.

". . . I was able to keep back certain evidence, you know," Robinson lied. In fact, he believed he had kept back nothing. He had prosecuted Leon Black as best he could, he felt, and he had been dismayed when the verdict was acquittal.

Pat wanted more, and tried some other theoretical cases. "A drug bust . . . would you be able to tell us?"

"Yeah, I'd be able to tell you at the time whether I could help," Robinson said. He knew he was falling into their pocket. It was the worst feeling of his life. He knew then that he had made a terrible mistake coming here. Now he knew what these men looked like, and he knew that if they were ever caught he might have to testify against them. He knew what happens to people who become witnesses against the Mafia. He knew that the government makes efforts to protect such witnesses, and often that protection doesn't work.

"If you're gonna help us," one of the Mafia men said, "what do you expect from us?"

"Money, man. Lots of money. That's what I'd expect," Robinson said. That might make them think harder about whether they really wanted him.

"You gonna put a price on everything?" Frank demanded. "When it comes to the point between you and I, I'm sure you stand a lot higher than I do. But *I* think we're both interested in the same thing—money." He drew out the cash box and cracked off two crisp $100 bills. "Let me give you this because at least you came today. . . ." He placed the two bills on the counter.

The prosecutor stared down at the bills. Rico zoomed the camera in for a closeup and as the conversation continued, the fingers of the prosecutor's hand eventually appeared on the monitor screen and came gently to rest on the notes, pinning them delicately with the fingertips.

Robinson told them he had problems in helping them get confidential information. "We got a pretty big office. A lot of the guys have different responsibilities. Every case does not come across my desk, you see. If a case comes across, that's the easy one. I can do anything I want with it. It's easy enough to find a reason. You can set a case for trial and not tell the witnesses. And you come into court and the judge says, 'You ready?' You say, 'No, I'm not ready. My witnesses—' The judge says, 'Bang!' That's the end of it. That's easy." It was a fact in D.C. Superior Court that some judges, faced with crowded court calendars, would cancel cases when prosecutors were unable to come up with their witnesses on trial day.

The talk swung back again to what Robinson had done for Loretta. Would she squeal on him, Paccione asked. Robinson assured them he was safe: "She doesn't even understand what went on. She couldn't prove anything."

"Well, she tells Pasquale stories all the time," said Frank.

"What's she tellin' Pasquale?" Robinson asked. "You might as well tell me."

"She says you did help," Frank said.

"Well, she does," Robinson said ruefully at one point. "She has a mouth on her. That's one thing. . . . See how many people in the world she's already told!"

"But a lot of 'em, they brag—talk bullshit," Frank reassured him at this time.

"I helped Loretta for nothing in a situation where it was easy for me to help her," Robinson said.

"You're telling me that you did certain things?" Frank Paccione probed relentlessly.

"Well, I had the case set up so that they just couldn't convict the guy, that's all," Robinson lied. Frank gently pushed the money on the counter toward Robinson.

They talked some more and then Robinson said, "Let me say this—what I'm gonna do now, now that I got your pitch and I understand—let me ask you this: Roughly how often do you think you're gonna be comin' to me?"

"Not often," Frank said.

Good, Robinson thought. By then I'll be in New York.

"We're not gonna be comin' to you for little things," Frank added. "I don't want that. Because to me you're too valuable."

"Let me be honest," Frank said, preparing to lie some more. "This is like a test. I know what you did. You're telling me what you did. Loretta tells me what you did. I don't know. I'll accept that. . . . I may not call you for three months. . . . It can't be a regular thing, because you've got your own work to do."

"That's my job," Robinson agreed, picking the money off the counter. "That's what I'm concerned about. That's one of the things I want to think about. What I want to do now that I understand where you're coming from . . . I wanta sit down and decide whether I wanta play ball with you or not. I got your offer and I want to think about it." Now he had the money in his hand. "If you'd rather keep this until I make my mind up, that's up to you. Frankly, I might call back and say, 'Look, I've thought it over —too much risk to me, to my career and it's not worth it to me.' Okay?"

"I think that's good," Frank said.

"I'll think it over and I'll let you know if I'm gonna play ball."

They asked him to retrieve some information about a woman named Marion Toye.

"She's got problems, and she can't do the job she's supposed to be doin' because of the problems," Frank said. "And it's givin' us heat."

"I'll get the information fast if I decide to do it, but I'm concerned about it and I'm gonna think it over. I'm gonna think it over, that's what I said . . . " Robinson repeated, seeking enough room so that he could play them along until he left town.

"But I would also hate to think that you're putting me on," Frank replied, trying to pressure Robinson into a decision. "Sure you gotta be concerned. Remember what I tell you about money. Money is no object. No object. Take it. But remember—the sky's the limit. And if you think sometimes that I didn't give you enough or Pasquale didn't, you tell me. Or if there are times when you need help, when you get a cramp, I don't care if you've helped me, but you call me. The same way I can call and say I need a little help."While Frank talked, Robinson was fitting the money into his wallet.

The conversation started to flag. Robinson had the money; he was now staring past them, his face completely still.

"Anything else—is it just that you're not sure or is something bothering you?" Frank asked solicitously.

"No, it's just that I'm not sure."

"You got any other problems, anything I can help with?"

"Not at the present time, no."

"That's just a small token now," Frank said ."I didn't want to embarrass you with that."

Robinson felt awkward; he believed he had been standing for moments without saying anything.

"If I can get this girl out," he said suddenly—"supposing I can spring her—what's that kind of job worth to you?"

Frank shot back: "What do *you* think it's worth—two thousand?"

"Yeah, I would say that," Robinson agreed.

"I'll tell you what—you get that thing set up the way you want. . . You think that's what it's worth, I'll have it here. No questions asked."

A few moments later, Robinson headed for the door.

The gang stole to the windows and watched Robinson walk back down 25th Place toward Bladensburg Road, the same path the thieves took. The other customers came from the ghetto, driven by their heroin compulsion. But here was an upper-crust white professional, paid much more than the police to put criminals in jail.

We gave you a choice and you just made the wrong one, Franzino thought. He was sure Robinson now was a prosecutor of criminals who had himself just become a criminal. Going after him never bothered any of the lawmen after that.

On the way back to his office, Robinson wrestled with himself, thinking at first he would go lay the two hundred dollars on his supervisor's desk and tell everything, and then remembering Loretta Butler. He had lied about her up to now, and they would want to know why. It was worse now than if he had leveled with them the first day.

He figured out a different path. He would tell his supervisor nothing and he would tell the Mafia he couldn't help them. And in a few more weeks, he would be gone. That was the best way, the safest way.

Frank Paccione stood before the phony mirror at P.F.F. Inc. "Okay," he said in his brisk way, "Special Agent Richard A. Genova, using the fictitious name Frank Paccione—"Pasquale interrupted, taking over from his FBI colleague, "The time is now one twenty-two P.M. The money delivered to Mr. Donald Robinson, assistant United States attorney, was two hundred dollars."

The men replayed the tape several times before they were satisfied that Robinson had been studying not the mirror but the nudes.

Don Campbell, the veteran prosecutor whose Major Crimes Section had been handling all P.F.F. cases since October, had spent an uneasy morning worrying about Robinson. He and the P.F.F. men had decided to pick the name of a P.F.F. customer to feed Robinson as a plausible test of his corruptibility. Together, they had chosen to give him Marion Elizabeth Toye, who had sold them a gun. Now Campbell waited to find out whether Robinson had in fact shown up at the warehouse. Bob Lill called in the early afternoon and gave him all the details of Robinson's visit. But, Lill cautioned, Robinson seemed uncertain as to whether he would actually go through with checking out Toye's status in return for the $200.

Campbell hurried from his fourth-floor office to give this information to Silbert. Campbell used a shortcut between the offices that took him through a room where secret grand jury records were filed. There he saw a man whom he recognized, but whose name he didn't know.

"I'm Don Robinson, an assistant prosecutor," the young man was saying to the secretary. Campbell stopped dead in his tracks. "Would you check the files on a defendant named Marion Toye?"

Campbell drifted out the door and rushed on to Silbert's office.

Robinson swept through Marion Toye's records with a mounting sense of relief. He could find no charge pending against her and at 2:26 P.M. called Pat to report this. But Pat suggested that perhaps she was on parole. Robinson never stopped to question how the Mafia could have been so mistaken about a friend. No danger signal went off.

He went back to the file and exactly one hour later called the warehouse. "She's on parole. It's outta my hands," he said. "There's nothing I can do," he told the man he once knew as Pete Smith but who he now knew was Pasquale Larocca.

"Fine," said the fence.

That's the end of it then, Robinson figured. He wasn't proud of what he had done, but he hadn't done anything wrong for the money, he was sure. And he was certain he would never have to do anything more. They had as much as told him so. He was going to be all right.

They called him from the warehouse the next day. Another name. "Milton Glover—we want you to help us. We want you to do what you can for him."

Robinson was almost sick with distress. They have got their hooks into me, they have me in their pockets. Just as quickly, he realized that the government lawyers might be tapping his phone, picking up all the calls he had not reported. So he called P.F.F. from another phone and told them he would telephone them from his desk and say he wanted nothing more to do with them. That would deceive anyone listening in. Now he was using the truth as a lie—he really *didn't* want to have anything to do with them.

In giving Marion E. Toye's name to Robinson, the prosecutors had inexplicably chosen a person who had no charges pending against her. They later realized this had not been a sufficient test of Robinson's willingness to provide information to the 'Mafia." So they chose Glover, a man who had been arrested in a drug case and was the subject of a grand jury investigation).

Robinson did nothing about Milton Glover. On February 10 they called and asked if he had looked into it. "No, I haven't been able to."

"Well, you know we're kind of interested in it. When do you think you would get back to us?" By the end of the week, Robinson heard himself say. Soon he had retrieved the Milton Glover file from court records and was studying it, knowing he must give them something. They had said they wanted information to feed Glover's lawyer. He decided to take them the date, time, and place of the arrest, figuring that such basic public information would not undermine the prosecution of the case. It sounded good to him as he sat in the safety of his office in the cavernous century-old Pension Building, in the heart of Washington's sprawling judicial mill. But on February 13, as he climbed the stairs in the frigid warehouse, seconds away from confronting the bearded gangsters of P.F.F., he knew he didn't have enough information for them and that he would have to make something up to keep them happy.

He got inside and began sparring with Pat, telling some things that weren't true, and some things that were. And then he passed on privileged information from the federal grand jury that only a prosecutor could know—that Milton Glover was about to be indicted by the grand jury. Robinson wasn't happy about doing this, but he figured he was the only one who would find out.

The lawmen were satisfied that Robinson had just committed a crime. Pat moved to complete the transaction in his usual way—by paying as little as possible.

"For your troubles . . . would a hundred be okay?" he asked.
Robinson drew himself away. "NOOO WAAAYY!"
"No? Why?" Pat demanded.
"Well, let's see. . . . What I've given you is something that a

lawyer might use to get a case knocked out," Robinson argued. "I say five . . . five bills!"

Fear had brought him to the warehouse, Robinson believed, fear of what the mob would do to him if he didn't come. But confronted with Pasquale Larocca's currency he had succumbed to greed. He was asking for $500 simply because it was $400 more than what was offered.

Pat opened the cash box. "What I'll give you is twenties, okay?"

"Uh-huh," Robinson said. "That's good." He watched, his face a mask of indifference, as Pat pulled out the money. The bills were brand new. "Are they in sequence, by the way?" Robinson asked.

"Yeah, I'm afraid so," Pasquale said. "I've got hundred dollar bills here if you'd care to have them."

"No, that's okay," Robinson said. "Just so I'll know because I'm gonna take 'em out of sequence." It was just one more in the string of precautions to protect his career. Now, he thought, if he could just make the lies hold up a little longer, he would be safely out of town, free from his own corruption; he could start life anew—beyond the grasp of Pasquale Larocca, this threatening underworld figure who had hooked him. And at least he would have the $500 for his troubles.

Pat snapped out the bills. Robinson would be a fitting trophy for their operation, like the bear rug.

Robinson put the money into his wallet.

"Thanks for the information," Pat said, shaking hands.

"Okay, good. As soon as I got anything further, I'll be in touch with you," Robinson said.

"All right, fine," said Pat, buzzing him out the door.

As Robinson left the warehouse he began sorting out where he stood. He knew beyond doubt that he was deep in the pocket of Mafia men, that he was a corrupted man. Somehow they had frightened him into it, he believed. Regardless, the nightmare would soon be over because in three weeks he would leave Washington to take the promising new job as a senior prosecutor in upstate New York. He drove back to his office, figuring that no one would ever find out what he had done.

Later that afternoon the United States Attorney for the District of Columbia, Earl J. Silbert, sat before videotape equipment in his locked third-floor office in the courthouse and watched Robinson take the $500 from Detective Patrick J. Lilly.

Monday, February 16, was a federal holiday in honor of George Washington's birthday, and the courts were closed. Robinson ran a family errand that day, driving forty-five miles to the Busy Corner Chair Shop, near Waldorf, a small town in rural southern Maryland.

Months before, the Robinsons had ordered a new dining-room table and eight chairs, handcrafted from oak by the shop owner, Marvin Stauffer, a taciturn Amishman who described himself as "fifty-fifty, farmer and furniture." The table and chairs were ready and Robinson was there to pay for them. It was a proud moment—Beth's family had patronized Stauffer for years, and now the prosecutor was starting to collect the unique pieces for his own family. Using the money he got at P.F.F., Robinson paid the bill—$417 plus tax.

15

Marion Elizabeth Toye knew a good thing when she saw it. Even though these men in the P.F.F. warehouse never returned a pistol she had loaned them, they were a good source of money, and she believed they had powerful friends; they were good people to know.

Toye had met the Mafia men through Loretta Butler, who claimed (with no substantiation at all) she had been sleeping with one of them and had been paid $500 for bringing them a district attorney.

Toye took a pistol to P.F.F. at Loretta's urging in January. The weapon belonged to someone else, but Loretta assured her she could pawn it and get it back later.

Once inside, Marion found a gun pointed at her face; a man named Pat loaned Loretta some money, and warned her to pay it back because he had fifty hits and one more didn't make any difference. One of the first things Pat asked Toye, after he got her name, was whether she tricked.

"I do a little bit—take my phone number down."

"Give a head job?" Pat asked.

Toye smiled. She understood these men, "Well, it could be arranged."

Toye, slim and bespectacled, a thirty-year-old lesbian and heroin addict, sold them her friend's gun, and answered the questions. She told them that she sold dope, she was on parole, and had got in a car accident, and wasn't working and lived alone, just her and her little poodle, in Southwest.

One of the lawmen behind the partition began muttering.

"Who's that back there?" Toye asked.

"That's Angelo," Pat said. "Man, you know every time they see beautiful women, they go ape-shit. They like to see a little tits, you know . . . that kind of shit."

"Oh, I got some nice tits," Toye said.

"Yeah, I'm a titty man, too," rumbled one of the other men behind the wall.

"Well, we plan on having a party because I'm trying to get big in the organization," Pat said. "I want my friends to meet my boss." Toye had a drink of wine. "You can bring me two of those rare bitches out of New York," she said, pointing to the *Playboy* foldouts in front of the hidden camera.

"Solid," Pat said. "We'll bring a couple of girls down for you, Toye, and we're gonna have the best of booze and drugs and everybody will get a door prize."

Toye figured they would help her. They had mentioned that they already had a D.A., and maybe one of their lawyers had the power to get the people downtown to stop messing with her, trying to violate her parole. As she left she reminded the men that she was only pawning the gun and wanted it back. They quickly agreed, but later told her they had sent it to New York. It was a standard excuse for holding on to evidence.

Toye left the place convinced and soon told one of her best friends, Ida Mae Logan, more often known as Margaret Jackson, or Ida Mae Jackson, or Ida Mae Watson. "Ida, I know these people—they got machine guns—they got to buzz you in and they take anything from you. Checks, credit cards, anything," Toye said.

"Toye, stop your damn lyin'."

"Ida, I swear!"

Her persistence set off a slight tingling in Ida's stomach. "Toye, you know what, I got a check home for almost seven hundred dollars. Now you take me over there and sell it." They went on January 23, 1976.

This was the first step in a chain of events that would end with Ida's husband agreeing to be a hit man for P.F.F. and confessing to an unsolved murder.

"Is that you, Toye?" a voice shouted at the top of the warehouse stairs.

"Yeah, man."

"Your friend with you?"

"Yeah." The door swung open.

"What's your friend's name?" the bearded man behind the counter asked.

"Ida." For that answer, Toye received a subtle foot stomp from her companion.

"Ida what?"

Ida told them her last name was Logan, which it in fact was, but she felt it was a perfect alias because she used other names all the time. She thought: You say Ida Logan on the street and nobody knows who the hell you're talking about. Nowhere in the world can you find Ida Logan anywhere.

The men in the warehouse knew exactly who she was. Angelo knew her as Ida Mae Watson, of a family already familiar to many city policemen. Some of them had pioneered in using portable, battery-powered electric drills to pierce car-door locks in seconds; they would then hot-wire the ignition, drive the car to an alley, and strip its tires and accessories in a few moments. Angelo figured that many Washingtonians were riding on "Watson tires."

"Ida, this is Pat; he's all right," Toye said. "Pat, Ida is all right and she's a helluva booster; she can bring you whatever you want."

Pretty soon they were hassling over how much the check was worth. Pat finally agreed to give Ida $60 for it, plus a $40 loan. Then he said, "Don't forget, we're having this big party and I want you to bring some girls."

"Oh yeah, you want these women over here for the party," Toye joked, nodding at the foldouts.

Angelo stepped out from the back room.

"Is that the titty freak?" Toye asked.

"Yeah, he loves titties," Pat said.

"I got some pretty titties. They ain't as big as the pictures, but they all right."

She stepped back and spread her coat and suddenly pulled up her sweater, exposing small breasts. "Are these titties worth anything?"

Ida paid no attention to Toye. She believed *she* had found a good thing and was busily jabbing at Pat.

"I'm the best fence in the city," Pat assured her.

"I'll damn well find out," Ida shot back.

"Yeah . . . you will," the counterman said, smiling.

Toye seemed despondent that no one was paying attention to her, and she pulled up her sweater again. "I said, 'Ain't as big as the pictures, but aren't they worth anything to you . . .' Jus' a mouthful, that's all you need."

Angelo bellowed.

Outside, Ida yammered how she didn't believe this was the Mafia, since those people were supposed to do things in secret and kill anyone who found out.

But Toye cut her off and made a joke out of Ida's apprehension. "Ida," she said, "it's for real."

Deceiving Ida Watson-Jackson-Logan was a tribute to the skills of the men in the warehouse. She was a quick read of people and at age thirty-two a veteran hustler. She had boosted (shoplifted) and sold drugs, had given birth to a child at the age of thirteen and had taken up with a drug dealer who bought her a new car, furniture, and shoes from Garfinckel's instead of Baker's or Chandler's. Ida spent years in jail, federal penitentiaries, and drug programs. Under the Narcotics Administration Rehabilitation Act she had to report to government clinics for counseling and urine specimens to check for heroin. Her parole hinged on it. She believed some of the counselors were whores and addicts themselves, and Ida knew of women who had foiled the urine test —even under close observation—by flicking some salt from the palm of a hand into the specimen bottle. Ida referred to the NARA act as "The Ugly Act."

Hustling was Ida's way of life. With little education and no decent job experience, she probably couldn't make more than $75 or $80 a week as a hospital cleanup worker or a waitress, she figured. That wasn't enough. What if she saw a couch that cost a lousy $300, for instance, and knew she couldn't get it without waiting three or four paychecks? Just coming out of the penitentiary, she didn't want to bus dishes or make beds. You do that for two or three years in jail, you don't wanna bus no dishes when you come home, she felt. There were other ways. She knew how to handle drugs and stolen things, and when an opportunity came along she moved. It looked like she could make some money from this guy Pat.

Over the next two weeks, Ida's husband, George (Sonny) Logan, badgered her for more information about the warehouse and these so-called Mafia men.

"It is unbelievable," Ida told him.

He had to see for himself. He had a stolen check he had bought on the street for $10, and a pistol that didn't work to sell to the men in the warehouse. The pistol had no clip, but he decided to take it along to see how smart they were.

Sonny didn't believe this type of operation could be right here in the federal city, the nation's capital, with the Bicentennial and all, right under the eyes of the FBI and the ATF and the the XYZ and all of them.

"How ya doin', how ya doin'," Pat said to him when he walked into the warehouse with Ida on February 4, 1976. Sonny was thirty-six years old and a native of Washington and thought he had seen everything until this—two bearded men holding what looked like machine guns, and boasting they were down from New York to organize the city, and would buy about anything he brought in. Sonny reached for the bottle of Jack Daniels, poured himself a glass and drank it straight down, not even bothering to wipe his mouth. Ida, wearing a floppy knitted hat pulled over her ears, was all smiles.

Pat paid $30 for the gun and 20 percent, or another $22, for the stolen check. Sonny swept the bills across the countertop. He was a hulking man, large-boned, broad-shouldered and could have passed for a light-heavyweight boxer. Sonny couldn't believe that these men were dumb enough to buy a gun without a clip.

"You came out good," Ida said to him, beaming. "You came out better than I thought you were gonna come out." To the men in the warehouse, this was simply incident number 555—until Sonny Logan confessed to an unsolved murder. Pat, fingering the pistol, asked him if he was afraid to use it.

"Hell, no," Sonny shot back. "Yeah, I done some things—between me and you, you know—I done some things and I had some things done to me. I been a convict, if that's what you wanta know." Sonny figured he'd better talk good to this Mafia man.

"What's the best thing you pulled off—the best thing?"

"Man," George said, "you know how people come up missin'. . . ."

Pat was on the scent. "Look, my boss in New York, he's hirin' twenty thieves to do various work; they'll be paid a weekly salary —people to do hit work—they will be paid bonuses, five, ten, fifteen thousand. . . . Have you taken anybody out?"

Sonny, shifting his feet, thought hard on this one. For about ten or fifteen seconds he said nothing. What was he going to tell them? Pat spoke up again. "Have you ever killed anybody?"

"Yeah."

"Tell me about it."

Ida could feel the anxiety building within her. Something wasn't right, she thought. It ain't Pat's business. He ain't here for nothin' but to buy somethin'. All over the world, she thought, fences don't care how you get it—all they do is want it. This man was getting too personal. She started babbling—whatever came to mind—to try to change the subject.

"Ida, there you go bein' a businesswoman again, never havin' no fun," Pat said, smiling at her. Then he turned to George again.

"I want a guy not afraid of anything. Not afraid to take a knife and stick it in somebody and slit 'em. Shoot 'em and walk away. I've killed fifty people, okay? And I've never served time on any of 'em. I've been outta jail within twelve hours. . . . Now, tell me about it."

"Well, you know a guy knocked off . . .," Sonny said. He was into it now. "We used to work together . . . it was in the paper . . . you know, that one on Kenilworth Avenue—Parsons."

"What's his first name," Pat interjected. Ida thought about elbowing Sonny in the stomach.

"Gilbert Parsons," he said. Ida felt like *she* had been elbowed in the stomach. Everybody started talking at once, each falsely trying to explain something.

Sonny had dealt drugs with Gilbert Parsons and for a while even roomed with him. Two months earlier, Sonny had read in the papers how Parsons had been found dumped off Kenilworth Avenue in suburban Maryland with bullet holes in his head. Sonny told friends that he was shocked by the murder.

Ida knew Gilbert, too, but claimed not to know anything about his death. Ida regarded Gilbert Parsons as kind of a Robin Hood of H Street, Northeast. He would take from people who had lots of dope—asking them for it at first and then sticking them up if they balked—and share it with other people. In his forties, he had been selling and using drugs for as long as she could remember. His veins were so collapsed that Ida had to stick the needle in for him, in places where the veins were still good, like his neck. Gilbert gave her things for that—like the stolen check that she had sold to Pat when she first came to the warehouse with Marion Toye.

Sonny had two more healthy shots from the whiskey bottle while he talked with the hoods. He knew quite a bit about Parsons's death and now he figured he would impress these men by saying he had done it. They might have some kind of job for him, or at least a good drug connection.

"I'm humble and I want to learn," he said. "Whatever you can teach me—okay. There's always somebody that knows something more, and in this business the more you know the longer you live."

Pat nodded his understanding. "When you make a hit," he said, "no broads, nothin' flashy. A fresh set of plates, you get out of town, fifteen hundred bucks—that's how you do it." Sonny gave them his home phone number, believing he could trust them now. He was chuckling to himself as he left down the stairs when Pat called out, "Next time you come back, man, bring the clip for it, hear?"

Outside, Ida was fussing. "Get yourself a damn cup of coffee," she sneered. It seemed to her that Sonny had been drinking too much. Ida didn't like the place anymore; didn't like the questions. She felt that she would never go back. Sonny, on the other hand, liked it. They had bought his broken gun. He just hoped that they'd stay around; he thought: I've got 'em hook, line, and sinker.

Sonny at age twelve had mastered the exchange rate of heroin like his friends on the street. Pretty soon he had turned his back on his parents and grandparents and their lives of work-a-day drudgery. He became a thief and dope dealer and caught a felony beef and a string of misdemeanors. At age thirty-six, he figured he had kicked heroin sixteen or seventeen times.

Sonny met Ida in 1966, after her main man got locked up. He always had dope and fancy clothes, and she began dealing with him and then sleeping with him. They were married while in a federal drug rehabilitation program at Lexington, Kentucky, and a year later, they had a child who was the first baby delivered at D.C. General Hospital to be born addicted to methadone.

Sonny was looking for a steady job, even if it was working for criminals, and the way the men in the warehouse talked, he might get one. So on February 17 he went back to P.F.F.

Pat was waiting for him. He wanted much more detail about the killing of Gilbert Parsons. "The guy you shot," Pat said. "The boss likes it. Tell me about the piece—what did you do with it?"

Sonny saw he was in trouble. Having lied before, now he made up something else. "I threw it in the east branch of the Potomac." He described in detail the two guns he said were used and said he shot Parsons six or seven times. The lawmen had read the police homicide report and it told pretty much the same facts. Listening to Logan, some of them were sure he was the killer. He even looked the part to them, with his close-cropped hair and menacing eyes, hunkered down in his turtleneck and leather jacket. Angelo, who had spent two years on the homicide squad, studied Logan's demeanor and concluded that he was guilty. Sonny's forearms tensed and his voice dropped when he told about Parsons. Mike Franzino chambered a shell into his shotgun when Logan walked into P.F.F. Angelo did the same with his Mossberg pump-action shotgun. The guns were normally loaded with two shells of Four-Shot, a special police load designed for wider spread and impact; and three shells of double-ought buck-shot, 32 pellets per shell. Either load could blast through the quarter-inch plywood false wall and blow apart the man standing in front of Pat.

Even though the shooting of a dope dealer like Gilbert Parsons cheered Angelo, he badly wanted George Logan. The way he figured it, if Logan had killed once, he could kill again and this time Angelo or some other lawman might be the dead man. Angelo's frustration sharpened when he allowed himself to re-member that the murderer he most wanted behind bars was right now free. This man had stomped an old man to death to get his Bulova watch and the money in his pants. Angelo had cracked the suspect into confession, but a judge barred the confession from evidence, ruling that it had been given under duress. The defendant was able to plead guilty to second-degree murder instead of getting the first-degree-murder conviction—and probably life imprisonment—that Angelo was sure he deserved. The murderer had been released recently. Angelo hoped he would run into him one day and that the man would try something. He'd nab him on the spot.

Now here was Logan, boasting of killing a man. Angelo fingered the trigger of his shotgun. Let him try something, he thought. Please try something. This time, there would be no plea.

George Logan wasn't the first to agree to be a hit man for P.F.F. Mike Franzino, in the running notes he took at the backup counter for the FBI, had recorded some thirty who said they would kill for P.F.F. Franzino was generally shocked that people volunteered to murder. Some of them, he believed, would have gone out to kill for fifty bucks. Mike had seen criminals portray themselves humbly to judges and police; he was surprised to see how different and bold they were when they thought they were among friends. The others in P.F.F., however—Angelo Lasagna, Tony Bonano, Pasquale Larocca, Bohanna La Fontaine, and Rico Rigatone—had worked undercover on the streets of Washington, and nothing surprised them. Tony Bonano, for instance, twice had had men point a gun at his head and pull the trigger only to have the gun misfire.

When George Logan confessed to an unsolved murder to prove his qualifications, the men behind the false walls itched to make the collar; instead they had to watch him walk away.

George was having his way now, the men in the warehouse told themselves. But in eleven days it would be their turn. "You be sure to come to the party," Pat reminded him. George smiled. Pat handed him a P.F.F. card and wrote in ink "8:15 P.M., Saturday, February 28." They planned for George to be one of the first to arrive.

16

As early as January Pat had come up with a new question for P.F.F. customers. "Hey, you gonna come to our party?" It provoked immediate interest.

On January 6 Richie Parker visited P.F.F. to transact a little more business with the Mafia fences who on December 4 had paid him for the hijacked truck full of Christmas toys. As he headed for the door with the money from his latest sale, Pat threw out his newest con. "You know, we're gonna have a party. . . . My boss is in Italy right now, but when he comes back, I'm movin' up in the organization, and there's gonna be a party. We're gonna invite all our best customers."

Richie stopped.

"There's gonna be the best broads, the best booze, the best shit, uh . . . uh. . . ." Pat counted the come-ons on his fingers. "Uh . . . drugs, and we're gonna have a door prize of at least fifty bucks for everyone that comes. . . ." Richie moved his elbows onto the counter and propped his head in his hands, grinning at Pat from beneath the black beret he was wearing low over his forehead.

"You gonna let me know when that date is?"

"Yeah . . . yeah."

"Gooood," Richie crooned. ". . . Luuuv parties . . . Luuuv door prizes!"

As he left, the room filled with laughter.

The lawmen had talked for months about ending Operation Sting with a party for their customers—featuring door prizes of handcuffs. The idea had tantalized them since the previous September, when they first heard it from Frank Herron of the New York City police. Their thoughts ripened during the months of contact with criminals who bragged how they had been preying on citizens and duping policemen and judges. In idle moments, the lawmen imagined how the felons' faces would look when they learned who they had been dealing with.

In late January Lill and Arscott started meeting in their stuffy offices with other police and FBI officials to map out the safe roundup of the hustlers, hookers, creepers, muggers, robbers, junkies, hijackers, burglars, and pickpockets who were P.F.F.'s regular customers. They chose the fourth Saturday in February for the party, giving them a month to get it ready. FBI agent Ed Leary, considered a paperwork genius in the Washington Field Office, was assigned to write up a plan that would cover the movement of every lawman on February 28.

A formidable task. As many as two hundred Sting suspects might come, many of them armed. They had to be arrested quickly and whisked away so that others would arrive unaware. Once in custody, the suspects would have to be stripped and searched, fingerprinted and identified, charged, interrogated, and hauled to jail. Other lawmen would sweep the city for suspects who didn't show up. Speed was essential; word would spread fast that the event at P.F.F. was no party.

It was going to take hundreds of lawmen working together like a crack combat assault team to pull this party off, and the planners began to realize that even for Washington's law forces

—who had apprehended demonstrators by the thousands during antiwar protests in the 1960s—the Sting party was shaping up as the largest surprise mass arrest in city history. .

In early February Assistant Prosecutor Dan Bernstein began plowing through the raw P.F.F. police reports to turn them into formal criminal charges against the customers. All through January the supervisors had steadily added clerks and technicians to keep the customers' case jackets up to date. The number of helpers rose from a handful of people in the first two months to sixty by the end of January. Bernstein, who had handled the legal business for the operation, was staggered by the amount of paper. File cabinets bulged with information. Long days of work stretched ahead. He added an assistant to help distill the raw reports and prepare affidavits showing that there was sufficient reason to arrest the person. With such affidavits, the prosecutors could ask for arrest warrants from the United States magistrate. It was slow going, sifting out the strongest charges and converting them to the right form for the magistrate's approval. By mid-February Bernstein had added four other assistants to finish the work and get the warrants signed by the judge in time for the February 28 party.

Not everyone in The Hole wanted the operation to end. Some of them realized, as few deskbound supervisors could, that they had been accepted as Mafia in a city that had no Mafia and knew little of organized crime. They felt that their customers could walk them into any operation in D.C.—drugs, numbers, fencing, name it. Mike and Tony talked about going with the thieves outside the warehouse to make connections. They sensed a chance to penetrate the inner crime circles of Washington, learning who the real fences sold to and the identities of major drug dealers and other elusive criminals. Finding little support, they didn't pursue the idea.

Like many young officers, the men did not have a "father," an older street officer who looked out for them, to argue their views; or a "rabbi," a senior official who was their patron, to get the message up to the command level. For their part, the supervisors worried about the men's safety and the mounting P.F.F. caseload. Lill felt the men were played out mentally and physically from the cold, the bouts of flu that had struck in mid-January, and the sheer length of the operation. Besides, other major undercover projects awaited execution, and the United States attorney's office began grumbling that no undercover operation had gone beyond six months.

Toward the end, the senior chieftains of the P.F.F. project sat down once again at a full-scale conference. Week after week through the winter, as the evidence accumulated in the basement rooms of the Second District, the videotape had stacked up under lock and key at police headquarters, more than 110 reels bearing seemingly irrefutable proof of wrongdoing by more than two hundred people. It had been the most thorough, successful undercover investigation in their careers. They had avoided violence, and they were sure they had avoided entrapment. Their secret had remained secure. The FBI and city police had worked harmoniously in ways that no senior official had ever imagined. Now they were at the threshold of a final con that would deliver dozens of criminals peacefully and voluntarily into their hands for arrest, incarceration, and prosecution.

It was a sweet moment. Most of the P.F.F. customers had turned out to have long records of previous arrests and convictions. With the videotapes, the lawmen were sure they could put these professional predators behind bars for years to come. Pasquale Larocca and the other members of the warehouse gang had performed brilliantly. The Sting operation would be remembered for years, they thought. Now the commanders churned carefully through FBI-man Leary's sixty-five-page "work product," as the bureau called it, reviewing the details and making some revisions. When the conference was finished, they were confident they could do the job. The senior officials then approved the largest mobilization of police and federal agents connected with an undercover operation in the history of Washington. Seven hundred officers and agents would be used at the warehouse, the Fifth District, the central cellblock at police headquarters, and in the arrest and interrogation teams in order to ensure a successful end to Police-FBI Fencing, Incognito.

In the week before the party, the undercover men once again grabbed hammers and nail aprons to make alterations to their lair, this time to the two cavernous rooms that stretched away behind the upstairs offices. Dusty and littered with scrap lumber, these rooms had been the target range where the gang tossed throwing knives, darts, and SuperBalls. Within a few days, the men rearranged the rooms into processing areas for the guests they hoped to arrest at the party.

They knocked a hole in the rear wall of the P.F.F. offices and built a temporary wooden stairway from the main floor of the warehouse up to the new rear exit from P.F.F. Customers in custody would be led down this directly to the processing area instead of via the front stairs where they might meet an unsuspecting customer on *his* way upstairs to the party.

The men stapled black plastic drop cloths over two large storage racks they found in the back room to make dressing cubicles for the prisoners to strip in privacy. They stretched a stout chain between two metal posts and backed up to it long park benches borrowed from the U.S. Park Police, who patrolled the monuments and many public parks in Washington. Prisoners would be seated on the benches and handcuffed to the chain while they awaited the ride to jail. The lawmen planned to move them in U-Haul vans from a three-bay garage that had been built onto the rear of the warehouse years before.

One day while the men were busy in the back rooms unloading government desks and chairs for the technicians who would process the customers, a customer barged in unannounced. The lawmen had just set up the park benches where the arrested suspects would sit and Tony Bonano was holding a sheaf of arrest forms. "Is Pat around?" the thief inquired.

"Hey, what the hell you doin' down here!" Tony yelled. "You know you're not supposed to come down here unless you call."

"Well, I called and no one answered."

"That means you don't come down here! You wanna get cut off?"

Angelo picked up one of the throwing knives and hurled it past the customer. It stuck impressively into the door frame. The punctuation was effective. The customer back-pedaled and returned later. He never caught on to what the lawmen were preparing.

The men positioned the desks so that the customers would move smoothly from the identification tables to a strip-search, to the park benches, and then past a final control desk before crawling into the waiting vans. Sound equipment was set up near the temporary stairway for party music, and technicians installed a special stroboscopic light alarm for Pat to warn the waiting police process teams when customers were inside P.F.F.

Toward the end of the week, the men lined up their clothes for the party. Tony, Bohanna, and Rico settled on their own slacks and jackets or leisure suits. Angelo chose the lush powder-blue double-knit brocade dinner jacket with dark velvet lapels that his wife, June, had sewn for him to wear at their daughter Jeannette's wedding the previous spring.

Pat and Mike went to a shop in Prince George's County to rent tuxedos. Mike picked a blue one, and a ruffled shirt, but Pat was taking his time. "How do I look?" he would ask, twirling in one jacket after another in front of the tailor's mirrors. He finally settled on a maroon velvet tuxedo and a pink shirt with ruffled front and lace at the cuffs. "This'll do just fine," he beamed.

By Thursday, February 26, Richie Parker was desperate. He knew the P.F.F. men were police. One of his friends had recognized Pat (even though Pat had quickly become "sick" and excused himself), and when Richie heard this, all the nosy P.F.F. questions suddenly made sense.

He wanted to make a deal. The problem was, he didn't have anything to offer. When Pat answered the phone, Richie tried to be cagey. "I have knowledge of who you are," he said.

"Uh-huh," Pat responded.

"I mean, I didn't use it against you, man. So since I didn't try to hurt you—don't hurt me; I mean because I didn't do it, you know? . . . I mean I considered your position, so if there is any way possible, I'd like you to consider mine."

"Uh-huh."

Shit, Richie thought. He couldn't speak more bluntly because they might arrest him on the spot. But this way he was giving Pat too much room. He searched for a hold.

"Look . . . I know what's gonna jump off Saturday . . . the party and all . . . and I know you gotta do what you gotta do. . . ."

"Uh-huh."

God-*damn* it.

"I mean . . . I know the organization that you work for. . . . Isn't that right?"

"Well," Pat said, "let's suppose it is."

"Yeah!" Richie said, relieved.

"Yeah?" Pat replied.

Pat wasn't giving. Richie's hopes collapsed. Just before he hung up, depressed and frustrated, he said something lame, like he wasn't going to blow the whistle on them, so he would appreciate it if they didn't blow one on him.

Of course, he had told everyone he could find that they were the police. But his friends and street acquaintances wouldn't believe him.

On the same day, Cockeye stood in D.C. Superior Court to be sentenced for crimes unrelated to his visits to P.F.F.

"Your Honor," said his court-appointed attorney, Alan Soschin, "I've gotten to know Mr. [Cockeye] quite well. I've been representing him now for eight months, and during that time with me he has always been responsible. But for these criminal violations, which I'll address myself to in a moment, Mr. [Cockeye] it appears has finally achieved some degree of stability in the community."

Cockeye, about to be sentenced for the four crimes he had pleaded guilty to in December, was appearing before the same judge he had lied to then. He was prepared to lie again. Unknown to anyone in the court he had returned again and again to the warehouse in January and February to sell credit cards, blank checks, a passport, a radio, a television, a tape deck, savings bonds, a pistol, ammunition, a knife, and handcuffs.

As Superior Court Judge Fred L. McIntyre looked on impassively, Soschin took up the defense and talked at length about his client: he now had a wife, a house, a job and apparently was off heroin, Soschin said. "I would suggest in this case, Your Honor, to take into consideration the good or the positive that Mr. [Cockeye] had displayed over the last several months and use that to temper whatever sentence Your Honor is going to impose. . . . Mr. [Cockeye] had his hand in the till since he was a young person. He's begun to see the error of his ways and perhaps this is going to be his last brush with the criminal justice system."

Cockeye's wife testified that some of his problems were her fault because she put pressure on him to get a house. He had never had such responsibility before, she said. But the responsibility has helped him improve.

"What we have before us is a real con man," the prosecutor, Jonathan Marks, said, "a man who when the pressure comes on and the going gets tough straightens himself up—at least apparently from December to now—but who in the end is a man who just can't do anything other than commit crimes in order to support himself."

Cockeye said that he had never tried to con anyone. McIntyre said it was unpleasant personally, but that he had no choice except to give Cockeye a sentence he probably wouldn't like: a minimum of thirty-five months' imprisonment and a maximum of nine years and three months for four charges—burglary, attempted forgery, petty larceny, and receiving stolen property.

The U.S. marshals led him away. Cockeye would not be going to the party.

The next night, Friday, February 27, Richie went to P.F.F. figuring it was his last chance. As he stood in the street, looking up at the brick warehouse, Richie's nerves started tingling. There was always a chance his friend was wrong, that they really were Mafia. If he threatened them, they just might blow him away. Naw, they had to be the rollers. He had described the men in the warehouse to the real police months ago. Nothing had happened. That had to be proof.

But if he threatened to blow their cover, these men might lock him up, even though he saw himself as an innocent middleman in his warehouse transactions, kind of like a businessman. If they got angry enough, they might even kill him. They could do that, he believed. Who would arrest the police? It was up to him to bring it off, to choose his words carefully enough so they would let him go.

As he trudged up the stairs, he knew he had felt this scared only once before—at a time when he left the girlfriend of a man we'll call Crazy Ike in a tight spot and then had to go back and explain it to him. A robber had stuck up Richie and the girl while they were walking on 14th Street and Richie had run off. Ike was the kind of man who would hunt him down and shoot him for this, so the only thing to do was to try to talk his way out of it.

He went to see Ike and as he tried to explain, Ike kept asking questions and slowly twisting the cylinder of his revolver. Richie believed Ike was toying with him before the kill. So he asked to relieve himself, then sneaked out the bathroom window. Now Richie had the same sickening feeling.

The conversation inside was as awkward as it had been on the telephone. In case Pat was thinking about locking him up or shooting him, Richie stammered, he had a friend waiting for him down the block.

After a little talk, Richie wound up saying, "I know what's goin' down, I know what's happening. I never put your shit out on the street, so I hope I get a break."

Pat nodded. "We'll see you at the party," he said.

Richie knew when he walked out of there, that was one party he wanted to miss.

Friday, February 27, Police-FBI Fencing Incognito closed for the last time. The men had recorded more than 750 incidents since the October 1 opening. Two hundred and twelve persons had been identified as suspects, and the lawmen had already obtained warrants for the arrests of 181 of them. They had made cases against creepers, hustlers, burglars, stickup men, hijackers, corrupt letter carriers, a high school janitor, and a city welfare clerk. They were sure they had all the evidence they needed to convict one man of murder and another of violating his prosecutor's oath by taking a bribe. They had respected Herron's warnings, and there had been no trouble. The only injury was a wrenched back; the only shots fired were blanks, triggered in jest. They had developed leads on other crimes and learned names, addresses, and alleged specialties of dozens of other criminals, information that would be placed on file. Now, with the undercover investigation ended, all that remained was to have a good party.

17

The gang members arose in their suburban homes early on Saturday, edgy with anticipation. The hour of the Sting was near.

In Washington, blue-jacketed police were streaming toward Second District headquarters from station houses all over the city. Chosen at roll call a few days earlier, these "uniforms" were under the impression they were going to work overtime Saturday on a routine movement of D.C. jail inmates from an old building to a new one, which would require little more than a show of force from the police.

But when they arrived at Two-D, they found themselves herded into U-Haul vans and rushed through the light weekend traffic to a rear entrance of the Fifth District headquarters at 1805 Bladensburg Road, Northeast. Moved inside by tight-lipped sergeants, the new arrivals spilled into roll call rooms and assembly areas, and wandered the corridors of the station house, surprised by what they saw. Dozens of plainclothes federal agents were pouring into the building—from the FBI, Secret Service, ATF, and Postal Service, as well as police from suburban Montgomery and Prince George's counties. Senior police conducted inspections and federal prosecutors clustered in offices studying thick sheaves of paper and going over tactics. This was no simple prisoner move.

In mid-afternoon, Mike Franzino readied himself for the party. His wife, Laura, was relieved to know the operation was nearly over. For months, she worried every day about his safety, and had parried neighbors' questions about his job. The neighbors in the new community where they recently moved had turned cool, put off by the sight of Mike going to work in his fatigues, long beard, sunglasses and battered pickup truck.

Now, Franzino donned his blue tuxedo, climbed into the pickup and clattered away, aware of more than the usual number of stares from the neighbors. He had decided to discard the tie and leave his shirt open at the collar, as he imagined mobsters might. Later, he realized he had worn a T-shirt underneath that showed through the open collar. What self-respecting mobster would wear a T-shirt? He laughed at himself.

Finally, all the P.F.F. gang arrived, Pat and Mike in their party clothes and the others in work togs. They completed their party arrangements, draping a roll of green crepe paper from the steel roof rafters and stacking up three cases of beer and some whiskey behind a partition for the arrest teams.

The tempo picked up—U-Haul vans rumbled into the property yard next to the warehouse; downstairs, policemen began filtering into the back rooms. As they explored the building, their voices drifted into the P.F.F. office through the hole at the top of the makeshift stairs. After a while, several awed officers came up and toured the elaborate trap where the men had lived and worked for five months. They stood before the counter wide-eyed.

Arscott, Lill, and Lieutenant Arif Mosrie, the arrest team

supervisor, arrived. The evidence table behind the P.F.F. side door was removed to make room for the arrest teams. This door, just to the right of the counter, led to passageways behind the false walls and had been kept locked during the fencing transactions. Tonight it would be unlocked, and behind it would be six-man police teams, men who at a signal would burst into the office, make the arrests, and then herd the prisoners through the processing until they were carted off in the U-Hauls. The man chosen to lead these teams was Sergeant Richard "Hook" Traylor, a twenty-year career man who was a supervisor of the riot squad. Hook Traylor stood about six feet four in his boots and weighed well over 220 pounds without his flak jacket. His strength was legendary in the police department. Dressed in his combat boots, bullet-proof vest and riot helmet, and cradling a short-barreled riot gun as if it were a toy, Hook was the leading edge of the shock wave that would roll over the customers. Angelo knew he was the right man for the job: once Hook had picked him up and effortlessly launched him through a glass transom to get at a fugitive behind a locked door.

Mosrie rehearsed and timed some fake arrests. Pat rapped with two "customers"—Lill and Arscott—and then ordered his "heavies" to frisk them for weapons. Tony and Bohanna slid out through the side door and patted the men down, finding a pistol Arscott had hidden in his clothing. Tony and Bohanna left, and within moments Hook Traylor and an arrest team rushed into the room while Pasquale announced, "You're under arrest!" Herron had said the customers would go into shock upon arrest and peacefully follow police commands. But the P.F.F. men were taking no chances.

Arscott feigned resistance as part of the practice run. He continued to buck (shrug off the arrest teams) until Hook planted a forearm chop on the lieutenant that sent him hurtling against a wall across the room. The two supervisors decided they had done enough rehearsing.

As the afternoon ended, the P.F.F. men found themselves encircled by uniformed police who were badgering them for stories about the warehouse operation. The men recounted their deceptions—how they cheated the customers out of money, rattled their confidence with fake Italian and tales of murder; how they staged phone calls to "Mario in New York" and got thieves to reveal their names and addresses while signing up to be hit men for the organization. They described the recipe for spicy meatballs and how they had made a case against a federal prosecutor. The uniformed policemen scarcely believed what they were hearing. But the Mafia men reassured them that they would soon see for themselves.

By five o'clock there was nothing left but to wait. The time grated on everyone's nerves. Pat and Mike decided to go for a drive in a new undercover Cadillac they had rented for the night (New York license plates supplied by the FBI). They wheeled up to the 14th Street strip and cruised, eyeing the crowds on the sidewalks. Wherever they went, they gave the clenched-fist black-power salute. Some people waved and whistled back at them. They felt, with some pride, that the residents of the strip regarded them as high-class mobsters.

Meanwhile Tony and Angelo and the others went to a Holiday Inn a few blocks away where Arscott had rented them rooms. They tried to relax, stretching on the beds or wandering aimlessly from room to room, like a high school basketball team before a championship game. The time dragged by and at last it was time to dress for the party.

They showered, shaved, and carefully donned their fine clothes, buttoning the shirts over bullet-proof vests one last time. Ready at last, they filed outside and drove slowly back to the warehouse in *their* undercover Cadillac. As they turned onto 25th Place from Bladensburg Road, their hackles rose. Parked at the corner was an unmarked police surveillance van, and it screamed "Police!" at them. Another was parked across the street from the front door. Both would have to be moved—everything must look exactly as it had for five months.

The men pulled up to the front of the warehouse and got out. The night breeze carried a hint of spring down the sidewalk.

Angelo's ever-present cigarette flared in the darkness as they formed up and walked inside. Mounting the metal staircase, they felt their senses sharpening with excitement. No more drudgery, boredom, routine. This was their final performance.

They found a new table set up behind Franzino's backup counter out of sight of the customers. It was covered with two hundred pairs of handcuffs, together with plastic hospital identification bracelets.

Buoyed by the success of the operation over five months, the men told themselves that things would go well tonight. But nothing was sure; apprehension crackled. Although they had notified more than one hundred customers in the past two weeks, they had no idea how many would actually come and once there, how difficult the arrests might be.

Their tensions tightened as the office began to fill with senior commanders, led by Chief Cullinane. With him were Deputy Chief Thomas R. Estes, Inspector Herbert Miller of the Second District, Inspector Charles Monroe, who had helped write the application for a federal grant; and various other high-ranking officials whom the men knew from memos only. It was as much brass in one place as they had ever seen.

The P.F.F. gang could see some sergeants' faces pinch with jealousy. "This ain't such a big deal," one of the new faces said loudly. But when they trooped downstairs for a tour of the back rooms, they could see for themselves that it was a very big deal.

More than eighty lawmen were congregated in the two rooms downstairs, getting ready for the suspects. They were shuffling reams of government forms, their faces wet with sweat from tension, the heat of packed bodies, and last-minute confusion. Men were lined up at coffee urns, others were clustered in small knots, heads down, conferring. As the gang members threaded their way through the warehouse, the noise died down and they were aware of people staring at them. Now they felt like celebrities. Young faces atop starched collars and carefully knotted ties stood aside for these men in tuxedos. Prosecutors hovered here and there talking to plainclothes federal agents. Chief

Cullinane stood to one side of the room, and near him was Frank Herron, down from New York to watch the finale. Various supervisors wore felt armbands of green, white, red, or yellow denoting different echelons of control. In the midst of the churning groups, friends pushed forward to greet the gang members they knew, pressing warm handshakes on them.

The men went back upstairs and began working the phones, calling their customers once more to urge them to come to the party and bring others. And some of the customers themselves began calling in, reassuring the hosts that they were indeed coming to the celebration. One of these was George Logan, the man whom the P.F.F. gang believed was a murderer. He called to apologize because he was going to be later than his 8:15 appointed time. He was at home and just about to take a bath. George asked Mike if he should bring a suitcase to the party. They had talked of sending George to New York that night to interview for a job with the organization. Mike assured him he would need no luggage. "You'll be taken care of," Mike said. "Once you get here, everything will become clear."

It was 7 P.M. and nearly time for the party to begin. There was one last preparation. The men taped a large sign over the new stairs to the processing rooms: "Through This Door Walks the Dumbest Thieves in the World." Now they were ready. They believed it was going to be one big glass of champagne.

Someone turned on the music. The front-door alarm shrieked a warning, and upstairs Mike Franzino fixed his gaze on the hallway spy monitor near Pat. Heavily armed police were all around him ready to leap from ambush. The room of waiting lawmen tensed. The television monitor filled with movement—four men moving up the P.F.F. stairs, swaying and popping their fingers to the music. It's working, Mike thought. They really believe it. . . . They're coming to a party!

Rico focused his camera on the P.F.F. door, as he had hundreds of times before. A long-haired, disheveled white man suddenly peered through the glass.

"Hey, Rick, what's happenin', baby!" screamed Pasquale Larocca as he buzzed the door open. Richard David Nelson, Lowell E. Sale, William R. Blake, and James Edward (Jimbo) Henry walked into P.F.F. Inc. It was 7:32 P.M., February 28, 1976, a moment the Mafia men had been pointing toward for months.

"Hey, Rick, come on over here . . . hey, listen, step up here, we gotta talk business," Pasquale said. The "guests" smiled and leaned against the counter. Sale and Blake had sold Pat various things, including a shotgun with a barrel that could be removed to make it a sawed-off. Nelson specialized in hospital equipment and Henry brought in a sawed-off rifle and movie equipment.

"I gotta put protection to my boss so I gotta know if you guys are packing pieces," Pasquale said, waving them closer. "I've gotta have my two heavies come out here and check you. Once they've checked an' it's cool, you can go meet my boss, get your door prize . . . *Hey Tony, Bohanna!*"

The two detectives moved through the P.F.F. side door beside the fencing counter, stepping past Hook Trayler and six other cops. As he walked into the suspect area, Tony felt exposed. A lawman he barely knew with a shotgun stood behind the fake air vent a few feet away. If he shoots, I'm dead, Tony thought.

Nelson started toward the side door, heading for the music. Tony shoved him backward. Nelson stretched his long arms for the frisk.

"You got a piece?"

"Nah . . . ," the customer said dreamily. Bonano's hands pried from armpits to waist, ran around the pants at the beltline, turning the wastband over quickly to shake out any weapons.

"Got a knife?"

"In my boot. . . ."

Tony explored gingerly and found a needle and syringe wrapped inside Nelson's sock top. The oaf's really gone, he thought. Bohanna was frisking the others and stealing glances at the mirror. He likes to get on film, Tony thought.

All the while Pat's chatter bombarded them: "Hey, no prob-

lem! No problem! You get it back. . . . I take care of my people.
. . . Hey, step on up here. . . . Let's talk. . . ."

The men turned with their arms raised, bumping into each
other in the small room. Blake, a ponytailed thirty-five-year-old,
caught Jim Henry's elbow on his jaw and staggered back. What
imbeciles, Tony was thinking, as the months of frustration welled
up in him. On a previous visit, Sale had amused the lawmen with
his explanation of how he had avoided a trial in New York. He
was supposed to face drug charges, but had succeeded in post-
poning the trial by writing a letter informing the court that he
would be unable to attend because he had a terminal illness. He
wrote the letter on stolen stationary from the National Institute
of Health and signed a doctor's name. The court granted the
postponement, the lawmen learned. Following this line, Franzino
could see a time when the trial would be cancelled forever because the court would be informed on offical stationary that the
defendant had died.

". . . I think you're all right!" Pat jabbered. "Hey, step
around here . . . ." He waved them close to the counter. They
stared at him, half-smiling at this strange introduction to a blow-
out of a party. "Hey, you gonna have a good party!" Pasquale
crowed. "I wanna have a couple escorts come up here, okay?"

Instantly, Hook Trayler burst through the side door cracking
a shell into his riot gun, followed by six others also in flak jackets
and riot helmets. One grabbed Nelson by his collar and jerked
him backward. "Over there! Against the wall! Over to the left!"
they shouted.

The police shoved four men up against the cinder-block wall
opposite the counter in the suspects' area, and police crowded in
behind them, their hands searching, probing, pushing the
thieves' heads down as other lawman brought the manacles from
the table behind Franzino and slapped them on the men's wrists.
A policeman on each arm, the four were marched meekly through
the side door toward the back stairs.

The whole thing had taken three minutes. It was 7:35 P.M.,
and the party had just begun.

"Come on, baby!" Pat warbled. "Come on in!"

Bobby Ray Crawford walked into P.F.F. minutes after Sale and his three buddies had been whisked away. The lawmen hadn't seen him since December 15, when he had conned them into paying a thousand dollars for the fake machine gun. They had boiled on that ever since. Angelo grinned. He had had the headache of explaining the purchase to penny-wise bureaucrats. Pasquale gave Bobby Ray a big soul pop. "You got a piece on you?"

Crawford shook his head.

"Okay, two of my heavies are gonna check . . . you understand . . . ?"

"It's cool, man."

Angelo and Bohanna slipped into the room and began patting Crawford down.

"I wanna tell you you're gonna have a hot time tonight," Pat babbled. "You're really gonna jam once we start this party! You are gonna get fucked, I guarantee it! GUARANTEE IT!" He waved Crawford closer and the man leaned over the counter, smiling.

"Now listen, there's something else I want to tell you. . . . *You're under arrest . . .* !" Flak-jacketed cops poured into the room, hands grabbing. Crawford flew backward, his mouth open. They bent him over, frisked him and slipped on the plastic hospital identification bracelet and the handcuffs, chattering: "Be cool now . . . everything will be okay . . . rest easy. . . ."

Crawford went without a word. "It's trick or treat, motherfucker," a lawman said.

At 7:53 P.M., Pat hailed Maurice Hamilton through the door. "Hey! Come on in! You ready to jam?"

Maurice—a frequent warehouse visitor, part of a gang whose other members had once offered to kill two drivers they had abducted if Pasquale wanted them to—was a tall young man with an open face and warm smile. He laughed with Pat.

"Hey, listen . . . a piece, you got one on you?"

"No."

"Hey, Bohan! *Abadiche!*" That would become Pat's Italian for "Go search 'em."

Bohanna and Tony slipped through the P.F.F. door.

"Hey, Mo-reese, how you doin'?" Bohanna smiled. "If you got a piece, you put it on the table, you know. . . . We got a boss, and we don't want the motherfucker to get hurt."

"I understand."

When the detectives finished frisking, Pasquale grabbed Hamilton's right hand in a soul grip. "Hey . . . you win the door prize!" he exclaimed. "YOU WIN THE DOOR PRIZE!"

With his left hand Pat put his leather billfold under Hamilton's nose. "I'm a police officer. You're under arrest!"

For a frozen moment, Hamilton's eyes bugged at the silver badge affixed to the wallet. Then as Hook Trayler and his team lunged into the room, cracking the shotgun, Hamilton's head dropped on the counter, until Hook got a grip on his shoulder and shoved him against the rear wall. "Spread 'em!"

Hamilton leaned weakly against the wall, arms out, head down. "It's okay, cocksucker," said a lawman.

"Is he sick?" asked a cop.

Pasquale walked over to Hamilton. "Hey, Maurice, you okay, man?"

"Yessir. . . ."

"Hey, I wantcha to lay it down, because you ain't been no trouble and they're going to be good to you. . . ."

"Okay! Okay!" the hijacker whimpered.

As the police led him away, Pat gave him a couple of friendly pats on the shoulder. His voice, however, was ice. "You done a lot of shit, and I know it."

Audrey Clipper, mother of George "Sonny" Logan, arrived at her Northeast home after a long day as a domestic worker. "Where's Sonny?" she asked. Her mother reported that George had left a few minutes earlier. "Sonny got himself all perfumed and dressed up," she said. "He said he was goin' to a party!"

A party? That was strange. Sonny never went to parties before—he didn't like groups. This was troubling. Mrs. Clipper had raised George, her only child, and a number of foster children, and George was the only one who had given her grief. Although he was thirty-six, he spent many nights at home, and she tried as best she could to keep track of him. Mrs. Clipper got to thinking. She had received a couple of strange phone calls in the last week from a Mr. Pat Pasquale, as she recalled the name, and he had mentioned something about a party. The conversations had been brief and nasty; she ran over them again.

He had asked if Ida were there. "Where is she?" he demanded.

"She don't live here," Mrs. Clipper said.

"You're lying. She does live there. Who are you?"

"It's none of your business who I am. What do you want with Ida anyway?"

"She owes me money."

"Are you a bill collector?"

"No . . . I want my money."

"If you crazy enough to give her your money, you find her —and don't you call on my phone with your nasty mouth," Mrs. Clipper said, slamming down the phone.

A few days later, he had called back.

"Didn't I tell you not to call?" she had said.

"I want Ida."

"Ida don't live here."

"You're a liar," he said.

"I'm Audrey Clipper, and she doesn't live here," she said, preparing to hang up.

"Wait a minute, wait a minute, we're havin' a party and she's supposed to come and bring girls," Mr. Pat Pasquale had said.

"You'll have to call her—don't you call here with your nasty mouth."

"Don't you tell me what to do," she recalled him saying, and he hung up on her.

Had Sonny gone off to meet with that man? Mrs. Clipper

wondered anxiously. Ida might know, so now she called her son's wife for help. It was shortly after 8 P.M. "He's gone to meet the big boss. He comin' from New York," she said.

Mrs. Clipper could barely restrain herself. "Oh, so Mister Mouth is goin' to the party to see the big man, huh?" She regarded her son as a big talker and a big liar; there was no telling what he was getting into.

Ida said she wasn't going to accompany George to the party. "The girls have to put on a show. They want you to turn tricks and everything. I'm not gonna put on no show—besides, there's no money jumpin' off; I'm not goin'."

As the bewildered Mrs. Clipper listened, Ida told how P.F.F. worked. Mrs. Clipper thought a moment and spoke up. "You mean all that time, people standin' around in front of the phone booth, holding things, and no police came? . . . Ida, they have to be the police."

"They ain't the police," Ida argued. "The police don't act like that."

"Yes, they do," Mrs. Clipper insisted. "They got a whole lot of stuff in 'em."

"Naw," Ida said. "All them people who went up there, they'll never be able to get 'em, there were too many."

"Ida," Mrs. Clipper said, "they know each and every one of you."

When fugitive Tony Hendley arrived for the Mafia party, he showed Pat the handcuffs and that got him quickly inside, where he hoped to find drugs to steal. It was easy for Tony to smile and scheme at the very same moment. He had been winning by stealth for years. As a teenager he worked for a fast-food stand, sleeping with some of the girls there, borrowing from each, and then stealing from their cash registers when they weren't looking. He amused himself by serving hamburgers that had been dropped on the floor, and in the evenings he sometimes took home a case of meat.

Tony had twice talked his way out of tight spots during

recent chases. In Alexandria, Virginia, a young white man was closing in after Tony snatched a woman's purse. "You better be an Olympic star or something, 'cause I'm dead on you!" the man shouted, pounding after Hendley. "Look here, man," Tony shouted over his shoulder, "all you want is the pocketbook. You just give me a little distance and I'll let it go." The man agreed and slacked off. As the distance widened, Tony pushed his feet faster and faster. "You damned dirty nigger!" the man yelled, sprinting too late. Tony, spotting his friend and the getaway car in an alley, raced there. The pursuer followed and the two thieves beat him dizzy.

When police chased Tony from a bank for trying to cash a stolen government check, he jumped into a customer's car in the parking lot and ordered him to drive slowly away. He claimed to be caught shoplifting and persuaded the man to drive him in return for a promise to reform. The man warned him that shoplifters "face something like five or ten years."

"Yeah, I know, I'll never do it again," Tony said. "I appreciate you talking to me and trying to level with me." He had checked the rear-view mirror and the police were gone.

Tony Bonano felt sorry for the poor sonofabitch cop who had let Antonio John "Tony" Hendley get away from the Robbery Squad room; Hendley told how he had escaped, and the chief of police was listening.

As he was led past Bonano, his old manacle dangling under the new handcuffs, Hendley murmured, "Man, today is just not my day." Bonano and the others, after months of verbal sparring and improvisations, said nothing. Bonano figured it was a waste of time to say anything more to these people. He regarded Hendley and the others as incapable of carrying on any normal kind of conversation and didn't want to talk with them unless it was a means to trap them. He savored his satisfaction in silence. After the arrest, Second District Commander Herbert Miller noticed the sign "Through This Door Walks the Dumbest Thieves in the World" and ordered it taken down.

• • •

Now it was John Gaino's and Thaddeus McRae, Jr.'s turn. They popped in at 8:22 P.M., smiling and relaxed.

"Come on, baby!" Pat crowed.

"How you doin'?" Gaino replied, exulting in his own answer: ". . . All right . . . !" He and McRae had sold a sawed-off shotgun to P.F.F. on January 22, according to the case jackets awaiting them downstairs. McRae had been logged on sixteen visits to the warehouse. He was making one of his first appearances since they had put the police on him and then told him to stay away because he was too hot.

"Hey, Tony, Angelo, *abadiche!* Uh . . . *getem-in-dhoozgow!*"

Tony began frisking McRae. "Gotta make sure you don't gotta no heat," he said. "The boss'll get onna my ass. . . ." Gaino chuckled. "An' he'll kill me an' putta me inna box and throw me inna river."

"Hey, listen," Pat reassured them as the enforcers finished, "it's no problem. Okay?"

"Solid," said John Gaino, who was about to meet Hook Trayler.

Tony and Angelo headed for the P.F.F. door. "Hey, look, give 'em the door prize," Tony said.

"Yeah, the door prize," Pat replied, grabbing the men's hands in his own for a soul shake as the police surged through the door. Gaino flinched in terror at the sound of the shotgun cracking and reached to bat away the barrel of a snub-nosed revolver pointed at his ear by Arif Mosrie. One man grabbed Gaino from behind by his leather jacket and swung him like a sack of potatoes against the rear wall. A few moments later, the two men shuffled meekly out of P.F.F., en route to processing and jail.

"Hey, Dewitt, come on in, my man." Pasquale beckoned as Dewitt L. Robinson sauntered through the door, a toothy grin on his face.

"How's EVER'BODY?" Dewitt asked. He had heard about the party from street dudes some weeks before and after offering his services at the warehouse, had accepted a $100 advance to provide a string of prostitutes for the partygoers. Now three women followed Dewitt, wearing tight, low-cut evening dresses, and they fixed Pat with come-on looks. "Hey, Ce-LESTE!" Pat crowed, recognizing one of them. "Wow! Step right up, girls, STEP UP!"

Robinson laid a long flat object wrapped in cloth on the counter. Pat paid no attention. His stubby forefinger jabbed at the girls.

"Rose, Celeste, Cookie. . . ." He paused.

"Hey, we got three broads a'comin' to the par-tee . . . ," Bohanna shouted from behind the false wall.

Pat smiled warmly at the women. "The boss, he usually likes two chicks, but I might persuade him to take three. Do you mind suckin' a cock?"

The women gave him schoolgirl smiles, and shook their heads. "Oh, hey, listen, he's stayin' in Virginia," Pat barged ahead, making his cases, "Do you mind takin' the chicks across the line? Because you told me before that's a risk, right? Okay, you don't mind?"

Dewitt said he didn't mind.

"He's not too big, you know what I mean?" Pat said of his mythical boss. "Okay, good money. Good money." He had what he wanted—a possible white slave charge against Robinson, transporting women across state lines for purposes of prostitution; and acknowledgment by the women that they sold sex. Now he grabbed the object on the counter and unwrapped a 30–30 lever-action rifle.

"Dy-no-MITE! *Abadiche! Mya cigaretta!*" he exclaimed.

"Good merchandise," said Franzino.

"Hey, Angelo, look at this," Pat called. "A 30–30 Winchester. Basimo!" He held up the rifle and feverishly worked the lever, snapping the trigger. He gave the weapon to Angelo and turned back to rush the women through a search. "One thing, ladies, you got purses? I gotta put protection on the boss. Lay 'em up here." The women obliged, watching him uneasily.

Tony and Bohanna drifted into the room toward the girls.

"Can I check-a this? Oh my God!" Tony said, staring hungrily at Rose. She watched him, a wry smile on her face.

"Lissen, I wanta take you to meet the boss," Pat said. Tony and Bohanna headed back toward the P.F.F. door, barking softly at the women, "Arf arf."

"I want the one in the middle—" Mike said.

"—To get the door prize!" Pat added, giving the signal. He turned quickly to Dewitt. "How much do you want for the piece?" Dewitt was taken aback. He had apparently brought the rifle as a gift to the Don—he had asked nothing for it. Just then, the arrest team rushed into the room, shouting and cocking their weapons. Robinson looked stricken. The prostitutes glared disbelievingly at Pasquale Larocca as they were led away.

"Where you been, man? . . . lookin' good . . . you sharp tonight," Pasquale said to the tall young man in a smart white suit. "Hey listen, I gotta put a little protection on my boss. Hey, come on out here a minute, Tony. *Abadiche!* Check him."

Tony Bonano came out front, paused to admire the man's clothes, and gently lifted the back of the coat to feel underneath. "Oh, thissa nice threads," he said. "Don't wanna mess up your suit." As he ran his hands under the man's arms, Tony was momentarily struck dumb. There, standing behind Pasquale Larocca, in full view of the customer, was Chief Cullinane, dapper in a suit and tie, the badge on his lapel glistening under the fluorescent lights. Jesus Christ, Bonano thought. What was he going to say if the customer saw the chief of police standing behind Pasquale Larocca. He could almost hear the man saying, "Hey, isn't that the chief of police?" Bonano decided that he would tell him that the chief was on the payroll, too. But the customer never noticed.

This was the biggest police operation in years in Washington; Cullinane had come to be with his troops and make sure that it ran smoothly.

"Don' wanna mess up your suit," Bonano went on, patting

the customer's clothes back into place. "Geez . . . how much was-a this?"

"Uh, two-oh-five."

"That's beautiful," Pat shouted for someone to give this customer the door prize and the next thing that could be heard was the sound of a 12-gauge shell clanking into a chamber.

8:54:43

George "Sonny" Logan arrived thirty-nine minutes after his appointed time. It didn't matter. The men had scheduled people to arrive at fifteen-minute intervals so that they could control them better, but no one was adhering to the timetable. The arrests were quick enough to cope with the guests about as fast as they arrived. Pat called them at the phone booth when it was their turn.

"Hey, George . . . Man, that's a dyno-mite lookin' coat, *dyno-mite,*" Pat chirped. George was wearing a leather jacket and white shirt open at the collar.

Angelo went out to frisk him. "We don't want our boss to get it," Franzino explained. George nodded and said that he didn't want to get hurt either. If anyone was likely to cause trouble, this was the man, Franzino believed. Angelo drew his thumbs around the waist and began crumpling clothing; Sonny had voluntarily spread-eagled himself against a wall. "Hey, George," Angelo chuckled, "you make me feel just like a cop!" He longed to sink his fingers into George's neck and make the arrest himself. That —the collar—was the moment he relished, the peak of his power. After that, the fate of the George Logans belonged to the courts.

"Give 'em the door prize now," Franzino said. Sonny figured he had an in with these men; he would get a good job and wouldn't have to hustle so much any more. He was just about to reach for the bottle on the counter when they rushed him. Lieutenant Arif Mosrie put his .38 police special to the back of Sonny Logan's brain, grabbed his collar with the other hand, and shoved him against the wall. Sonny's expression never changed.

He believed he was going to be executed. Only gradually did it become clear that these men were the police. "Plead insanity, George," Tony Bonano taunted, referring to Sonny's earlier claims that he beat charges by pretending to be insane so that the judges would send him to mental hospitals instead of prison. "Tell 'em you're crazy," Angelo said.

Loretta Butler was in the warehouse only a matter of seconds before Pat pulled his badge. Although she was the woman who had brought them Assistant United States Attorney Donald E. Robinson, Jr., she received no favored treatment. A buxom figure in her leather jacket, Loretta tried to glare at Pat, but an officer quickly moved her to a wall. "We still love you, we love you," Pat mimicked, "and Donald wuves you, too." When she had gone, and the camera was turned off, Pasquale and his colleagues broke into a few lyrics from a song by Simon and Garfunkel:
"Well, here's to you, Mister Robinson, Jesus loves you more than you will know, woe-woe-woe, woe-woe-woe."

Thirty miles from the grimy warehouse, nestled into their cozy townhouse in suburban Gaithersburg, Maryland, Assistant United States Attorney Robinson, his wife, and two of their friends had just capped a long, relaxed dinner with one of Beth's specialties, strawberry cream cake. The three Robinson daughters and their friends' two daughters were lined up on the living-room sofa, quietly watching television. Robinson was filled with a torpid sense of well-being in these moments away from the deceptions he had woven at the courthouse.
Ding-dong!
He got up from the new dining-room table bought with P.F.F. money and walked toward the front door. Could it be someone come this late to look at their townhouse, which he had just put on the market?
Beth Robinson lounged at the table, savoring a warm recollection—the doorbell made her think of the soft spring nights

when neighbors' children punched the front bell and stared up at her, their faces eager: "Can Mr. Robinson come out and play?" He was the Pied Piper of the neighborhood, often calling the children out of their homes with his rich lilting voice as he stood at the entrance to their subdivision: "It's hide-and-go-seek at the Hideaway Farms sign."

Robinson opened the front door. A neatly dressed man with an intense face was peering at him. Four other men stood in darkness on the front lawn.

"Yes?"

"Mr. Robinson?"

"Yes."

"I'm special agent Thomas Easton of the FBI. I want to talk to you." Robinson felt his knees about to buckle. Easton stepped into the small front hallway, followed by the others.

"Sure, come on in," Robinson said.

"This is an important matter," Easton said. He was glancing at the children nearby. Beth Robinson was on her feet, hovering in the dining room, vaguely aware that something odd was going on.

"Come on downstairs, to the family room," Robinson said. His body felt numb and weightless as he led the way downstairs and stood before a couch, facing the five men.

"It is my duty to tell you that you're under arrest," Easton said.

"What's the violation?"

"Eighteen U.S.C. two-oh-one."

Robinson groped for the meaning of what Easton had just said. He knew these numbers in the United States criminal code. It was the section dealing with bribery. "Do you have a warrant?" Easton produced his papers and handed them to the prosecutor. Robinson felt himself dissolving. He collapsed backward on the sofa.

Beth's voice floated down the stairwell. "Robbie, is everything all right?"

"Do you have an affidavit on me?" he asked. He knew that such a document would contain details of the crimes he was charged with.

"Yes."

"Can I see it?"

They explained that they didn't have it with them, and would show it to him later. Robinson knew it had to do with Pasquale Larocca.

"We're going to put handcuffs on you," Easton said.

"The kids are up there watching television," Robinson said. "Do you really need to?"

"If you give us your word. . . ."

"I do. Can I take a minute to get myself together?"

"Go ahead." The lawmen seemed embarrassed.

After a few moments, Robinson headed upstairs. "I've got to go downtown on official business," he announced to Beth and their friends, brushing past them to the bedroom on the second floor, where he picked up his wallet and a light windbreaker. As he came downstairs, he felt as if he could awake from this at any moment.

"Are you driving?" Beth asked.

"No. . . . They'll drive. . . ."

He kissed her and the three children.

"What's happened?" she asked, her face wrinkled with apprehension.

"Something's come up, that's all," he said. Robinson stepped into the night. Beth closed the door against the cold.

When they got to the unmarked car at the curb, the lawmen cuffed Robinson's hands together in front and removed his pants belt. They positioned him in the back seat and lawmen piled in on either side. As they drove off, they tried to wrap the belt around his legs and thread it through the handcuff chain. But the belt didn't reach far enough and they couldn't truss him up.

"Where are we going?"

"Fifth District."

He knew the legal procedures, and this wasn't right. He was

charged with a federal crime, so they had to take him before the nearest federal magistrate. That meant Rockville, Maryland, a few miles away, not Northeast Washington. "It's wrong to do it this way," he protested.

No one answered him.

"Isn't there some other place besides Five-D?"

"No."

The lawmen began throwing inane questions at him.

"How long have you lived in your house?" . . . "You got nice restaurants out here. What's your favorite?" . . . "Your kids go to school out here? They like it? Like their teachers? Do *you* like their teachers?"

Robinson's head was spinning. He thought he knew what they were doing, a standard police technique to keep a suspect from collecting his wits. Easton thought of it as small talk that would make everyone more comfortable. He had already advised Robinson that it would be better if he didn't say anything.

"Hey, I would appreciate you guys leaving me alone."

They began telling loud jokes to each other. Robinson tried to piece together what had happened.

By 10 P.M., Fifth District police headquarters was crammed with Sting prisoners. Chaos reigned. The party arrests had gone much faster than the planners had anticipated, and now prisoners and their guards milled through the building, seeking interrogation teams free to question suspects and show them enough videotape to loosen reluctant tongues. Other police sat and groused. These were the specially trained and briefed arrest teams, chafing to get out into the city and chase suspects. The commanders had held them back to preserve the secrecy of P.F.F. Inc. as long as possible, and allow the customers to come to the warehouse on their own. The arrest teams would not be fully unleashed until nearly 2 A.M.

Another problem developed when two newsmen with inside information converged on the stationhouse to get the story. The lawmen had planned for the contingency. Two men allowed Pat Collins of WTOP radio and television to follow them around the city while they drove aimlessly in an empty U-Haul. Then they detained him on a back street and escorted him to Five-D, where senior commanders convinced him to sit on the story in order to protect the arrest teams.

Meanwhile, Larry Krebs, of WMAL radio and television, had positioned himself down the street from Five-D in his car, a Pontiac specially equipped with extra batteries to run cameras, lights, and recorders. Sitting in the vehicle, which was known to his mechanics as the Queen Mary, Krebs sipped coffee from his built-in urn, listened to the numerous police radios he carried, and kept track of the proceedings from a safe distance. He figured he had the story in hand and stayed until dawn, watching and recording.

Robinson was stunned at the sight of Five-D as he climbed out of the car. The building was awash with lights and policemen, U-Haul trucks were being emptied of their dazed cargo. The lawmen threw Robinson's jacket over his manacled wrists and led him to a back entrance. He could see faces staring out at him through the doors, people crowding around to look at him. Larry Barcella, Don Campbell and Silbert's top aide, Carl Rauh, were among them, their faces filled with contempt. Robinson felt nausea from the humiliation.

"We want to ask you questions," someone said. "Will you talk to us?"

"Yes."

They led him upstairs to an interrogation room and left a young, bored-looking cop as a guard. Robinson began clarifying his thoughts as he sat alone in the quiet room. He began to see what had happened and what was to come. The Mafia men had been arrested and had talked to the cops, throwing him in to get a better deal for themselves. He knew he had taken money, but there was plenty of reason for it, he felt. No matter what the Mafia said about him, Robinson knew he had a reasonable defense and it would be the sworn statements of a United States prosecutor against the testimony of criminals. From his experience, he was sure this would be suffificient for acquittal.

At 11:19 P.M., Robinson sat down with Easton to tell what he had done since December 29. The FBI man asked him every ten minutes or so whether he wanted a soft drink or coffee or needed to relieve himself. The interrogation lasted three hours and Robinson broke down several times. He revealed many things, but he never told agent Easton about Loretta Butler. That was one fact he meant to keep to himself.

When he finished his statement, the lawmen showed him the affidavit they had drawn up to get his arrest warrant. For the first time he read that the Mafia men were in fact the police and that they had videotaped his two visits to the P.F.F. warehouse. He asked to see the tapes.

When he saw himself taking money from Frank Paccione and Pasquale Larocca, Robinson wept. His mind ranged back through all the weeks he had been dealing with them, the strange connection between Pete Smith and Loretta, the barrage of telephone calls at his office and the threatening calls to Beth at home; how Silbert had refused to release him immediately from his job so that he could go to New York. All this time, he now told himself, they must have been planning out every step. They must have learned right at the beginning something damaging about him and Loretta and yet no one had told him. Instead they coordinated an attack against him. His astonishment at what they had done turned to outrage. They hounded me until I fell, he thought. That's called entrapment.

When the tape was finished, Robinson was led downstairs. He found Don Campbell standing in the throng and got him aside. "Can I see Earl?" Robinson was sure that if he could talk to Silbert, he could explain it all. And he wanted to ask the man he worked for how they could do this to him.

"No," said Campbell grimly. The head of Major Crimes then handed him a short letter on official stationery of the United States attorney's office informing Robinson that he had been fired.

•   •   •

Henry Daniel, Jr. pulled up in front of the P.F.F. warehouse in a late-model Lincoln, and turned his motor off. He scribbled something and tucked it under the windshield visor. Henry was a fence who had lost all his customers to P.F.F. He came over with the last customer. Tony Bonano and Angelo Lasagna had been watching from the warehouse, and when Bonano went out and escorted the customer in, Angelo grabbed the note from the visor. It was a map, showing where the front door of P.F.F. was and a rough sketch of the interior. Angelo figured Henry was setting them up for a ripoff, leaving a note for a friend who could sneak in with help from Henry.

"Where'd you park your car, man?" Pat asked.

"Down there," Daniel said.

"Okay, everything is cool. Come on; let's go get the door prize. Hey listen, come here. I want you to hear this—the funniest fuckin' thing happened—well, you're just not gonna believe it. Really. You're under arrest. That's right."

The telephone rang as the arrest team swooped in.

"P.F.F.," Franzino answered in his cold baritone. "Yes, you call from the corner. . . . Oh good, beautiful! Yes . . . we have two more customers. Hey, THE FISHMAN!"

Paul Roscoe Wills, who said he was known to police as the Fishman because he was slippery as a fish and kept eluding them, was about to be reeled in.

In the back room Angelo and Tony Bonano approached the handcuffed Henry Daniel. The others stood aside. "What was this for?" Angelo demanded, showing Daniel his note. "That's in case I disappear—people will know where I disappeared to," he mumbled. The two men walked away; they believed they knew his plans.

The customers sitting there could watch a nearby monitor and see other customers get arrested. "Wait till they see the soldiers," one handcuffed man chuckled while watching unsuspecting customers talk with Pat. Most of the prisoners said nothing. Some of the arrest-and-processing men, strolling about with coffee and doughnuts, occasionally tossed remarks at them. "Hey, George, helluva party huh?" They taunted George Logan. "How'd you like the party?" George kept his head down. They stared at him like he was an insect.

The only one who acted up was Albert Lee Colbert, known as "Big Al." Big Al used to call from places like Richmond, Va., and claim to have hijacked three trucks and be on his way, but he never showed up. Now on the park bench he wouldn't shut up. "This is the greatest thing in the world!" he screamed. "You had to have some kind of setup like this to get me!" His yelling was persistent, and he was a danger to tip off arriving customers, so some of the men in the backroom stuffed rags in his mouth and wrapped tape around his head until he resembled a mummy. Big Al awaited his turn, along with Henry Daniel and George Logan, and when about a half-dozen had been processed, they were loaded into U-Haul vans at the back and driven past the arriving guests to Fifth District headquarters.

At about 11 P.M. Karl Mattis arrived unexpectedly, to the delight of the men of P.F.F. He had been one of the originals in the warehouse, the supervisor until he injured his back lifting a typewriter in December. He had been on sick leave ever since, but had come to the party to congratulate his colleagues. Mattis was a soft-spoken man, but firm and fair, and had earned their respect. "Sit down," Pasquale said, pointing to an old wooden government-issue chair next to Mike Franzino's backup counter. "I'm going to make you a Don!" Mattis protested but the men would have none of it. For about an hour—until his back acted up and he had to leave—he played "Don Karlo." Pasquale urged the next few arrivals to "Show some respect for the Don," and at one point knelt and kissed Mattis's ring—his wedding ring, the only one he wore. "Hi, Don," one of the customers said. Another gave a black-power salute. Several waved. Mattis, a forty-three-year-old father of six, a suburban homeowner, a member of the Elks, American Legion, and Veterans of Foreign Wars, came to the party dressed in an inexpensive blue leisure suit his wife had bought him. He didn't know how to behave like a Don. He decided to improvise. "Bless you, my son," he said to the customers. He wondered if some customers might think he was a pope rather than a don. Seated there, a grim visage with his piercing blue eyes and slicked-back gray hair, perched between gun-toting Pasquale Larocca and Michael Franzino, Don Karlo was convincing enough.

Marion Elizabeth Toye had overslept and didn't wake up until shortly before midnight. Panicky, she called the warehouse. Pat told her it would be all right to come late. "We got the two girls for you out of New York," he told her. "Are you wearing something really sexy, something open at the front?"

"No, I got on a two-piece suit," she told him.

"Ah, you got to have something open, real sexy," he said. Toye laughed and headed on over to the party, still wearing the suit. She arrived with two men she had met at the phone booth, and standing there, slim and bespectacled in her suit, a short bush haircut, she looked almost like a man.

"Hey, hey, show a little respect for the Don," Pat barked, nodding toward the silver-haired Mattis.

"Hello," Toye said, waving. She thought the Don was cool.

"You look real nice," the cool man said. "Have plenty of fun."

Toye started to light a cigarette. "Put that away," Pasquale barked. "I don't want you to meet the boss with a cigarette in your mouth." (The arrest teams had complained about having to deal with lit cigarettes.)

"I want you to meet my boss," Pasquale said, and Toye started to take one step toward the door to go behind the counter and meet the Don when helmeted policemen charged out, their guns pointed at her. They pushed her up against a wall and frisked her. Benumbed, she knew nevertheless what was happening to her. As she was led to the rear of the warehouse for processing, she caught sight of Angelo. "You know, Angelo," she said, deadpan, "I really wanted your bod."

212

Angelo beamed. "You play your cards right, Toye," he said, never giving up the con, "and you still might get it."

One of the male customers arrested with Toye, Marcellous Paul Smith, didn't take it so well. He was one of the few arrested at a party to show any emotion other than shock. "This ain't no party, ain't no party," he whined over and over as the arrest team handcuffed him. "Ain't did nothin', ain't did nothin'," he complained. "What I did?"

"We got a warrant for you," one of the men on the arrest team said.

"For what?"

"You name it, we got it."

Tony Bonano couldn't restrain his sarcasm. "Hey, he ain't did nothing, you can let him go!"

As he was led away Smith continued to bleat, "This ain't no . . . hey, man, what's goin' on . . . this ain't no party, man."

"It's a surprise party," Pasquale smirked. The other men of P.F.F. picked up Pat's lead and burst into robust song: "WHEN THE MOON HITSA YOU EYE LIKE A BIG PIZZA PIE, THAT'S AMOR-E. . . ."

As the customers continued parading into P.F.F., the lawmen relaxed more. Five months of frustrating play-acting was finished. Now it was their turn to get even. This time they gave nothing. They were as cold in the heart as the predators.

Pasquale: "Hey listen, you know something funny? I heard the funniest fucking thing. It's funny as shit. . . . Hey, you're really gonna get tight! No problem. Hey, you're gonna get a big kick outta this. The door prize is just gonna astound you! It's gonna knock you on your ass! You know what? You're under arrest!"

Pasquale: (As the customer is led away): SHIT! GODDAMN! GET OFF YOUR ASS AND JAM!

Pasquale: "Hey, listen, you guys are special. Hey, you're gonna hear somethin' so fuckin' funny, I think you guys are going to love it. Now, we're gonna getcha the door prize, okay? I think you guys are gonna love this . . . I'm a police officer and you're under arrest!"

Lieutenant Arif Mosrie: "Up against the wall or I'll blow your brains out."

Pasquale: "Hey, now, listen, I got somethin' else. Hey, you gonna love this. It's a real trip. You want me to show you? I'm a police officer—"

Customer: "Oh my God, man . . . !"

Lawmen: *"When the moon hits your eye, like a big pizza pie, that's amor-e. . . ."*

Pasquale: "It's a joke! IT'S ALL A JOKE!"

Pasquale: "Come here, come here. Hey, listen, I want to tell you something. No hard feelings, but you're under arrest!"

Customer: "I'm feelin' sick . . . I'm sick. I'm dead."

Lawman: "Don't worry about it."

They woke up Eugene "Ike" Isaacs, one of the mailmen who stole from the mail. "Hey, Pat's givin' this party, and he was embarrassed you weren't there," Mike Franzino said in a 1 A.M. phone call.

"Oh, I'm sorry, I'll be right there . . . I'm gettin' dressed now," Ike said. He showed up in a leather suit topped with a leather cap.

"Hey, what about your uniform?" Pasquale said. Ike explained he had recently been arrested.

"Hey, you caught a fuckin' mail beef?" Angelo said. "What! From stealin' all those fuckin' checks? You didn't get me into it, did you?"

Isaacs: "No."

Pasquale: "Hey, you get a door prize. Listen, you caught a mail beef?"

Isaacs: "Yeah."

Pasquale: "You caught a lot more than that. You're under arrest! . . ."

As Isaacs was led away, Pasquale appeared to offer some

consolation. "Hey, listen, cooperate and maybe everything will go good for you," he said.

Ike nodded his head repeatedly, so much so his leather hat fell off and the officers leading him away trampled it. When he was out of the room Pasquale shouted sarcastically, "SURPRISE, SURPRISE!. . . and the men again burst into chorus, "WHEN THE MOON HITSA YOU EYE LIKE A BIG PIZZA PIE, THAT'S AMOR-E." They sang and sang, even after the camera was turned off.

By 3 A.M., the warehouse had fallen silent. No new customers had set foot inside for an hour. The last U-Haul had carried away the last prisoner. The party was over.

The P.F.F. men went downstairs for coffee with Arscott and Lill. Arrest forms, plastic cups, cigarette butts, crumpled evidence envelopes, and official forms lay everywhere. When the coffee cups were drained, they drove to the Fifth District to see the other end of the operation.

Arrest teams were arriving with sullen, handcuffed customers. Other teams, warrants in hand, were rushing into the night to find those who had missed the party. Police and prosecutors bustled along the corridors, shepherding prisoners from place to place as they headed from interrogation rooms to jail.

Lawmen all over the building stopped to congratulate the gang members. More than a dozen FBI men from the local office gathered around Mike, who had been away for five months. Now they knew what he had been doing. They loved it.

About 5 A.M. the detectives were marked "off the book"— dismissed for the day. Together with the federal men, they drove back to the Holiday Inn where they had a quick drink together and then fell exhausted into bed.

Mike was wakened an hour later by Bob Lill. "They got a question at Five-D and gotta talk to you. It's on my phone."

Mike stumbled into a pair of trousers and walked along the cold, outdoor balcony corridor to Lill's room so he could solve a tiny problem for an eight-hour-a-day man on the other end. He fell back into bed, thinking that this would not be much of a night. In three hours, he knew, he had to be awake and on his way to a press conference at Second District where all the city would learn what he and his colleagues had been doing for the last five months.

In Northeast Washington at 5 o'clock that Sunday morning, the telephone rang in the home of Audrey Clipper. It was Ida. The police were looking everywhere for her, she said frantically. Mrs. Clipper, bleary-eyed, concluded that the police must already have her Sonny; he hadn't come home yet, and she hadn't heard from him. As she talked with Ida she saw flashlight beams in her window, and the silhouettes of men coming to her front door. "We are from the FBI," she thought one of them said. "We're looking for Ida Mae Logan." They barged in, men in trenchcoats, shining their flashlights in the faces of children and Mrs. Clipper's mother and father, waking up the household, looking in the back yard. Apparently neither they nor this Pat Pasquale realized that Ida and Sonny had a room about a block away where they stayed from time to time. The telephone rang again and a policeman told Mrs. Clipper that they had George. They were holding him on some kind of check charge, she heard them say. The neighborhood dogs began barking. The men in trenchcoats looked a little longer, and then abruptly left. Mrs. Clipper tried to put the pieces together. The policeman on the phone had said Sonny had been arrested in some operation—he had a name for it—but she had never heard of it. He had called it Operation Sting.

18

February 29 dawned as typical slow-news-Sunday in Washington, with newspaper and television editors leafing through the Sunday supplements, sipping coffee, and wondering where they would find enough news for viewers that night and readers the next day. When word came that the city's law enforcers were going to make a major announcement, television and radio crews, newspaper reporters, and photographers rushed, as instructed, to Second District headquarters.

As the media people packed into the conference room, they found the city's top law enforcers sitting at a table: Police Chief Maurice J. Cullinane, United States Attorney Earl J. Silbert, and the chief of the FBI's Washington Field Office, Nick F. Stames. At about 11 A.M., Silbert stepped to the podium and started talking.

He began unfolding the mysteries of the five-month-long P.F.F., Inc., operation, ending with the party, where sixty people had been arrested. Another forty-eight were caught elsewhere in the city, Silbert said, and they expected to arrest an additional one hundred soon. The operation had cost $122,000, mostly federal grant money, and the lawmen had recovered some 3500 stolen items valued at $2.4 million.

Silbert praised the unprecedented cooperation between the local police and FBI, and promised that each case would be carefully monitored through the criminal justice system. Silbert had long maintained that local judges were too lenient in their sentencing and freed too many suspects pending trial, and he took this opportunity to point out that two-thirds of those arrested in Sting had committed crimes before, and that one-third were out on personal release or bond. He noted that Cockeye, a man with many convictions, had been released after serving only five years of a twenty-four-year sentence for armed robbery, and had since been arrested six times for forgery, burglary, and other crimes. He had been released each time from pretrial detention on his word that he would reappear in court voluntarily.

As Silbert, then Cullinane and Stames spoke, the six men who had worked in the warehouse for five months sat unobtrusively in the background. Exhausted, they were somewhat bewildered by the blitz. It pleased them to hear their superiors praise the operation, and they were delighted to know that theirs was bigger than anything pulled off in New York. But at the same time, they were not allowed to speak to the press, nor were they identified for the reporters. The idea of anonymity had some attractions to the P.F.F. gang. They could keep their undercover identities for future operations, and they and their families could be spared crank—or real—threats. But here was the press yammering for details and the men who knew all of it had to sit quiet while the top brass tried to tell what had happened in the warehouse. It was somewhat disturbing.

When the officials were finished, the journalists ran for the phones to tell their editors of this extraordinary Sting project. It was a rare Washington police story, one with drama and humor, a good-guys-over-bad-guys scenario, and success on an unprecedented scale. Never had the police and FBI cooperated to such an extent. It was said to be the most successful police undercover operation ever in Washington, and in the number of arrests en masse, the most successful in FBI history.

Photographers allowed into the Second District property room Sunday put on wide-angle lenses to take in the loot: 225 typewriters and calculators, 80 firearms, 70 television and stereo sets, 2 kitchen ranges, 1 microwave oven, 1 electrocardiogram machine, 1500 credit cards, 703 savings bonds, 1 set of candelabra, and hanging on a wall, 1 bear rug. P.F.F. also had bought 18 stolen cars and trucks, which had been returned to their owners.

Eddie "Angelo Lasagna" Seibert and Michael "Mike Franzino" Hartman cruised 14th Street on Sunday looking for customers who had escaped arrest. They found none, but did recognize a bearded black man with a leathery face whom they knew only by his street name, Kind Lovin'.

"Hey, Kind Lovin', thanks for all the help!" Mike said, giving him a black-power salute. Kind Lovin' looked stricken, and quietly turned around to see if others were watching. He had reason to look over his shoulder. The night before, Franzino had convinced him to find more P.F.F. customers and bring them to the party. After a three-hour search, Kind Lovin', claiming he couldn't find any, came to the party alone. The lawmen had to release him immediately because the misdemeanor warrant they had for him could not, under Washington law, be served on Sunday. Now, Angelo and Mike figured, Kind Lovin' would have to do some fast talking to the people he had tried to recruit for the P.F.F. party. Kind Lovin's expression seemed to confirm his desperation. The two lawmen were delighted. He could go ahead and spend Sunday with his friends; they planned to arrest him on Monday.

By Sunday afternoon, former Assistant United States Attorney Donald E. Robinson, Jr., had been without sleep for thirty-eight hours. After the interrogation, had been carted off to the

Montgomery County Detention Center in Rockville, Maryland. When he got home in mid-afternoon, out on bond, he wondered if it hadn't all been a dream. Then he remembered he was scheduled to teach on Monday night. He would be in no shape to make a public appearance. He called a man he considered one of his best friends, Assistant United States Attorney Joseph Guerrieri, and asked him to go to his office and give the teaching materials to a friend and the court cases to a secretary. Guerrieri offered consolation and when he had hung up, called his superiors and reported Robinson's request. Silbert had already placed the office off-limits as part of the investigation. Robinson went to bed that night wondering who his other friends were, or if he ever really had any.

Late Sunday, Maurice Tyrone (Monk) Sams, another suspect, danced at a friend's house. Monk had sold some stolen savings bonds to P.F.F. and had an invitation to go to the party. He was smarter than that. The main reason he didn't go was that he knew they weren't Mafia in the warehouse. They kept saying the Don from New York would be there, but he knew that wasn't nuthin' but some stuff. Monk believed there had been only one don in the world and that was Don Corleone, and Monk knew he was dead. He had read it in a paper somewhere and had seen *The Godfather,* Parts I and II, and furthermore, he had heard it from some Italians he met in Lorton prison. Monk was also suspicious about another thing: he had never been to a party where people were told to come at different times.

Though he knew this wasn't the Mafia, Monk had gone to P.F.F. just the same to sell things.

Now he was laying low at a friend's house. Several couples were there, everybody having some drinks, listening to the O'Jays, the Ohio Players, Aretha Franklin, just dancing, bumping, having a nice time, talking. Late Sunday evening, the hostess turned on a little color TV.

Monk saw newsfilm of a group of people, many in party clothes, getting onto a big police bus. "Man!" Monk shouted, "that's the warehouse! Turn the record player off! Let's turn this up!"

The announcer unfolded a sketchy tale of a vast undercover law-enforcement investigation operating for months at a warehouse in Northeast Washington. Monk's jaw dropped open. The television crew showed a police wagon ferrying well-dressed prisoners from the Fifth District to the central cellblock. "Man," Monk jabbered excitedly, "there's a gigantic police bus at the Don Corleone's Mafia party, the P.F.F., FBI, so and so, oh man! I done got away. . . . Don't you know I was supposed to be at that party?"

The others were laughing like he was crazy. "Yeah," he said, "I had an invitation for nine o'clock." He showed them a yellow slip of paper, torn from Pasquale Larocca's legal pad. "Man," Monk said, "them people was *rollers!*"

Monk was exhilarated. He had finally beaten the law. Right under their noses he had escaped the party. He began laughing. Someone put on another record.

After a few moments, Monk's smile began to fade. Doubt gripped him—the rollers had his name. He had shown them his driver's license and his personal bond papers. What if they came looking for the people who had missed the party? Nah, he thought, too many people went to that warehouse. That's probably why they had that party, because there were too many dudes to track down. Besides, he had only been an agent, a middleman anyway; he was selling the savings bonds for someone else. He hadn't really done anything wrong.

Shortly before midnight, the worried Monk called home. A relative told him excitedly, "the FBI just left here; they been in here twice. They kicked the door in, came in, looked under the mattresses, all up on the roof, all out the back with their shotguns drawn—"

"Wait a minute," Monk interrupted. He couldn't quite grasp all that—didn't want to really, and to prevent that he tried to focus on the most puzzling part of what he had just heard. "With their shotguns drawn? Who I done killed?"

Monk's mother grabbed the telephone. "What you got your-self into now, boy?" she said. "You 'bout to worry your poor grandmother over there. You know she's already sick!"

"Mom, I ain't doin' nothin'," Monk wailed. "I don't know why the FBI lookin' for me, and their shotguns drawn. What I done did that is so bad; I didn't kill anybody."

When he hung up, Monk's doubts had given way to fear. He stayed at a friend's house that night, but he did not sleep.

On Monday morning the story was played across the front pages of *The Washington Post,* and in the afternoon *Star.* There were rich descriptions of some of the ruses and tricks used by the lawmen, and later, intriguing pictures of the modishly dressed, bearded P.F.F. men with their comic-opera fake Italian names and the strange weapons they had bought over the months—shotguns the size of pistols, and rifles that folded for easy, concealed carrying. Television news shows highlighted the P.F.F. project, and the media clamored for interviews with the lawmen.

That same day, Tony Bonano, Mike Franzino, and Bohanna La Fontaine returned to The Hole, suspecting they might find some customers who hadn't got the word. About 11 A.M., Johnny Douglas Bush, also known as Johnny Valentine, strolled in. He had been there before and was bringing in some stolen government checks. While the hidden camera rolled once more, Johnny Bush jabbered about how he was out on bond for armed robbery in Delaware and had stolen the checks from an Alexandria mailbox.

"I don't remember you—who brought you in here?" Franzino barked, handling the counterman's role.

Johnny Bush mentioned Gloria Hardy, a familiar visitor to P.F.F.

"Oh, yeah, Gloria." Franzino smiled. "I heard she got jammed [arrested] over the weekend."

"Yeah, man, some police thing," Johnny said.

Franzino held up a copy of that morning's *Washington Post* and pointed to the headline atop Page One: *Police, FBI Arrest 108 in Fake Fence Project.* . . . "You read about this?"

"Yeah, I wondered whether it was you all," Johnny Bush said, running his finger along the headline.

"Yeah, it was," Mike said, pulling out his badge and a gun.

In the early afternoon Fred Johnson came in with some credit cards he said he had stolen from a woman in Bladensburg, Maryland, the night before. This time, Tony Bonano, Mike, and Bohanna lined up on their side of the counter and gave the customer the third degree; the only thing missing was the light pulled low over his head. They asked what he had done and how he had done it, and as Mike pulled out a legal pad and started taking notes, Johnson supplied his name, address, date of birth, even his Social Security number.

"Do any armed robberies?" Mike asked.

"I stuck up befo'," Johnson said, telling how he had got off on two other armed robbery charges.

"Did ya do 'em?" Tony asked.

"Yeah." Johnson told of robbing and then shooting a man in the stomach when the victim chased him.

"Momma-ma-mia!" said Bohanna.

"Do you want a job with us?" Tony asked.

Johnson nodded.

"You sound like the kind of guy we want; I'm gonna call the boss and let you talk to him." Tony dialed Arscott. "Hey, I got a guy here who doesn't know who we are. . . ." He handed the phone to Johnson. "The boss wants to talk to you personally."

"Yeah?" Johnson said into the phone.

"You must be the dumbest guy in the world," Arscott said.

Johnson looked mystified. "This is Lieutenant Robert Arscott of the Metropolitan Police and you are under arrest." Johnson's mouth opened slowly. Mike leveled his derringer at the customer and showed his badge. "Come get him, Bohanna."

•   •   •

Richie Parker heard the police knocking on his door. He was on the second floor at the time. He had sometimes wondered whether he would jump out the window if the police ever came for him and now he knew the answer. In an instant, he was down on the ground and sprinting for the woods behind his home.

He heard them shout and his stomach sank. He started to run faster until he heard the unmistakable sound of a shell being racked into a rifle breech—*ca-clank!*—and one second later he had stopped.

Goddamn it, he thought. He knew he had done something wrong, but he reasoned that the circumstances had forced him to go into that warehouse. He had to have money somehow. He said nothing.

At the warehouse Monday, the men received an agonized call from Kind Lovin', the customer Mike and Angelo had greeted warmly on Sunday morning. "I'm in hidin'," Kind Lovin' wailed. "That stuff yesterday was the last straw! They out to kill me and you gotta do something!"

"I got an idea," said Franzino. "Why don't you give yourself up?"

Audrey Clipper read the Monday newspapers and began to grasp Operation Sting. But she couldn't understand why so much had been written about it; the big headlines suggested to her that someone had robbed Fort Knox. She couldn't see her George getting wrapped up in anything that significant. He was involved in drugs and he was a liar, she believed, but nothing more serious than that. That afternoon, Sonny called her and said he had been charged with murder.

Meanwhile, Monk Sams, who had been too smart to go to the party, called his mother's house from the Washington Hospital Center, where he was receiving therapy for a slowly healing finger he had crushed on the job weeks before. A strange voice came on the phone: "Maurice Tyrone Sams?"

"Yeah man, why do you all keep messin' with me?" Monk cried out. He felt like bawling. "I ain't bothered nobody. I got a government job, I work every day, you understand. I ain't been doin' no wrong. Why do you all keep bothering me, coming over here kicking my grandmother's door in, disturbing her, about to make her have a heart breakdown and everything."

"All we want to do is talk to you, Mr. Sams," the voice said calmly. "We have a warrant for your arrest. Give yourself up— we're going to get you anyway."

"Well, c'mon and get me, man. I'm up here in the doctor's office getting my physical therapy. By the time I have my therapy you all should be here."

He went back to the therapy room and cried. Here it goes again. Would he be released on personal bond, or have to go to jail? He had five convictions for robbery, attempted robbery, assault, petty larceny, things like that, and had spent about eight of his thirty-two years in confinement. Now all these police wouldn't let him live his life.

He was arrested and taken downtown for questioning by Secret Service agents. Man, I must be a big-time gangster, Monk thought. He understood them to say that if he cooperated 100 percent, they would help him with the judge. But even though he told the truth from A to Z, as he put it, he still couldn't come across with the facts they wanted, like who had forged the bonds or exactly who he got them from.

Late Monday they took Monk to the central cellblock at police headquarters. The bed was flat steel with holes in it, no mattress or pillow. A dry sandwich to eat and coffee like dishwater. Half the prisoners were from the party. Some cried; many were young junkies. There was muttering and cursing about killing Pat and Mike if they ever saw them again. A bald man, let's call him Crystal Ball, declared the P.F.F. trickery was probably illegal and for sure it was entrapment. He wanted to blow up the warehouse and Monk wished somehow he could.

Monk's cellmate was a big man, sitting listlessly on the floor with his elbows propped on the bunk. Monk knew him from somewhere in the life. It was Sonny Logan. Sonny said he had made up some story about killing somebody and now the rollers had given him the beef. "Man, I was jokin' with them," Sonny wailed. All night long he had seizures from heroin withdrawal.

By Tuesday Sonny wasn't feeling much better, but he concluded he'd get out of it. He was sure this Lieutenant Arscott he'd been hearing about had conspired with the undercover men to perpetrate a crime against him. He thought they suffered from delusions of grandeur and he felt sorry for himself.

Mrs. Clipper went to Superior Court and learned that Sonny had been charged with the murder of Gilbert Parsons. She watched a judge appoint a lawyer for her son. "Sonny confessed to murder and it's on tape," she told the lawyer during a recess. He wheeled out of the courtroom and loped unhappily for the bullpen in the basement.

About midday, marshals manacled Monk and some others together and took them from the central cellblock to the District Court's basement bullpen across the street. "Here come the party boys," a marshal jeered. "Did you have a nice time?"

Monk said he hadn't been at the party, they had to get an arrest warrant to find him. It bothered Monk to be regarded as one of the dudes stupid enough to go to the party.

He had heard that U.S. Magistrate Lawrence Margolis, who was handling preliminary Sting hearings, was nasty. "Out of sixty people involved in that party, all sixty went to jail," a guard exaggerated. "The lowest bond he gave was twenty-five hundred dollars." Monk felt sick. No way I have a chance, he thought.

A court-appointed lawyer, Paul G. (Lefty) Evans, came in and introduced himself. "The Bail Agency has recommended personal bond," he said. Evans, a compact man wearing a tweed jacket, moved from courtroom to courtroom picking up assignments to handle impoverished defendants such as Monk Sams.

Monk voiced his doubts: "One of the fellows told me Margolis is a man with no understanding. Don't give no law or justice."

"Don't worry," Evans said. "Personal bond is already recommended. I called your parole officer; they said they aren't going to 'violate' you. You're all right. You're going out today."

But the prosecutor, Neil Kaplan, had a different idea, telling Margolis he had a very strong case against Monk, including a confession. He said Monk had an "absolutely horrible record, including five convictions." Monk shuddered and peeped at his mother, who was sitting in the courtroom staring out a window.

The Secret Service agents he thought had promised to appear for him because he had cooperated weren't there. Monk jabbed Evans in the ribs. "Man, tell 'em I'm not on trial. What they bringing all my record and stuff up for. . . . This is a political thing, we automatically guilty."

Margolis, a man with a fleshy face and a prim manner, was studying the D.C. Bail Agency report. "I'm going to set bond at five thousand dollars surety," Margolis said.

Monk was stunned—five thousand bucks cash! He hissed to Evans: "Man, there ain't no way I can make it! I got a wife and two kids out there! They suffering day in and day out! I got a three-year job working for the D.C. Water Department. . . ."

"That will be all," Margolis said. Marshals approached to walk Monk back behind bars. At that moment, Monk Sams wanted to take a chain to Lawrence Margolis's head.

By Thursday, March 4, the demands for interview with the P.F.F. gang were intense, and the LEAA, which had funded much of the project, found itself inundated with requests from other cities for "Sting" information. Reporters wanted to know much more about an operation that served up spicy meatballs, threatened snitches, and bagged a prosecutor and a murder suspect. Harried police officials staged another press conference featuring the undercover men. But the commanders warned the newsmen not to use the real names of the P.F.F. gang.

Some of the policemen couldn't understand this. Hartman (Mike Franzino) and Lilly (Pasquale Larocca) had been identified in the newspapers by reporters who found their names on court affidavits, and nothing had happened. The men saw no reason any more why they shouldn't share in the limelight. A cop can shoot a man and the next day his name will be in the paper for everyone to see, one of them observed. The use of their real names became a subject of strain between the men and the top commanders. Soon, there was more strain over publicity.

In the next few weeks, interview requests and lucrative book and movie offers showered down on them from various places. They heard the names of Jack Webb, Warren Beatty, Paramount Pictures, and Dell-Delacorte books. The lawmen began dickering. Lill, Hartman, and Seibert, as federal agents, were prevented from taking money for telling about their official duties. But there were no such regulations on the city police, and they negotiated a $200,000 contract with Dell-Delacorte for a book.

Meanwhile, Silbert and FBI Director Clarence M. Kelley were urging Cullinane to muzzle his men and curb pretrial publicity that could jeopardize the prosecutions of Sting defendants. Further, some of the scouts who had worked in P.F.F. during the first few weeks of the project had talked with a lawyer about getting a cut of the book money for themselves. The detectives who had been in The Hole for five months were just as determined to keep them from any significant share. This presented Cullinane with a serious morale problem.

Just as the detectives were envisioning how to spend their money, they were summoned to the chief's office and Cullinane proceeded to tell them that he was sorry, but if they wanted to write a book, they first had to resign. The men huddled over the next few weeks to try to decide which of them would resign and go forward with the book. Three offered to end their careers, but they couldn't agree on how to split the money. While their discussions continued, Dell-Delacorte canceled the contract—the publishers were wary of the chief's gag order and the uncertainty among the men.

Leslie Waller, an author selected by Delacorte to write the Sting story, was not enthusiastic about the project anyway. He had talked at length with the men and decided that since they caught no big crooks or organized-crime figures, the Sting was little more than a Band-Aid operation. And he flew off to Italy to complete work on a home there.

The P.F.F. men, who had so carefully controlled the events in the warehouse for five months, now found that they controlled nothing. Instead, they were assigned to the back rooms of the Second District, where they endured the tedium of processing evidence and following up on investigations. Meanwhile, Lill and Arscott, the two P.F.F. supervisors, began traveling around the country to appear before rapt audiences of law enforcers to tell them how they could launch their own Sting projects.

Earl J. Silbert, the most powerful local law-enforcement official in the District of Columbia, also saw the fruits of the Sting project slipping from his grasp.

Despite the videotape and careful preparation of cases, some of the prosecutors thought the judges were giving the Sting defendants light sentences. Beyond that, it seemed to make no difference whether the suspect had committed one offense or twenty—the sentences were the same.

Judges were issuing concurrent sentences, meaning prison time for two or more crimes was to be served simultaneously. The sentences, with time off for good behavior, were averaging about a year, and judges were ruling in such a way that the city's liberal parole board could release prisoners almost at will.

Further, Silbert found he had neither the time nor the manpower to carry out his promise to monitor each case carefully through the criminal justice system. He immediately found himself involved with a second Sting operation, known as G.Y.A., which stood for "Got Ya Again." This operation was attracting dangerous criminals and needed top-level attention. It also was painfully time-consuming to build the cases from the P.F.F. project. Silbert's men were running into bureaucratic hurdles among city and suburban law-enforcement agencies, and within the city's police districts. A theft could occur in one district, and the victim could live in another, and the item could be fenced in a third. District commanders balked at sending their own men to work on a crime that would be counted as solved by the commander of a rival district. The very ill that Sting had been designed to remedy—useless rivalry among lawmen—had come back to haunt the Sting cases.

Silbert became so diverted from the P.F.F. cases that he lost track of Cockeye. This was the man Silbert had singled out to reporters as an especially troublesome criminal who somehow always managed to slip through with small penalties.

Cockeye maintained his resourcefulness. He faced a formidable problem: already jailed on February 26 on various non-Sting charges, he now had an additional fifty-six felony and misdemeanor offenses lodged against him from the P.F.F. operation. So he turned to an old adversary for help.

"Is this the same John Gill who was the prosecutor?" Cockeye drawled over the telephone one spring night.

"Well . . . yes . . ." John Gill, relaxing at home from his private law practice in Rockville, Maryland, was dumfounded to hear Cockeye's voice. As a federal prosecutor in 1970, Gill had sent Cockeye away for eight to twenty-four years for armed robbery It can't be the same man, he now thought. It's only been six years, and I put him away for at least eight! There was no way he could know that Federal Judge Gasch had reduced Cockeye's minimum sentence to five years because he had been a model prisoner.

"I don't think I should represent you," Gill said. "I was the guy who put you away!"

Cockeye said that didn't matter, he just hoped Gill was as good a defense attorney as he had been a prosecutor.

He was. Gill began plea bargaining with an assistant federal prosecutor. Soon, Gill, Cockeye, and the prosecutor stood before U. S. District Court Judge Aubrey Robinson to report agreement on a negotiated plea, just the thing Silbert, Campbell, and Bernstein had hoped to curb with the Sting videotapes. In return for Cockeye's plea of guilty to five P.F.F. felony charges, the prosecutor agreed to drop the remaining fifty-one other charges.

230

Gill told Judge Robinson that he once had thought Cockeye was "the worst possible type of person," but had since come to regard him as "an intelligent, civil human being," and he asked the judge not to give up on his client. Robinson sentenced Cockeye to a minimum eleven years in prison; he could be eligible for parole in about four years. For his part, Cockeye went to prison disgusted that he hadn't been sentenced to a drug rehabilitation program.

Months later, Silbert was dismayed to learn that one of his assistant prosecutors had let the slippery Cockeye strike just one more bargain.

"I never would have done that!" the United States attorney declared. "He is a horrible criminal."

Part of the reason Silbert lost track of Cockeye was because he was busy directing the prosecution of Donald Robinson. Silbert felt a burning moral duty to convict Robinson, and he put two of his most experienced prosecutors on the case. They toiled through the summer putting their facts together, and by the time the trial opened in early September, the government was able to wheel in its case material in a supermarket shopping cart.

Robinson moved to upstate New York with his family. He hired a team of lawyers from the prestigious Washington firm of Edward Bennett Williams—David Povich, assisted by Robert Watkins and Kendra Heyman. The trial opened in early September before Judge Gasch. The courtroom was dominated by a twelve-foot-high screen, on which the prosecution projected the two videotapes of Robinson's visits to P.F.F. and his negotiations with Pasquale Larocca and Frank Paccione.

Confronted by the tapes, Robinson wept and admitted that he had taken money at P.F.F. But his attorneys, building an entrapment defense, insisted that Robinson was coerced by the lawmen into committing the crimes. At the end of the trial Robinson took the witness stand and withstood the prosecutor's attempts to splinter his testimony. He had a plausible explanation for his every action.

He had dealt with P.F.F. only to cover up his involvement

with Loretta Butler, he testified. Although he admitted he was "in their pocket" by the second visit, he maintained he never intended to be. He said the lawmen had badgered and frightened him into coming into the warehouse. In the end, the jury agreed, acquitting him of the two bribery charges and the two obstruction of justice charges that were lodged against him. Robinson went back home and resumed practicing law in a relative's firm.

Unlike most other Sting defendants, Robinson had never been convicted of a crime, and consequently it was difficcult for the prosecutors to prove that he was predisposed to commit one —a standard legal attack on an entrapment defense. While the court-appointed lawyers frequently had many Sting cases to juggle, Robinson's lawyers were able to concentrate all summer on his defense. The legal work cost him more than $50,000. Months later, Robinson said that because of what "they" had done to him, he himself would never again want to be a prosecutor.

George "Sonny" Logan was brought to trial twice for the murder of Gilbert Parsons. His defense maintained that Logan was only lying about the murder to try to impress some Mafia people. The first jury was deadlocked and a mistrial declared. A second jury acquitted him. But Sonny didn't escape: he pleaded guilty to selling Pat a pistol and was sentenced to two to eight years. In prison, Sonny Logan believed that the police had made him a scapegoat for their failure to get organized crime members.

Maurice "Monk" Sams and Loretta Butler were put on probation.

Richie Parker and Tommy "Tee" Brisbon each received sentences of five years and could be paroled in about two. Stan Robinson, the man who embezzled the truckload of Christmas toys, pleaded guilty to embezzlement and received seven years; under the Federal Youth Corrections Act, he can be released at any time. Robinson worked as a guard at the Smithsonian Institution between his arrest and sentencing.

Charges against Ida Mae Watson-Jackson-Logan were dropped. Marion Toye received an eighteen-month term for selling a gun; Bobby Turner was sentenced to two to six years for violating the National Firearms Act and was not charged with selling stolen cars. Prosecutors withdrew the charge against Kind Lovin'; she became eligible for parole after serving six months.

Maurice Hamilton, a truck hijacker, was charged with carrying a firearm during the commission of a felony, carrying a pistol without a license, federal kidnap, armed kidnap, interfering with commerce—robbery and armed robbery. He was released on his personal recognizance and two weeks later, on March 18, 1976, was arrested in suburban Maryland in connection with the armed robbery of a Safeway store. He was released on $10,000 bond there and was arrested a few days later in the District of Columbia for carrying a pistol. He was then held without bond. In June he was allowed to plead guilty to one of the six Sting charges—armed robbery. He was sentenced to five to fifteen years in prison and ordered to an institution where he would receive drug therapy.

Although he was disgruntled with the sentences, Silbert realized that they were about average, especially in the cases of addicts who were thieves. He knew he couldn't make a public issue of it. He could go to war with judges over light sentences for murderers, rapists, and robbers—but not thieves.

Some of the lawmen felt that Donald Robinson should have been convicted and George Logan should have been jailed for a long time and that people like Maurice Hamilton should never get out. They watched in disgust as one prosecutor after another trooped into and out of the same case. At times they saw a new prosecutor rushed into a case at sentencing without knowing anything about the defendant.

"We're lawyers, not administrators," said Don Campbell, the Major Crimes chief, in acknowledging the officers' complaints.

But there was more to be said. While almost all the Sting defendants were allowed to plead guilty to only a fraction of the charges against them, the judges in most cases could have imposed enough penalty to keep the defendant locked up for most of a lifetime. But locked up under what conditions? The prosecutors knew and the judges knew that the prisons where the defendants were to be punished and rehabilitated were snakepits.

For their part, some of the lawmen drew satisfaction that most of the Sting defendants were sent to the city's correctional facility at Lorton, Virginia. They regarded this institution as one of the worst prisons in the country—in their view, a fitting location for the criminals they chased. It is a place where men get raped and men get killed, and many of the rest live in fear.

Lorton is a sprawling collection of red-brick buildings circled by barbed wire and tucked into isolated hills along the southern border of Fairfax County, Virginia, about twenty-five miles from Washington. It is a place, inmates explained, where prisoners stole the Coke machine from the administration building, dragged it outside, and smashed it open; where the inmates stole the purses and wallets of the visiting teenage choir one Sunday; where a benefit performance of a circus was called off because the props disappeared; where the cupcake man used to drive up to the commissary to make deliveries—until he returned one day to find his van empty.

Other prisoners spend many hours studying law books in search of angles that will get them back on the streets. They have their own terms for their sentences: a five-year penalty is a *buffalo* (after the buffalo nickel); two consecutive five-year terms is a *double buffalo;* two five-year terms running concurrently is a *buffalo running wild;* a ten-year term is a *dime;* and in the rare instances when a prisoner gets a life term, he can report to his friends, "Man, I got it *all.*"

It is also a place where the best inmate jobs pay next to nothing; where prisoners learn to keep lockers empty because they will be broken into; where pimps sell services of homosexuals for $10 or a pack of cigarettes. Heroin is available, smuggled in by visitors or tossed over the fence for money.

Some of the P.F.F. lawmen believe that if it weren't for police, order in Washington would quickly give way to rule of the strong. At Lorton, according to inmates, the strong do rule. Guards are unarmed so that prisoners won't attack them and take their weapons. Prisoners say the guards avoid breaking up or preventing fights between prisoners. Inmates who believe they are marked for assault take turns guarding each other on watches during the night and believe that if attacked, they would find safety only if they could somehow get to the office of the captain of the guards and lock themselves in. Then they might have a chance.

Weapons are abundant, stored in dormitories or hiding places on the grounds. A brick inside a sock becomes a blackjack; a toothbrush ground in a pencil sharpener becomes an icepick; a razor blade embedded in a pencil becomes a knife.

More than anything else, many men there are preoccupied with sex. Most of the violence is the result of homosexual conflict.

Cockeye saw a man stabbed to death during dinner at Lorton in 1970. Someone fell upon the hapless fellow with a butcher knife while he walked to his table. The victim tried to stagger away as the attacker plunged the knife in again and again. He died on the dining-room floor. The argument was over a homosexual, "the girlfriend" of the attacker. The victim had lent the "girlfriend" a coat and the attacker didn't like it. "If she needs a coat, I'll give it to her," he said. They argued and the dispute ended in the cafeteria.

All this was understandable to Cockeye.

According to two inmates who spent much of the early 1970s at Lorton, some men like full lips, or certain shapes of legs or the shapes of other parts of the body. Some men look "damn near" like a woman—and wear wigs and dresses they make in the tailor shop or smuggle in from outside, and they have names like Shirley and Barbara. Some are homosexuals by choice and allow themselves to be sodomized or raped for a pack of cigarettes for themselves or their pimps. More often, men are forced or conned into homosexuality. The veterans know all the signs.

Inmates are constantly studying one another to see who is weak: Does he drink his coffee right down, like a man, or does he blow on it and wait for it to cool? Does he towel off in the showers unmindful of others, like a man, or is he shy and does he try to hide his swipes (genitals)?

Many eyes watch a new arrival in the shower. If an older man sees a young man in the shower trying to hide his private parts, the veteran will walk right in and bump into him. If the young man does nothing, the older prisoners may rape him on the spot. If the young man refuses to submit, then the man on the hunt can say he could tell there had been others. If the young man denies it, then the old man can taunt him, and demand evidence. If the young man were foolhardy, he bent over to show his proof and the attack would be instant. Another dude could walk by and say, "I'm next."

Now and then a new arrival saved himself by smashing at an assailant as a man should, one of the prisoners explained. The others would know because the older man would show up one day with a black eye and a broken nose and everybody would realize they "weren't playin' no more."

Once a man was raped or sodomized, the word got out and others came around, the two inmates said. If the young man bucked, he could get hurt and feared getting killed. The person thus became a "fuckboy." Maybe he began to like it, or he just went along because he didn't want to get hurt.

As men lived by the con on the street, so they lived by the con at Lorton. One inmate knew a man who loaned a coat to a young man and then secretly stole it back later and hid it from the victim. This older man, a veteran prisoner, later asked the victim for the coat back and when the young man said it had been stolen, the veteran warned him, "Man, you know that coat belongs to Jimmy. . . . But that's all right, I'll try to take care of it. I'll try to talk to the dude."

Then he came back, saying, "Damn, that dude wants his coat." Knowing the victim was broke and in a spot, the veteran suggested that "Jimmy's chest is heavy," or that "his rocks are in the pond and somethin's gotta be done about it. So what are you gonna do?" The victim protested and the veteran eased his fears, telling him, "Say, man, I ain't gonna let him do it. . . . I'm gonna be right there. . . . Just let him put it between your legs, that's all, it'll just be slickleggin'. I won't let him put it in there."

236

Then, while the veteran stood guard, Jimmy greased up and put it right in there. When the victim realized this, it was too late. "He just got fucked," said one inmate. He screamed and when Jimmy got through with him, he tried to get up and was crying. But then it was the veteran's turn while Jimmy did the guarding. "Just stay right there," the veteran said. "Don't even move." After that, the word got around. There were no secrets at Lorton.

Prisoners at Lorton are raped, mugged, knifed, or piped if they pose real or imagined threats, or if they have something someone else wants, or for no particular reason at all.

On one prisoner's first day at Lorton, he saw a bed on the walk outside his dormitory. When he got inside, he realized that it was his bed and everybody was watching him. He didn't know who had done it, but if he did nothing, the word would get out that he was weak and more abuse would surely follow. If the guilty party, however, believed that the prisoner *knew* who had done it, the guilty party might fire on him, figuring to preempt retaliation. The prisoner didn't know what to do, but let his instincts take over.

"Now the judge has sent me down here just like he sent everybody else down here and I'm tryin' to do my time like everybody else," he said. "Because my name tag wasn't on my bed, I won't take this as anything personally against me. I'm gonna go out on the walk, get the bed, and put it back with my name tag on it. Anybody who touches my bed from there after, you know, I will take it as bein' personally disrespectful to me and I will deal with it accordingly. I don't know who did it and I don't want to know who did it."

No one bothered him there again, perhaps because some of his friends came up to support him and potential enemies saw that he had the power.

The prisoner got another test in the long lunch line. A man cut in front of him and let about thirty of his friends in. Danny stepped in front of the leader.

"Hey, chump, you don't want to walk in front of me," the

leader said. The prisoner turned around and saw the other dudes start to form a semicircle around the leader. This man looks strong, the prisoner thought.

"Well," he said lightly, trying to avoid a confrontation but maintain a strong image, "you got all your buddies and I ain't about to wait for you and all your buddies when I was right behind you. The best you can do is get in front of me."

The leader said that was solid; he wound up first, followed by the prisoner and then the thirty friends. The prisoner ate comfortably.

In prison Danny says he has at last learned his lesson. His addiction had obscured good judgment, he says, and the existence of P.F.F. prompted him to look for things to sell rather than looking for work.

One of his main problems, he now believes, is that he lacks a "marketable skill." He is looking for a way to attend Antioch Law School in Washington, D.C. His worries center around the fact that his GI Bill benefits expire next year and he wonders how, on the day he finally gets out of prison, he is going to pay for his education, which, he hopes, "will place me beyond the reach of criminal influences."

In August 1976 Eddie Seibert drove from Washington to Baltimore to buy a bomb from an assassin. He was through with Angelo Lasagna of P.F.F. Inc., and was now posing as a Mafia hit man from New Jersey. Seibert had heard that Cockeye had pleaded guilty to only a few charges out of fifty-six, but he tried not to dwell on it. The prosecution of the Sting cases had gone to hell in his view; the U.S. attorneys were disorganized and unable to press the cases properly that he and his colleagues had worked so hard to make. But he knew from sixteen years in police work that if he let it bother him, he would go nuts.

People break rules and laws all the time anyway, he reasoned. He saw it everywhere, beginning with Little League baseball, where he had been an umpire for ten years. Participants were constantly bending and breaking the rules to win. Just recently someone had pointed out that the star pitcher for the opposing team was pitching without the required rest between starts. Umpire Seibert strolled over to talk with the team's manager. "Did you pitch this boy yesterday?" he asked.

"I don't make mistakes," the manager said indignantly. "Team, have you ever known me to cheat or make a mistake?"

"Oh, no, sir!" the boys said.

Seibert said he hadn't walked all the way over there to be impressed with the manager's power over the boys. "Did you pitch him yesterday?" he repeated. The manager said no. But the boy then stood up and admitted he had. Seibert walked away.

He had a vague notion that there was a sweeping disregard for law and morality in the country and that it was in some way connected to the deterioration of family and church life. He saw himself as one of the palace guard, trying to protect what he believed was right, in the face of an uncaring public and an inept criminal justice system. That's why he tried not to think about justice too much. There was none, he believed, not so long as laws were written by lawyers for lawyers and all it took was smart lawyers to walk the guilty out of court.

He had to keep going, he said to himself, because if he didn't, who else would? He dismissed the outcome of the P.F.F. cases with one of his favorite multi-use descriptives: "Tough-shinski!"

A few hours later, he bought a bomb.

KALAMAZOO VALLEY
COMMUNITY COLLEGE

Presented By

Lana Mason